P9-CFV-288

IN MEMORY OF:

Ransom and Ann Oetzel

PRESENTED BY:

Mr. and Mrs. Terry Oetzel
and
Family

Women's Almanac

10/00

Women's Almanac

VOLUME 3:
Culture

Edited by Linda Schmittroth
& Mary Reilly McCall

U·X·L ®
AN IMPRINT OF GALE

REF.
305.4
WOM

Women's Almanac

Edited by Linda Schmittroth and Mary Reilly McCall

Staff

Julie Carnagie, *U•X•L Associate Developmental Editor*
Carol DeKane Nagel, *U•X•L Managing Editor*
Thomas L. Romig, *U•X•L Publisher*

Shanna P. Heilveil, *Production Assistant*
Evi Seoud, *Assistant Production Manager*
Mary Beth Trimper, *Production Director*

Margaret A. Chamberlain, *Permissions Associate (Pictures)*

Pamela A. E. Galbreath, *Art Director*
Cynthia Baldwin, *Product Design Manager*

Linda Mahoney, *Typesetting*

Library of Congress Cataloging-in-Publication Data

Women's almanac / edited by Linda Schmittroth and Mary Reilly McCall.
  p. cm.
Includes biographical references and index.
ISBN 0-7876-0656-1 (set: alk. paper); ISBN 0-7876-0657-x (v. 1);
ISBN 0-7876-0658-8 (v. 2); ISBN 0-7876-0659-6 (v. 3)

1. Women—Miscellanea. 2. Women—History—Miscellanea.
  3.Almanacs. I. Schmittroth, Linda. II. McCall, Mary Reilly.

HQ1111.W73 1996
305.4'09 — dc20

96-25681
CIP

This publication is a creative work fully protected by all applicable copyright laws, as well as by misappropriation, trade secret, unfair competition, and other applicable laws. The editors of this work have added value to the underlying factual material herein through one or more of the following: unique and original selection, coordination, expression, arrangement, and classification of the information. All rights to this publication will be vigorously defended.

Copyright © 1997   U•X•L   An Imprint of Gale Research

All rights reserved, including the right of reproduction in whole or in part in any form.

™ This book is printed on acid-free paper that meets the minimum requirements of American National Standard for Information Sciences—Permanence Paper for Printed Library Materials, ANSI Z39.48-1984.

Printed in the United States of America

10 9 8 7 6 5 4 3 2

This book is dedicated to some of the leaders of tomorrow—
Sara Schmittroth and the members of Girl Scout Troop #1399:
Stephanie Cetnar, Jackie Douglas, Laura Hendrickson,
Ashley Jenkins, Sheena Maggard, Margie McCall,
Jayla McDavid, Monti Miller, Erin Morand, Rachel Morand,
Rameka Parham, Courtney Phillips, and Amy Yunker

Contents

Bold type indicates volume number.
Regular *type* indicates page number.

Volume 2: Society

Reader's Guide

Women's Almanac features a comprehensive range of historical and current information on the life and culture of women in the United States and around the world. Each of the 25 subject chapters in these three volumes focuses on a specific topic relevant to women, such as education, civil rights, and social concerns. The *Women's Almanac* does more than highlight the accomplishments of women in a variety of fields, time periods, and cultures. It offers insight into history and attitudes, so that readers can understand just how remarkable some of these accomplishments truly are.

Additional Features

Women's Almanac contains biographical boxes on prominent women relating to the subject being discussed, sidebar boxes examining related events and issues of high interest to students, more than 200 black-and-white illustrations, and 20 statistical tables. Each of the three volumes also contains a glossary of terms used throughout the text and a cumulative subject index.

Acknowledgments

Special thanks are due for the invaluable comments and suggestions provided by U•X•L's *Women's Almanac* advisors:

Annette Haley, Librarian/Media Specialist at Grosse Ile High School in Grosse Ile, Michigan; Mary Ruthsdotter, Projects Director of the National Women's History Project in Windsor, California; and Francine Stampnitzky, Children's/Youth Adult Librarian at Elmont Public Library in Elmont, New York.

Special thanks also is extended to the panel of readers, whose comments in many areas have strengthened and added insight to the text: Marlene Heitmanis, Kathleen Reilly, and Robert Reilly. Marlene Heitmanis is the coordinator of an at-risk program at a Michigan middle school. She holds bachelor's and master's degrees in teaching and an education specialist degree. She commented on the appropriateness of the text and the reading level. Kathleen Reilly holds a bachelor's degree in anthropology and a master's degree in teaching English as a second language. She commented on grammar, culture, and feminist issues. Robert Reilly holds a doctoral degree in English. He is a professor emeritus of the University of Detroit, where he taught American literature for 33 years. He commented on grammar, literature, history, and philosophy.

Thank you, too, to Teresa San-Clementi for fine tuning the fine and applied arts information, and to Bob Russette for theater and Broadway musical information.

Comments and Suggestions

We welcome your comments on *Women's Almanac* as well as your suggestions for topics to be featured in future editions. Please write: Editors, *Women's Almanac,* U•X•L, 835 Penobscot Bldg., Detroit, Michigan 48226-4094; call toll-free: 1-800-877-4253; or fax: 313-961-6348.

Photo Credits

The Granger Collection, New York: Suffragettes (top); **Corbis-Bettmann:** ERA demonstration at Lincoln Memorial (bottom); **AP/Wide World Photos:** Benazir Bhutto (left).

Photographs and illustrations appearing in *Women's Almanac* were received from the following sources:

Corbis-Bettmann: Volume 1: pp. vii, 17, 34, 67, 99, 119, 137, 170; Volume 2: pp. 252, 359, 391, 412; Volume 3: pp. 534, 591, 595, 677, 744; **AP/Wide World Photos:** Volume 1: pp. xiii, xvii, 23, 50, 54, 59, 66, 88, 93, 101, 104, 114, 139, 146, 154, 177, 181, 183, 197, 213, 215; Volume 2: pp. 246, 257, 259, 270, 271, 273, 275, 277, 278, 279, 283, 284, 290, 302, 303, 315, 321, 331, 334, 335, 337, 361, 366, 376, 380, 383, 387, 410, 433, 438, 441, 442, 443, 467; Volume 3: pp. 507, 512, 518, 537, 549, 552, 558, 560, 561, 565, 566, 587, 593, 601, 604, 611, 612, 627, 629, 631, 637, 638, 649, 653, 654, 686, 705, 706, 709, 725, 730, 736, 740, 749, 751; **UPI/Corbis-Bettmann:** Volume 1: pp. xxvii, 61, 75, 110, 138, 140, 186, 194, 195, 219; Volume 2: p. 422; Volume 3: pp. 632, 731; **Archive**

Photos: Volume 1: pp. 16, 77, 106, 121, 164; Volume 2: pp. 244, 316, 324, 333, 392, 417; Volume 3: pp. 674, 692, 693, 728; **The Granger Collection, New York:** Volume 1: pp. 30, 37, 168, 173, 201; Volume 2: pp. 289, 323, 327, 350, 415; Volume 3: pp. 521, 523, 701, 726; **The Bettmann Archive/Newsphotos, Inc.:** Volume 1: p. 102; **Courtesy of National Aeronautics and Space Administration:** Volume 1: p. 107; **Reuters/Corbis-Bettmann:** Volume 1: pp. 112, 143, 151; Volume 2: p. 425; Volume 3: p. 562; **National Archives and Records Administration:** Volume 1: p. 169; **Courtesy of The Library of Congress:** Volume 2: pp. 245, 249, 251, 329; Volume 3: pp. 579, 597, 662, 713; **Photograph by Freda Leinwand:** Volume 2: pp. 405, 475; **Spencer Grant/FPG International:** Volume 2: p. 299; **Photograph by Gary Cameron. Reuters/Gary Cameron/Archive Photos:** Volume 2: p. 313; **Roy Morsch/The Stock Market:** Volume 2: p. 436; **Abarno/The Stock Market:** Volume 2: p. 445; **1996 Paul Barton/The Stock Market:** Volume 2: p. 449; **Martin Rotker/Phototake NYC:** Volume 2: p. 454; **Gary Buss 1994/FPG International:** Volume 2: p. 458; **Ed Carlin/Archive Photos:** Volume 2: p. 463; **Phototake Kunkel/Phototake NYC:** Volume 2: p. 465; **Culver Pictures, Inc.:** Volume 3: p. 501; **Fotos International/Archive Photos:** Volume 3: pp. 503, 624; **Popperfoto/Archive Photos:** Volume 3: p. 509; **Copyright 1969 by Maya Angelou. Reprinted with permission of Random House, Inc.:** Volume 3: p. 517; **AFP/CorbisBettmann:** Volume 3: p. 538; **Photograph by Don Hunstein:** Volume 3: p. 541; **Bob Douglas/Michael Ochs Archives/Venice CA:** Volume 3: p. 554; **Painting by Andy Warhol. Reproduced by permission of The Andy Warhol Foundation:** Volume 3: p. 619; **Photograph by Frank Capri. SAGA 1993/Archive Photos:** Volume 3: p. 645; **University Research Library, University of California at Los Angeles:** Volume 3: p. 652; **New York Public Library:** Volume 3: p. 659; **Archive Photos/Lambert Studios:** Volume 3: p. 691; **Photograph by C. Love. Courtesy of Faith Ringgold:** Volume 3: p. 696; **The Metropolitan Museum of Art, The Alfred Stieglitz Collection, 1949 (52,203):** Volume 3: p. 703.

Words to Know

A

Abolition: A movement in American history (1775–1864) in which people (abolitionists) worked to legally end the practice of slavery.

Activist: A person who has a strong belief and takes action to make that belief become an accepted part of society, either through law or government policy.

Agenda: A set of goals that a person or group tries to complete.

Allies: Nations or groups who fight on the same side during a war.

Anchor: In the television news media, the person who either narrates (tells) or coordinates (organizes) a program on which several correspondents give news reports.

Apartheid: An official South African policy that denied blacks and other nonwhites equality with whites in politics, law, and the economy.

Artifacts: Objects made by human beings, especially tools and utensils, often studied by later societies.

Astrology: The study of the stars and planets in the belief that they have an influence on events on earth and in human affairs.

Autobiography: A factual story that a person tells about his or her own life.

B

Baptism: In many Christian churches, this is the sacrament of joining or being initiated into the church; it usually involves the pouring of water over the new member to symbolize the washing away of sin.

Barbarians: People who do not behave in accepted civilized ways. For instance, the French and German tribes that overran Rome in about A.D. 400 were considered barbarians by the Romans.

Blockade: The use of ships, planes, and soldiers to seal off traffic to and from a coastline or city. The blockade cuts off the enemy's supply of food and weapons.

Blueprint: A written plan or drawing for how something should be built.

Boycott: The refusal to purchase the products of an individual, corporation, or nation as a way of bringing about social and political pressure for change.

C

Cabinet: A select group of people who advise the head of government.

Campaign: With reference to politics, an action undertaken to achieve a political goal.

Capitalism: An economic system in which goods and services are exchanged in a free market and are priced according to what people are willing to pay for them. Companies producing those goods and services are privately owned.

Censorship: The examination of filmed or printed material to ensure there is nothing objectionable in it.

Census: An official count of the population, conducted in the United States every ten years.

Chauvinist: A person who believes in the superiority of his or her own gender.

Choreographer: A person who creates the pattern of steps for a dance.

Christian: A person who believes that Jesus Christ is God, and that he lived on earth in human form.

Civil Rights movement: A social movement of the late 1950s and 1960s to win equal rights for African Americans.

Civil disobedience: Nonviolent acts that disrupt the normal flow of society, such as bus boycotts and sit-ins.

Civilian: A person who is not in the military.

Classic: A literary work of such quality that it continues to be read long after its original publication date.

Clearinghouse: A central location for the collection and sharing of information and/or materials.

Coeducational: An adjective describing an educational system in which both boys and girls (or men and women) attend the same institution or classes.

Code of law: A written list of rules that apply to all people. Laws can be enforced by the ruler or the government, and those who break the law can be tried and punished.

Collage: An art form that combines many different media and which may include paper, fabric, objects, text, and glass or metal.

Colonial period: The time in U.S. history between the first permanent English settlements in the early 1600s to the signing of the Declaration of Independence in 1776 when America was considered a colony of England.

Colonist: A person who settles in a new land and declares that the new land belongs to an already existing country.

Combat: The actual fighting that occurs during a war, including hand-to-hand fighting between soldiers, fights between pilots in planes, and fights between enemy ships.

Commission: An order for an artist to create a piece of art for a wealthy patron.

Communism: A form of government whose system requires common ownership of property for the use of all citizens. All profits are to be equally distributed and prices of goods and services are usually set by the state. Communism also refers directly to the official doctrine of the former Soviet Union.

Concerto: A musical composition for an orchestra that features one or more solo instruments.

Conservative: This term describes a philosophy or belief that the status quo, or the current system, should remain unchanged unless a very good argument is put forward for the change. Conservatives tend to prefer a small federal government and careful spending of public money.

Convention: A formal meeting of an organization's members.

Credit union: An organization somewhat like a bank that is owned by its members.

Crossover: A recording or album of one particular style, such as gospel or rap, that also becomes a hit on the popular music charts.

Curricula: All the courses of study offered by an educational institution. The singular form of the word is curriculum.

D

Dark Ages: The period (450–900) after the collapse of the Roman Empire, when violence, ignorance, and superstition was common.

Debut: Pronounced day-byoo; a first performance. An actor or dancer opens her career with a debut performance.

Delegation: A person or group of persons elected or appointed to represent others. A delegation to a national party convention represents all the voters of the state from which it came.

Democracy: A system of government in which the people elect their rulers.

Desegregate: To open a place such as a school or workplace to members of all races or ethnic groups. Desegregation usually happens after laws are passed rather than as a result of voluntary action taken by an institution.

Developed countries: A category used by the United Nations for countries that have extensive industry and a high standard of living. Developed countries and areas include all of North America, Europe, parts of the former Soviet Union, Japan, Australia, and New Zealand.

Developing countries: Countries that are not highly industrialized. Developing countries include all of Africa, all of Asia except Japan, all of Latin America and the Caribbean, and all of Oceania except Australia and New Zealand. Also known as the Third World or less developed countries.

Discrimination: Unfair practices, laws, or treatment of certain people based on a person's social class, gender, or race rather than on the person's merits.

Displaced homemakers: Women whose primary activity has been homemaking and who have lost their main source of income because of divorce, separation, widowhood, their husband's inability to work, or long-term unemployment.

Doctrine: A set of beliefs that guides how a person views the world and how she or he behaves.

Documentary: A nonfiction (true-to-life) film that tries to present information in a dramatic and entertaining way.

Domestic and decorative arts: The type of knowledge thought appropriate for young women in European society from the Dark Ages to modern times. These arts include caring for and beautifying the home, child care, gardening and food preparation, and self-improvement through art and music.

Dowry: Money, property, or goods that a bride's family gives to a bridegroom or his family at the time of a wedding.

E

Embassies: The buildings that governments maintain in foreign countries to conduct diplomatic business.

Endowed: To be provided with income or a source of income. Sometimes wealthy people endow colleges, providing the school with a source of income. The college then does not have to rely entirely on tuition payments.

Enlightenment: A period of cultural richness in Europe during the eighteenth century that called for critical examination of previously unchallenged doctrines and beliefs.

Evangelical: An adjective that refers to the Gospels of the New Testament in the Bible; an evangelist seeks to win converts to Christianity by teaching about the Gospels.

Exodus: A massive moving of people from one area to another.

Exploited: The act of using a person or resource without permission or without adequate payment.

F

Feminism: The belief that women are equal to men in terms of physical and mental ability, and that women's accomplishments should be equally praised in history and society.

Forum: A group that conducts an open discussion.

Frontier: The edge of known territory or what is considered civilized territory. When the Europeans first came to America, they considered the land west of the Appalachian Mountains the frontier. Next it was the land west of the Mississippi River. Finally, the frontier was the territory west of the Rocky Mountains.

Front line: The site of a battle where two sides meet to fight.

G

Gender equity: Fair treatment of both men and women.

Genre: A type of literary form, such as a poem, story, novel, essay, or autobiography. Sometimes genre refers to the groups within a literary form. For instance, novels may be historical, mystery, thriller, spy, or romance.

Great Depression: A period of economic hardship in U.S. history, from 1929 to about 1940. Many companies went out of business, and many people were without jobs.

Greco-Roman: Relating to both ancient Greece and Rome.

Guilds: Formal organizations of skilled workers that dominated trade and crafts in the Middle Ages (500–1500). Young people were apprenticed to guild members, who taught them a skill. Guilds had rules about days and times a business could be operated, prices that could be charged, and the number of new apprentices taken on each year.

I

Illiteracy: Illiteracy is defined differently in different countries. Sometimes it means the ability to read and write only simple sentences. In some countries, people who have never attended school are considered illiterate.

Immigrant: A person who leaves one country and settles in another.

Impressionism: A style of painting made popular in the late 1800s in France. Impressionists watched how light illuminated forms and then used color to create that image. Their work was very different from that of traditional realist painters, who represented scenes with great accuracy.

Incest: A sexual act between closely related people such as a father and daughter, a mother and son, a sister and brother.

Income: Money received by persons from all sources. Some of these sources can include wages, payments from government such as welfare or Social Security benefits, and money received from rental property.

Indentured servants: A person bound by contract to work for another for a certain length of time; during the early period of American history, both black and white indentured servants were commonly used and were usually forced to work for seven years before they gained their freedom.

Industrial Revolution: A period of history that began in England about 1750 and lasted until about 1870. The period was characterized by great growth in business and cities and greater dependence on machinery and inventions, which replaced hand tools and individual labor.

Inflation: An economic term referring to a rise in the cost of living. In an inflationary period, the cost of goods and services rises faster than wages increase.

Information Age: A period of time when a country's economy depends more on the exchange of information than on the production of goods.

J

Judaism: A religion based on belief in one God and a moral life based on the teachings of the Torah, or the Old Testament of the Bible.

Judeo-Christian: The religious tradition that forms the basis of the Christian churches. It includes the belief in one divine God and the need to live a good life in order to reach eternal salvation in heaven after death.

L

Labor unions: An organization of workers formed to bargain with employers over wages, hours, and working conditions.

Liberal left: A political belief that the federal government has a duty to make changes happen in society. Liberals favor government managed health care and social programs and strict environmental regulations.

Literate: The ability to read and write.

Lobby: In politics, the act of trying to persuade an elected or appointed government official to favor a particular policy. Washington, D.C., has thousands of lobbyists who argue for causes such as gun control.

Lyricist: The person who writes the words (lyrics) to a song. Many lyricists work with a composer, who creates the music to go with the words.

M

Mainstream: The beliefs and customs of the majority of society.

Maternity leave: Time off from work to have and care for a baby.

Medieval: An adjective that refers to the Middle Ages, which took place in Europe from about 500 to 1500.

Middle Ages: The period (500–1500) when the struggle for power gradually resolved itself into the creation of kingdoms ruled by a king and his noblemen. The period was a highly religious one, and learning and the arts reappeared as the times of peace lengthened.

Midwife: A trained health-care worker, most often a woman, who assists during childbirth and cares for newborns.

Militia: Civilians who join together to form an unofficial army, usually to protect their homes from invasion by an enemy.

Minimum wage: A payment per hour that is set by the government; employers cannot pay their workers less than the minimum wage.

Mural: A painting done on a wall. During the Renaissance (1450–1600), murals were done on wet plaster. Modern murals are often done on the cinder block walls of public structures or on the brick of a neighborhood building.

N

Network: A large chain of interconnected radio or television broadcasting stations.

Networking: The sharing of information and resources among a group of individuals in the same profession or interest area.

New World: The term used to refer to the North and South American continents. The Europeans (from the Old World) "discovered" the Americas in the late 1400s, and claimed the land for their king back home. The New World became colonies of the Old World.

Nontraditional: A new or different way of thinking or acting. For example, nontraditional jobs for women still include being a mechanic or the head of an automobile manufacturing plant.

O

Obstetrics: The branch of medicine concerned with pregnancy and childbirth.

Order: An official religious group dedicated to a specific purpose.

P

Pacifist: A person who is opposed to war or any use of force against another person.

Paganism: A religious system that does not accept the existence of one true god. Instead, pagans may worship animals, their own ancestors, or nature.

Parliament: An assembly of representatives, usually of an entire country, that makes laws.

Patent: A grant made by a government to an inventor that gives only the inventor the right to make, use, and sell her invention for a certain period of time.

Patriarchy: Social organization marked by the supremacy of the father in the clan or family, the legal dependence of wives and children, and the tracing of descent through the father's side of the family.

Pension: An amount of money given to a person by an organization on a regular basis, usually after a person retires. Career military people receive a pension from the U.S. government.

Philanthropists: Wealthy people who donate to charity or who try to make life better for others.

Philosopher: A scholar who is concerned with the principles that explain the nature of the universe and human thought and behavior.

Picket lines: To picket is to stand outside a place of employment during a strike. A picket line consists of more than one person picketing.

Piecework: Work paid for by the piece. Today this type of work is still done by women in the home, as a "cottage industry."

Policies: Plans or courses of action of a government, political party, school, or business intended to influence and determine decisions, actions, and other matters.

Political prisoners: People who are without legal rights and are held by a government that has no right to imprison them.

Poverty: The condition of being poor. The U.S. government defines poverty according to levels of money income that vary by age and family size.

Preparatory: Relating to study or training that serves as a preparation for advanced education. College preparatory classes prepare a student to handle college-level work.

Prodigy: An extremely talented child who shows an understanding or ability far beyond his or her age.

Producer: One who supervises and finances a public entertainment.

Progressive: A political or social belief that existing systems and organizations should be reevaluated from time to time and that new ways of doing things should be adopted if they are better.

Prohibition: A law, order, or decree that forbids something.

Public interest: A phrase used to identify concerns that affect the public as a whole.

R

Racism: Discrimination based on race.

Rape: The crime of forcing another person by spoken or implied threats of violence to submit to sex acts, especially sexual intercourse.

Ratification: The political process of passing an amendment to the U.S. Constitution. In the United States, thirty-six states must approve an amendment before it is passed into constitutional law.

Renaissance: The period from about 1450 to about 1750 that saw a great flowering in knowledge of all kinds, including the arts, sciences, music, literature, and philosophy.

Representative: In politics, a type of government in which people have the right to vote for their rulers. The rulers in turn represent or look after the interests of the people.

Rhetoric: The art of using language in a persuasive way that is not necessarily supported by facts.

S

Sacred: Something or someone that is holy or associated with a religion.

Saint: A person who has been officially recognized through the process of canonization as being worthy of special reverence.

Scholarly: Related to advanced learning.

Segregated: Separated or apart from others. Sex-segregated schools have either all boys or all girls; usually refers to government laws and social customs that keep white and black people apart.

Seminary: A school. The term is used today to mean a school for the training of priests, ministers, or rabbis. In the past, it referred to a private school of higher education for women.

Sex discrimination: Treating a person differently based only on his or her sex.

Sexism: Discrimination based on gender.

Sexual harassment: A practice that implies a person will lose his or her job, scholarship, or position unless he or she is willing to trade sexual favors.

Social government: This general phrase refers to some modern governments that believe they must play a strong role in protecting their citizens' health, safety, and educational systems. Other governments believe that individuals in the society must contribute and protect these things.

Socialism: An economic system under which ownership of land and other property is distributed among the community as a whole, and every member of the community shares in the work and products of the work. Socialists may tolerate capitalism as long as the government maintains influence over the economy.

Speakers' bureau: People within a group or club that give speeches regarding the group or club's goals, mission, or activities to an audience.

Stereotype: A distorted, one-sided image of a person or idea. Stereotypes include the strong, silent hero and the dizzy, blond heroine.

Steroids: Chemical compounds that may be useful for treating some medical conditions, but are sometimes misused by athletes to enhance their performance.

Still-life: A type of painting in which the subject is not moving. Flowers and fruit are favorite subjects of still-life painters.

Stream of consciousness: A writing technique that reflects the thought process of a character. The writing may include sentence fragments, unconnected ideas, and confused thinking. The technique is used to give the reader insight into how a character feels and makes decisions.

Strike: A refusal by employees in a particular business or industry to work. The goal is usually to force employers to meet demands for better pay and working conditions.

Subordinate: The idea that one person is less valuable or important than another. For instance, slaves are subordinate to their masters, and they must obey them. In some societies women are still subordinate to men.

Suffrage: The legal right to vote. In U.S. history, it usually refers to the movement to gain a woman's right to vote in elections of officials to public office.

Sweatshop: A factory in which employees work long hours for low wages under poor conditions.

T

Technology: Using the ideas of science to make tasks easier. Technology began with the invention of stone tools. The development of computers is one of the most important recent advances in technology.

Temperance movement: A social movement in the United States that started in the early 1870s in the West. Its goal was to make liquor production and consumption illegal.

Theology: The study of God and religious writings.

Tour of duty: The amount of time an enlisted man or woman spends in the military. Usually tours of duty or "hitches" run from two to four years.

U

Underrepresentation: The inadequate or insufficient representation of a certain group of people. For instance, in the 1960s, women and people of color were underrepresented on the police forces of most American cities

Universal suffrage: The right of an entire population, regardless of race or sex, to vote.

V

Vaudeville: An early form of American musical theater that was a collection of separate acts with no connecting theme.

Further Reading

A

Adair, Christy, *Women and Dance: Sylphs and Sirens,* New York University Press, 1992.

Agonito, Rosemary, *History of Ideas on Woman: A Sourcebook,* Perigee Books, 1977.

Alcott, Louisa May, *Work: A Story of Experience,* Roberts Brothers, 1873, reprinted, Viking Penguin, 1994.

Anderson, Bonnie S., and Judith P. Zinsser, *A History of Their Own: Women in Europe from Prehistory to the Present,* Harper & Row, 1988.

Ash, Russell, and Bernard Higton, *Great Women Artists,* Chronicle Books, 1991.

B

Basinger, Jeanine, *A Woman's View: How Hollywood Spoke to Women, 1930-1960,* Alfred A. Knopf, 1993.

Beauvoir, Simone de, *Le Deuxieme Sexe,* Gallimard, 1949, translation published as *The Second Sex,* Knopf, 1953.

Blos, Joan W., *A Gathering of Days: A New England Girl's Journal, 1830-32: A Novel,* Scribner, 1979.

Boston Women's Health Collective, *The New Our Bodies, Ourselves: A Book By and For Women,* Touchstone Books, 1992.

Bowers, Jane, and Judith Tick, eds., *Women Making Music: The Western Art Tradition, 1150-1950,* University of Illinois Press, 1986.

Brennan, Shawn, ed., *Women's Information Directory,* Gale Research, 1993.

C

Cantor, Dorothy W., and Toni Bernay, with Jean Stoess, *Women in Power: The Secrets of Leadership,* Houghton Mifflin, 1992.

Carabillo, Toni, Judith Meuli, and June Bundy Csida, *Feminist Chronicles: 1953-1993,* Women's Graphics, 1993.

Chadwick, Whitney, *Women, Art, and Society,* Thames and Hudson, 1990.

Clapp, Patricia, *Constance: A Story of Early Plymouth,* Lothrop, Lee & Shepard, 1968.

D

DeWitt, Lisa F., *Cue Cards: Famous Women of the Twentieth Century,* Pro Lingua Associates, 1993.

E

Edwards, Julia, *Women of the World: The Great Foreign Correspondents,* Houghton Mifflin, 1988.

Evans, Sara M., *Born for Liberty: A History of Women in America,* The Free Press, 1989.

F

Fallaci, Oriana, *Interview with History,* Houghton Mifflin, 1976.

Faludi, Susan, *Backlash: The Undeclared War Against American Women,* Crown Publishers, 1991.

Farrer, Claire R., *Women and Folklore,* University of Texas, 1975.

Fernea, Elizabeth Warnock and Basima Qattan Bezirgan, eds., *Middle Eastern Muslim Women Speak,* University of Texas Press, 1977.

Fischer, Christiane, ed., *Let Them Speak for Themselves: Women in the American West, 1849-1900,* E. P. Dutton, 1978.

Fisher, Maxine P., *Women in the Third World,* Franklin Watts, 1989.

Fox-Genovese, Elizabeth, *Within the Plantation Household: Black and White Women of the Old South,* University of North Carolina, 1988.

Fraser, Antonia, *The Warrior Queens,* Alfred A. Knopf, 1989.

Fraser, Antonia, *The Weaker Vessel,* Alfred A. Knopf, 1984.

Friedan, Betty, *The Feminine Mystique,* Dell Publishing, 1963.

G

Gilden, Julia, and Mark Friedman, *Woman to Woman: Entertaining and Enlightening Quotes by Women About Women,* Dell Publishing, 1994.

Goodrich, Norma Lorre, *Heroines: Demigoddess, Prima Donna, Movie Star,* HarperCollins, 1993.

H

Haskell, Molly, *From Reverence to Rape: The Treatment of Women in the Movies,* Holt, Rinehart and Winston, 1973.

Hymowitz, Carol, and Michaele Weissman, *A History of Women in America,* Bantam Books, 1978.

K

Kosser, Mike, *Hot Country Women,* Avon, 1994.

Kraft, Betsy Harvey, *Mother Jones: One Woman's Fight for Labor,* Clarion Books, 1995.

Kramarae, Cheris, and Paula A. Treichler, *Amazons, Bluestockings and Crones: A Feminist Dictionary,* Pandora Press, 1992.

L

Lerner, Gerda, *The Creation of Feminist Consciousness: From the Middle Ages to Eighteen-seventy,* Oxford University Press, 1993.

Levey, Judith S., *The World Almanac for Kids: 1996,* World Almanac Books, 1995.

Lobb, Nancy, *Sixteen Extraordinary Hispanic Americans,* J. Weston Walch, Publisher, 1995.

Lunardini, Christine, Ph.D., *What Every American Should Know About Women's History: 200 Events that Shaped Our Destiny,* Bob Adams, Inc., 1994.

M

Macdonald, Anne L., *Feminine Ingenuity: Women and Invention in America,* Ballantine Books, 1992.

Maio, Kathi, *Popcorn and Sexual Politics: Movie Reviews,* The Crossing Press, 1991.

McLoone, Margo, and Alice Siegel, *The Information Please Girls' Almanac,* Houghton Mifflin, 1995.

Mead, Margaret, *Male & Female: A Study of the Sexes in a Changing World,* William Morrow, 1977.

Mills, Kay, *A Place in the News: From the Women's Pages to the Front Pages,* Columbia University Press, 1991.

Morgan, Robin, ed., *Sisterhood Is Global: The International Women's Movement Anthology,* Anchor Press/Doubleday, 1984.

Moses, Robert, and Beth Rowen, eds., *The 1996 Information Please Entertainment Almanac,* Houghton Mifflin, 1995.

N

Nelson, Mariah Burton, *Are We Winning Yet?: How Women Are Changing Sports and Sports Are Changing Women,* Random House, 1991.

Netzer, Dick, and Ellen Parker, *Dancemakers: A Study Report Published by the National Endowment for the Arts,* National Endowment for the Arts, 1993.

P

Paterson, Katherine, *Lyddie,* Dutton, 1991.

Pederson, Jay P., and Kenneth Estell, eds., *African American Almanac,* UXL, 1994.

Post, Elizabeth L., *Emily Post's Etiquette,* 14th ed., Harper & Row, 1984.

R

Ranke-Heineman, Uta, *Eunuchs for the Kingdom of Heaven: Women, Sexuality, and the Catholic Church,* Viking Penguin, 1991.

Rubinstein, Charlotte Streifer, *American Women Artists from Early Indian Times to the Present,* Avon Books, 1982.

Ryan, Bryan, and Nicolas Kanellos, eds., *Hispanic American Almanac,* UXL, 1995.

S

Schmittroth, Linda, ed., *Statistical Record of Women Worldwide,* 2nd ed., Gale Research, 1995.

Schneir, Miriam, ed., *Feminism: The Essential Historical Writings,* Random House, 1973.

Sherr, Lynn, and Jurate Kazickas, *Susan B. Anthony Slept Here: A Guide to American Women's Landmarks,* Times Books, 1994.

Sklar, Kathryn Kish, *Catharine Beecher: A Study in American Domesticity,* W. W. Norton: 1976.

Smith, Robert, *Famous Women: Literature-Based Activities for Thematic Teaching, Grades 4-6,* Creative Teaching Press, 1993.

Stratton, Joanna L., *Pioneer Woman: Voices from the Kansas Frontier,* Simon & Schuster, 1981.

T

Taylor, Debbie, *Women: A World Report,* Oxford University Press, 1985.

Trager, James, *The Women's Chronology: A Year-by-Year Record, from Prehistory to the Present,* Henry Holt and Company, 1994.

Trotta, Liz, *Fighting for Air: In the Trenches with Television News,* Simon & Schuster, 1991.

U

Uglow, Jennifer S., ed., *The International Dictionary of Women's Biography,* Continuum, 1982.

U.S. Bureau of the Census, *Historial Statistics of the United States. Colonial Times to 1970,* U.S. Dept. of Commerce, 1975.

W

Witt, Linda, Karen M. Paget, and Glenna Matthews, eds., *Running As A Woman: Gender and Power in American Politics,* The Free Press, 1994.

Wright, John W., ed., *The 1996 Universal Almanac,* Andrews and McMeel, 1995.

Z

Zientara, Marguerite, *Women, Technology & Power: Ten Stars and the History They Made,* AMACOM, 1987.

18

Literature

"This place I am from is everything I am as a writer and a human being."

—Leslie Marmon Silko

History abounds with examples of the contributions of women to the arts, especially literature. Unlike politics, law, business, medicine, and higher education, literature has long been a field open to women, most likely because writing is a private act, taking place in the privacy of one's home or office. While women throughout history were discouraged from entering public life, they have been less restricted in their private activities.

This chapter focuses on the contributions of American women to literature, history, scholarly study, and popular writing. Through novels, poems, plays, letters, speeches, and articles, these women helped shape American thinking on a variety of personal and social issues. Also included in this chapter are sections on how fairy tales help shape our thinking, and how some of the best-loved children's classics have been written by women.

The chapter begins with the writings of colonial women (from the mid-1600s) and goes through the 1990s. Also included

Timeline: American Women Writers

1650 Poet Anne Bradstreet becomes the first American woman whose work is widely read.

1773 Poet Phillis Wheatley becomes the first well-known black author in America.

1784 Hannah Adams, who wrote about religion and history, is the first American woman to become a professional writer.

1851 Susan Warner becomes the first American author to write a book that sells one million copies. The book, about a motherless child, is called *The Wide, Wide World*.

1852 Novelist Harriet Beecher Stowe publishes *Uncle Tom's Cabin*. Her depiction of slavery helps set the stage for the American Civil War (1861–65).

1852 Poet Emily Dickinson's first work is published.

1871 Sarah Orne Jewett publishes her first book of short stories about her home state of Maine.

1904 Writer Ida Tarbell publishes an exposé about the Standard Oil Company.

1908 Playwright, biographer, educational commentator, and lyricist (songwriter) Julia Ward Howe is the first woman elected to the American Academy of Arts and Letters. Her most famous work is "The Battle Hymn of the Republic," a song that became the anthem of the North during the Civil War.

1920 Novelist Edith Wharton becomes the first woman to win a Pulitzer Prize, for her novel *The Age of Innocence*.

1923 Edna St. Vincent Millay becomes the first woman to win a Pulitzer Prize for poetry. Willa Cather wins a Pulitzer Prize for her novel *One of Ours*.

1936 American novelist Margaret Mitchell publishes *Gone with the Wind*.

1938 Novelist Pearl Buck becomes the first American woman to win a Nobel Prize for literature.

1950 Poet Gwendolyn Brooks wins a Pulitzer Prize for *Annie Allen*. She is the first African American woman awarded the prize.

1976 Asian American writer Maxine Hong Kingston wins the National Book Critics Circle Award for her autobiography, *The Woman Warrior*.

1993 Novelist Toni Morrison becomes the first African American woman to win the Nobel Prize for literature. African American poet Maya Angelou reads an original work at the inauguration of U. S. President Bill Clinton.

is an overview of the writings of European, Asian, African, Australian, and South American women.

Colonial Writers

America's colonial period began with the settlement of the Jamestown (Virginia) Colony in 1607. It ended when the United States began to operate as a country about 1787, the time the U.S. Constitution was published. Colonial life in America varied depending on where one lived. Cities such as Boston, Massachusetts, Philadelphia, Pennsylvania, and Richmond, Virginia, were sophisticated centers of business, learning, and culture. Around them clustered towns and farms, giving many people access to the benefits of city life. But many other Americans lived in remote (distant) areas that were isolated and where change happened slowly. The frontier, the mountains, the Canadian border, and the rural South, all provided a different life experience.

American writers were quick to see and capture the many different lifestyles of Americans, even as early as the colonial period. Writers were influenced by more than where they lived. Their view of the world was also shaped by their education, their religion, their wealth (or lack of it), and their experience of culture. For instance, a man living in Boston might be fairly wealthy, attend the newly opened Harvard University, and have a Puritan (a religion with very strict morals and code of acceptable behavior) view of the world. However, a man living in Rich-

Memoirs of a Medieval Woman

Margery Kempe of Norfolk, England, wrote one of the first autobiographies to appear in English. She was born in 1373, married, became the mother of fourteen children, and made a pilgrimage (journey) to the Holy Land (Israel). Her writings have been collected and published under the title *Memoirs of a Medieval Woman*.

Another colonial writer of influence was Phillis Wheatley. Wheatley was born in Africa and taken as a slave to America. She lived with the prosperous Wheatley family in Boston and, unlike many other slaves, was treated well. She learned to read and write, and published her first poem in 1773, when she was fourteen years old. While she was not the first black author in America, she was the first to be published. In one famous poem, she describes her capture in Africa:

> Should you, my lord, while you pursue my song,
> Wonder from whence my love of Freedom sprung,
> Whence flow these wishes for the common good,
> By feeling hearts alone best understood,
> I, young in life, by seeming cruel fate
> Was snatch'd from Africa's fancy'd happy seat . . . .

Phillis Wheatley became the first published African American author.

ed to be an example of a good Puritan housewife (meek and religious). Bradstreet wrote about her life in journals and poems. Her first book, published anonymously in London, was called *The Tenth Muse Lately Sprung Up in America; or, Several Poems, Compiled With Great Variety of Wit and Learning, Full of Delight . . . By a Gentlewoman in Those Parts.* A second collection, published posthumously (after her death), showed how Bradstreet's poetic voice had matured, how she had developed her own writing style, and how her views of a woman's role in society had broadened.

Another colonial woman who left her mark on society was Abigail Adams. In colonial times, people communicated mainly by letter, and some of these letters have been preserved to tell us the story of the writer's life and concerns. Adams was a prolific letter writer. Many of her letters were addressed to her husband, John, who was away from home, helping to form the new American government. John Adams would eventually become the second U.S. president, and Abigail Adams would serve as first lady. But while America was still moving toward a break with England, Abigail Adams wrote her husband:

> Emancipating [freeing] all nations, you insist upon retaining absolute power over Wives. . . . If particular care and attention is not paid to the Ladies, we are determined to foment [start] a Rebellion, and will not hold ourselves bound by any Laws in which we have no voice, or Representation.

But John Adams did not take his wife's advice and include equality for

mond might also be wealthy, but would attend the new William and Mary College and have a less rigid view of religion. Unlike the man in the North, this Southern man might feel that slavery was acceptable and that the government should have little influence in a person's life.

The Writers

One of the earliest American writers was Anne Bradstreet of Boston. Bradstreet was born in England and immigrated to the Massachusetts Bay Colony in 1630. Her husband was an important leader in the community, and Bradstreet was expect-

women in either the Declaration of Independence or the U.S. Constitution. This failure to address the status of women is ironic. One of America's reasons for rebelling against England was England's refusal to allow American representatives to sit in Parliament (an assembly of persons that makes the laws of a nation). The cry in America was "no taxation without representation!" Yet when Abigail Adams suggested that her husband help guarantee the same rights of citizenship to American women, he and the other founding fathers ignored her. This blatant exclusion continued to bother women and eventually led to Elizabeth Cady Stanton's Declaration of Sentiments in 1848. Stanton's document, based in part on the ideas that Abigail Adams had expressed so many years before, was the beginning of the American Women's Suffrage (right to vote) movement.

While Abigail Adams was calling for women's rights, novelist Lydia Maria Child turned her attention to the rights of black Americans. Child, who was a white woman, was writing in the 1830s, when slavery was a legal institution and practiced throughout much of the United States. In 1833, she became the first American to publish a book that publicly called for an end to slavery. Before the publication of *Appeal in Favor of That Class of Americans Called Africans,* Child had been a respected Boston author of many books on different topics. After her *Appeal* was published, she found many doors closed to her but nevertheless continued to work for an end to slavery.

Writers of the Civil War

Two generations separated the heroes of the American Revolutionary War (1775–81) and those of the American Civil War (1861–65). Men who had fought against the British at Yorktown (Virginia) and Saratoga (New York) watched as their grandsons battled each other at places like Gettysburg (Pennsylvania) and The Wilderness (Virginia). What could have happened in the eighty years between the wars to create such regional hatred and set North against South?

Actually, the seeds of the Civil War were present when the United States were formed. In the 1770s, much of America was still agricultural (devoted to farming). However, there were already signs that the North would become an industrial center and the South would continue to rely on slavery to operate its plantations (large farms). The founding fathers sidestepped the issue of slavery, agreeing to allow the South to keep the practice. Another issue was how much power the federal government would have over the states. The North favored a strong central government, while the South favored strong states' rights. The two sides continued to debate this issue in Congress in Washington, D.C., right up until the Civil War began in 1861.

The Writers

Among those writing against this backdrop of northern versus southern interests was Harriet Beecher Stowe.

Stowe was an abolitionist (antislavery crusader) as well as a writer. When the Fugitive Slave Act was passed in 1850, Stowe began to write a novel she published as *Uncle Tom's Cabin; or, Life Among the Lowly*. The Fugitive Slave Act allowed slave owners to track down runaway slaves in other states. In Stowe's novel, the hero was Uncle Tom, an elderly slave who was sold away from his wife and endured much harsh treatment at the hands of his new master. Stowe's book was first published in a serial format (chapter by chapter) in an abolitionist newspaper. However, when it was published in book form, it ignited a huge debate in America and even in Europe over the evils of slavery. Stowe's book caused such an uproar that President Abraham Lincoln called her "the little woman who made this great war." He was referring to the Civil War.

Another author to publish in serial format was Louisa May Alcott. Alcott was the author of the beloved children's classic *Little Women*. *Little Women* told the story of how the March family coped during the Civil War, when their father was serving as a chaplain (minister) in the Union (Northern) Army. The story of Meg, Jo, Beth, and Amy was continued in two later books called *Little Men* and *Jo's Boys*. Alcott's earliest writings, mostly historical romances and adventures, were published in serial format in magazines. Her later books revolved around family relationships and the way young people grow to maturity through their experiences.

One of America's great poets, Emily Dickinson published her first poem before the Civil War, in 1852. Unlike Stowe and Alcott, Dickinson did not write about the great issues of the day. Instead, her thoughts turned inward. She lived quietly in her family's home in Amherst, Massachusetts. Dickinson had very definite (and very unusual for her time) opinions about what was important in life. In one poem, she describes how we select friends based not on rank or money but on how closely their interests resemble our own. Because Dickinson refers to the soul in the poem as "she," many people believe that she is describing herself:

The Soul selects her own Society

Then—shuts the Door—

To her divine Majesty—

Present no more—

Unmoved—she notes the Chariots— pausing—

At her low Gate—

Unmoved—an Emperor be kneeling

Upon her Mat—

I've known her—from an ample nation—

Choose one—

Then—close the Valves of her attention—

Like Stone—

Other types of private writing were popular before and during the war. Letter writing continued to be a major form of expression. Diary or journal writing also became popular as people found themselves isolated from family and friends because of the war. Diaries became places where people could confide their experiences, hopes, and fears. They also helped ease the loneliness suffered by women and men alike as they spent months or even years apart. Today, as we read these diaries, we gain a sense not only of the personality of the writer but of the tremendous times through which they were living.

One such writer was Mary Boykin Chesnut, whose husband and father were both Washington, D.C., politicians before the outbreak of the war. When South Carolina seceded (broke away) from the Union (North) in 1861, Chesnut's male relatives went away to war. She was left behind to run the family's plantation, as were many other Southern women. Chesnut's diary was published as *Mary Chesnut's Civil War* in 1884. Excerpts from her diary were featured in *The Civil War,* the much-acclaimed television documentary by filmmaker Ken Burns.

On January 16, 1865, Chesnut wrote:

My husband is at home once more—for how long, I do not know. And his aides [military staff] fill the house, and a group of hopelessly wounded haunt the place. And the drilling [training] and the marching goes on. . . . A month ago my husband wrote me a letter which I promptly suppressed after showing it to Mrs. McCord [a family friend]. He warned us to make ready–for the end had come. Our resources were exhausted—and the means of resistance could not be found. It was what we could not bring ourselves to believe.

The issue of women's rights and roles was a heavily debated subject in this period. One woman chose to document the contributions of women to American history and used these contributions

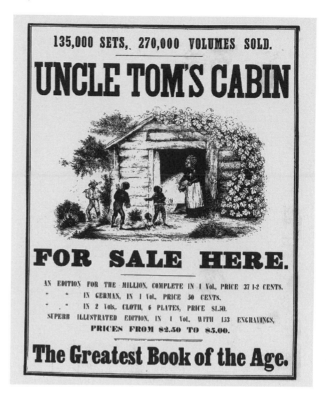

Poster advertising Harriet Beecher Stowe's Uncle Tom's Cabin.

as an argument for better treatment. She was Elizabeth Lummis Ellet, and her books include the three-volumes *The Women of the American Revolution* (published in 1848), *Domestic History of the American Revolution* (1850), and *Pioneer Women of the West* (1852).

The Age of Extremes

After the Civil War, the United States embarked on a period of huge change. The era of big industry was born, and with it came the Age of Extremes, which lasted from about 1880 to World War I (1914). Men became millionaires through industry and business (J. D. Rockefeller started Standard Oil, Andrew Carnegie ran the steel industry, Andrew Melon was the big name in banking, and Cornelius Vanderbilt became the richest man in America through railroads). As a result, the gap between the very rich and the very poor widened.

At the poor end were the millions of immigrants who flocked to America from Europe. They were attracted by jobs in the growing industries in large U.S. cities. Others came to lay the railroad lines that helped conquer the West. It was a time of great energy, both social and political. Men, however, continued to run politics, government, and business. Women, working outside the home in larger numbers than ever before, became concerned with workers' rights, the poor, education, and public health care. Not surprisingly, much of the writing done during this period focused on the hard life of the poor and success stories of poverty-stricken immigrants who worked hard and made a name for themselves in America. Diaries and novels continued to be popular literary forms, but new forms such as "muckraking" (social criticism) and speeches joined their ranks.

The Writers

One of the most popular children's authors in America is Laura Ingalls Wilder. Her novels trace her family's journeys from the *Little House in the Big Woods* (Wisconsin) through homesteads in Kansas, Minnesota, Iowa, and the Dakota Territory. The nine books, which are largely autobiographical, describe life on the American frontier, including experiences with Indians, plagues of locusts, and prairie fires. Wilder's books cover the period from 1870 to 1889, when the final taming of the American West was taking place. Railroads cut across huge sections of the American plains, the Indian Wars were coming to an end, and the days of the cowboy were numbered. Wilder's works, while they focus on her family and their relationships with each other, do bring to life the great changes occurring during this time.

Some homesteaders (people who traveled West to receive land to farm) kept travel diaries as they journeyed to their new homes. Others wrote letters back home, describing their life in the West. One woman homesteader was Elinore Rupert Stewart, who wrote in *Letters of a Woman Homesteader:*

> I realize that temperament [personality] has much to do with success in any undertaking, and persons afraid of coyotes and work and loneliness had better let ranching alone. At the same time, any woman who can stand the beauty of the sunset, loves growing things, and is willing to put in as much time at careful labor as she does standing over the washtub, will certainly succeed.

Another diarist of the West was Isabella Bird, who wrote *A Lady's Life in the Rocky Mountains.*

When it came to political speeches and organizing, few could surpass Mary Harris "Mother" Jones. This Irish immi-

The television show Little House on the Prairie *was based on Laura Ingalls Wilder's novels.*

grant was best known for the help she gave coal miners who were struggling for better working conditions. But she also had a soft spot for children, possibly because she had lost her own young family to malaria. Jones wrote about child labor (the use of young children in factories): "Little girls and boys, walked up and down between the endless rows of spindles, reaching thin little hands into the machinery to repair snapped threads. They crawled under machinery to oil it. They replaced spindles all day long; all night through."

In part because of public reaction to the words of organizers such as Jones, the U.S. Congress passed laws that restricted the number of hours that children could work and at what age they could begin to work.

Other women challenged American society in a vocal and public way. They, along with their male colleagues, were called "muckrakers." Muckrakers were a new breed of journalist who wrote about social ills and the disgraceful conduct of America's rich and ruling class. Among the most famous of the muckrakers was Ida Tarbell. Her 1904 book about Standard Oil and John D. Rockefeller changed history. Her description of Rockefeller's illegal business practices led the U.S. Supreme

Court to break up his huge company because it was a monopoly. (A monopoly is a business that controls its market, unfairly shutting out other competitors.)

About this time, writers who captured the "local color," or flavor and concerns of particular geographic regions, were also becoming popular. One such writer was Sarah Orne Jewett, who was born in Maine in 1849. She published her first book of short stories in 1871 and continued to write about the oceanside villages and farming communities of her home state. Another writer with a regional flavor was Kate Chopin, who wrote novels about the French-Creole society of her native St. Louis, Missouri.

Other writers were addressing the unique experience of some of America's ethnic groups. Lola Rodriguez de Tio, a Puerto Rican-born American, became one of the first Hispanic women to win publication in the United States. De Tio, a short story writer and a playwright, wrote about the immigrant experience in America. She and other Hispanic writers of the time are given credit for helping to preserve the oral tradition (the use of stories and songs to keep track of and pass on a culture's traditions and values) and culture of the Puerto Rican community.

World War I and the Lost Generation

World War I began in Europe in 1914; however, the United States did not enter the conflict until 1917. The war grew out of the assassination (murder for political reasons) of Archduke Francis Ferdinand, heir to the Austro-Hungarian throne, by a Serbian nationalist. A nationalist is someone who believes strongly in the independence and greatness of his or her own country. When Austria declared war on Serbia, many other countries were bound to join in because they had treaties with the warring nations. Before long, Germany and Turkey were allied on the side of the Austro-Hungarian Empire. On the other side were Serbia, England, France, Russia, and Italy.

At first the United States refused to become involved, even though it did have strong ties to England. Although Americans considered the conflict a European war, the Germans changed that with their practice of unrestricted submarine warfare. When they torpedoed a ship carrying many American passengers, the United States declared war. Altogether, the United States sent 4.3 million soldiers to fight in Europe. It was a terrible war, with trench fighting, blinding mustard gas, and huge casualties (injuries and killings). America and her allies (Serbia, England, France, Russia, and Italy) finally won the war, and peace was declared in 1918. A total of 65 million men on both sides had been called to serve during the war. Of this number, 8.5 million were killed. The victors blamed German for starting the war, and they made her and her allies pay huge fines. These fines helped to bankrupt Germany and set the stage for a worldwide depression (economic slowdown) in the 1920s and 1930s.

Many people regard the First World War as the start of the Modern Age because it was the first war to be fought with motorized equipment and long-range guns. It also revolved around the idea of nationhood (single countries) instead of empires (groups of countries). Some writers call it the Great War because it led to an end of hope and optimism among people. The huge death rate and the hundreds of miles of destruction in France and Germany were testimony to the power of modern warfare. As a result, many novelists and poets wrote about the sense of loss they felt.

The Writers

One such poet was Edna St. Vincent Millay. Millay, a native of Maine, gained fame with the publication of her first poem, "Renascence," in 1912. She won a Pulitzer Prize in 1923 for *The Ballad of the Harp-Weaver* and other poems. One of Millay's favorite forms was the sonnet, a 14-line poem. In a passage from this sonnet, she talks about a sense of loss:

> But the rain
> Is full of ghosts tonight, that tap and sigh
> Upon the glass and listen for reply,
> And in my heart there stirs a quiet pain
> For unremembered lads . . .

Millay is also noteworthy because she was a role model for other women of her time. She lived independently in New York City, she supported herself financially, she was well educated, and she favored short skirts and form-fitting evening gowns. In short, she was a modern woman.

Edith Wharton was a woman writing in the same period as Millay who took a somewhat more conventional (traditional) approach to her private life. Wharton was married and lived off and on at expensive European health resorts with her often-ill husband. They were part of wealthy Boston society when they lived in America, and Wharton published her first short stories in American magazines.

Wharton's novels were concerned with the struggles that people go through to attain wealth and status in society. Many of her characters are newly rich Americans who travel to Europe, only to find that European society will not accept them no matter what they do. Wharton was the first American woman to receive a Pulitzer Prize for fiction. She won it in 1920 for *The Age of Innocence,* a novel describing the manners and restrictions of society, especially as they affect the lives of women.

Willa Cather, born in Virginia and reared in Nebraska, received a Pulitzer Prize for literature in 1923. Her first writings were poems, newspaper stories, and magazine articles. Later she turned to novels in which she told the stories of the immigrants among whom she had grown up in Nebraska. Her major characters are women who struggle to survive against the harshness—drought, fire, locusts, loneliness—of prairie life.

Gertrude Stein is known as the "grandmother of the modern movement." She was born in Pennsylvania but lived most of her adult life in Paris, France.

Stein was one of the most famous of a group of writers who preferred to live in Europe. She originated the phrase the "lost generation" to describe the disenchantment (loss of hope) that young people felt after World War I ended. Stein used dialect (speech of a particular group or region) in the dialogue she wrote for her characters and experimented with telling stories in different ways. She was influenced by the new art of cinema (moviemaking), which used quick cuts between scenes to tell two stories at once. Stein wrote both fiction and nonfiction, including a book that described what it was like to live in Paris while the city was occupied (taken over) by the Germans during World War I.

The Great Depression and a New Deal

The Great Depression of 1929 to 1940 left millions of people out of work and helped bring about a worldwide economic crisis. In the United States, factories and shops closed their doors or laid off workers. Some of the workers took to the road, looking for work in different towns. Others stood in bread lines and at soup kitchens, looking for a meal. Missions and churches were overflowing with families who had lost their homes because they had no money to make house payments. In the summer of 1930, a drought bankrupted farmers from Virginia to Arkansas and many of them, too, took to the road in search of

work. It was a time of great hardship and great migration.

When the stock market crashed in 1929 and set the Great Depression in motion, there were no government programs in place to help the poor or unemployed. By 1932, when Franklin D. Roosevelt was elected president, twelve million people (1 in 4 Americans) were out of work. Roosevelt ran on a political platform designed to change that. He began a series of programs designed to give Americans a "new deal." As a result, many laws were passed in 1933 to help relieve widespread poverty. This was the first wave of New Deal legislation, which provided money for unemployment insurance and pensions, established laws that set fairer wages and hours, and ended child labor.

Two other events greatly changed American life during this time. The Eighteenth Amendment (Prohibition) was passed in 1919. Prohibition made it illegal to purchase, manufacture, possess, or transport liquor (alcohol). The amendment was not repealed until 1933, by which time a whole underground liquor industry had developed. These makers and sellers of illegal whiskey created the era of gangsters and police shoot-outs that were popularized in movies and books. In 1920 came the Nineteenth Amendment, which granted suffrage (the right to vote) to women.

A whole new generation of writers was influenced by the aftermath of the war, the depression, and challenge to legal authority. The war led many people to become pacifists (antiwar). The depression created a new social consciousness as people heard daily of the suffering of their fellow Americans. The atmosphere of lawlessness encouraged many to reexamine all types of order and authority.

The Writers

Among the more famous of the women writers of this time was Katherine Anne Porter. In many of her short stories and novels, Porter focuses on life in the South (she was born in Texas). She examines the system of justice in the South, especially as it relates to poor people and black people. One of her works, *Ship of Fools,* uses the stories of a shipful of passengers to comment on Germany's move toward Nazism (Hitler's political party).

Lillian Hellman, one of America's most famous women playwrights, was active during this period. Hellman was also born of Jewish parents in New Orleans, Louisiana. As an adult, she moved to New York to be close to the Broadway theater district. Her dramas examine the movement within American politics to suppress personal liberty in favor of law and order. Her other themes in plays such as *The Little Foxes* and *The Children's Hour* depict family relationships and the life of the modern woman. Hellman was writing at a time when the American stage was dominated by male playwrights. Nonetheless, she wrote her plays and found producers for them. Hellman was famous for being direct, outspoken, and truthful.

Lillian Hellman

Another outspoken woman of the times was Dorothy Parker, who became famous for her witticisms such as "Men seldom make passes at girls who wear glasses." Parker wrote reviews of plays and books for New York newspapers and magazines. She also wrote short stories, poems, and sketches.

Along with Parker, Anita Loos and Clare Booth Luce were the other outspoken women writers of the day. Loos wrote Hollywood movie scripts and was known for her sense of humor and satire. Luce, a playwright, eventually went on to become a representative to Congress and later an ambassador to Italy.

Hellman Says "No!" to Joe McCarthy

In addition to being renowned as a playwright, Lillian Hellman is also famous for refusing to testify before the House Un-American Activities Committee in 1952. After World War II ended in 1945, many Americans feared that communism would spread to America. This fear helped Senator Joseph McCarthy gain great power in government. McCarthy claimed to have had a list of 205 U.S. government officials who were members of the American Communist Party. He also drew up a list of 418 authors whom he claimed used communist ideas in their writings. Many Americans were willing to be suspicious of members of the arts community because they knew that new ideas often spread through books, music, and plays. Because McCarthy's accusations unsettled many throughout the United States, he and his colleagues were able to create a committee in the U.S. House of Representatives which made actors, writers, and artists—as well as high-ranking government officials and other politicians—testify on their alleged activities in the American Communist Party.

The committee hearings helped create a "blacklist" of names of Americans accused of being communists. When the list was published, these people could not find work. (Whether they were really communists at all is still argued.) Hellman was ordered to testify before the committee and to name the names of her communist friends. She refused. She claimed that the committee hearings were illegal and a witch hunt and wrote to the committee to explain her refusal to testify:

"I am most willing to answer all questions about myself. . . . But to hurt innocent people whom I knew many years ago in order to save myself is, to me, inhuman and indecent and dishonorable. I cannot and will not cut my conscience to fit this year's fashions."

Hellman's refusal to testify, along with the courageous defiance of many others, helped bring the McCarthy Era to a close. But by the time the U.S. Senate had finally censured (criticized) Joe McCarthy in 1954, hundreds of Hollywood (California) and Broadway (New York) careers had been ruined.

Another writer with international ties was Pearl Buck, who became the first American woman to win the Nobel Prize for literature, in 1938. Buck was born in West Virginia but spent much of her life in China, where her parents were religious missionaries. Buck's short stories, essays, and novels explore the differences and similarities between Oriental (Eastern) and Occidental (Western) life and thought. Buck's second novel, *The Good Earth,* was the story of a Chinese peasant family. It won a Pulitzer Prize in 1932 and became one of the bestselling books in the United States. Over her lifetime, Buck wrote more than one hundred books, many of which helped interpret Chinese life and beliefs for Western readers. She wrote, "The minds of my own country and of China, my foster country, are alike in many ways, but above all, alike in our common love of freedom."

The tradition of writing about a particular region or group continued during this period. Eudora Welty and Margaret Mitchell were typical of a new breed of writers emerging in the South. These writers explored how the past still influenced their lives.

Welty grew up in Jackson, Mississippi, when segregation (separation of people by race) was in full force. Blacks and whites attended different schools, lived in different neighborhoods, and worshiped at different churches. Welty's writing career spanned five decades, from the 1930s to the 1970s. She won a Pulitzer Prize in 1973 for her novel called *The Optimist's Daughter.*

Margaret Mitchell is the author of *Gone With the Wind* (1936), one of the bestselling books of all time that was made into an equally famous film. Her novel tells a story of the "old South," before, during, and after the Civil War. Her heroine, Scarlett O'Hara, manages to cope with the loss of several fortunes and several husbands. What worries her

Vivien Leigh portrayed character Scarlett O'Hara in the film version of Margaret Mitchell's Civil War saga Gone With the Wind.

most is losing her beloved Tara, her family's plantation. Through Scarlett, Mitchell explores how strongly Southerners are tied to the land and an old way of life.

Another regional writer was Josephina Niggli, a Hispanic short story writer whose work was published in Mexican American magazines. Her themes include how difficult life was for Hispanic farm workers in the Southwest during the Great Depression.

African American writers such as Zora Neale Hurston were also helping black Americans find a voice in popular culture. A folklorist, Hurston's specialty was finding and writing down the stories kept alive through the black oral tradition in America, and she is known for her ability to hear and reproduce local dialects and accurately portray various religious rituals. Among the stories she retold are the Uncle Remus tales, and her most famous novel is *Their Eyes Were Watching God.*

World War II and Its Aftermath

World War II broke out in Europe in 1939 when Germany invaded Poland. Since England was allied to Poland, England quickly declared war against Germany. France and Russia came out on the side of England, while Japan and Italy sided with Germany. Soon the war had spread to the Pacific region and into parts of the Middle East and Africa. The United States, however, did not enter the war until 1941, when the Japanese bombed the U.S. naval base at Pearl Harbor in Hawaii.

The war ended the worldwide economic depression because the demand for war equipment, weapons, uniforms, and medical supplies put industry back on its feet. Soon the United States was supplying the ships and aircraft that would help England stay in the war as it fought Germany, virtually alone, through the end of 1941. France, like Belgium, Holland, Greece, and the rest of Europe, had quickly fallen into German hands.

The threat of the spread of German Nazism had troubled Americans for many years. The Nazis were a political party headed by Adolf Hitler that came to power in Germany in 1933. They held racist views, claiming that members of the Germanic "Aryan" race were superior to Jewish or black people. The Nazis systematically persecuted Jews, killing more than six million by the war's end.

After Hitler came to power, he rebuilt and rearmed his country. By 1939, Hitler began to invade the countries he wanted to become part of a German empire. Back in the United States, Nazism had already become a topic of books, poems, plays, films, and newspaper and magazine articles.

The war had another impact on the United States. With so many men marching off to war, factory and office jobs were open to women. Women also began to serve in the military in increasing numbers, mainly in office support staffs and in medical positions. They also drove jeeps and flew supply planes.

After the war ended in 1945, Americans settled back into a fifteen-year period of peace and prosperity. The economy boomed, and life in the suburbs (the residential area outside a major city) became the American dream. At least it was the dream for white middle-class Americans. African Americans, though, still suffered from racial discrimination and more black authors were writing about that experience.

The Writers

One such author was Gwendolyn Brooks, who was born in Chicago, Illinois. She won her first award for poetry in 1943, and a Pulitzer Prize for her poem *Annie Allen* in 1950. Her topics were city life, children raised in poverty, and the black experience in segregated America. "My dreams, my works, must wait till after hell," she writes in this poem, about the difficulty of maintaining hope for a better life:

I am very hungry. I am incomplete.
And none can tell when I may dine again.
No man can give me any word but Wait,
The puny light. I keep eyes pointed in;
Hoping that, when the devil days of my
  hurt
Drag out . . . in such heart as I can manage,
Remember to go home . . .

Marianne Moore was another prize-winning poet from this era. Moore was raised in Pennsylvania but eventually lived in New York City where she worked as a literary editor. She began publishing her poems in 1924 and won the National Book Award and the Pulitzer in 1952 for her *Collected Poems*. Moore was best known for experimenting with new patterns of rhythm.

The Diary of Anne Frank

One of the most famous writers in the world was a German girl named Anne Frank. Frank died in 1945, when she was just fifteen years old. She is famous for the diary she kept while her family lived in hiding for two years from the Nazi police, who were looking for Jewish families like Anne's to be sent to concentration camps and either put to work or killed. The time was World War II (1939–45), and Frank's diary was set in Holland, where her family had fled after the Nazis came to power in Germany. The Nazi police did, however, find the Frank family, and Anne died in a concentration camp about three months before the war ended. Her diary was found and published as *The Diary of Anne Frank.*

In the area of popular fiction, the war brought about several new genres. One was the military adventure novel, and another was the espionage or spy novel. Many of these spy novels featured the Russians (communists) as bad guys and the Americans (believers in democracy and freedom) as the good guys. One popular espionage writer was Helen MacInnes, who wrote several dozen novels during her career.

Another famous writer of this time was Flannery O'Connor, who was born in Georgia but whose novels were set in

Gwendolyn Brooks with one of her books of poetry.

II working in London. She immigrated to America in 1948 and was soon writing poems in American English. She is best known for her experiments with free verse (unrhymed poetry).

One of the most successful playwrights of this period was African American Lorraine Hansberry. Her play, *A Raisin in the Sun,* first appeared on stage in New York in 1959. It went on to become the country's first sustained (long-running) drama about black life.

The Women's Movement and Beyond

The publication of Betty Friedan's groundbreaking book *The Feminine Mystique* in 1962 is said to have launched the modern women's movement. Many people believe that the women's movement died a natural death after women won the right to vote in 1920. However, history shows that this is not true. As we have seen, women writers (and some men as well) continued to explore and challenge the role that women played in society. With Friedan's book came a vision and a voice. Women who read *The Feminine Mystique* readily identified with Friedan's description of a sense of emptiness and a loss of self that many women were experiencing. Friedan and other women who agreed with her were called feminists. These women believed that this emptiness was the result of women losing their identity as a sepa-

Tennessee. O'Connor, who died at the age of 39, wrote in a style known as Southern Gothic. Her short stories and novels featured dialogue written in the local dialect, as well as unusual characters and events.

Some of the better-known poets of this time include Sylvia Plath and Denise Levertov. Plath is most famous for collections of poems and her autobiographical novel *The Bell Jar.* She lived a short, unhappy life as the wife of English poet Ted Hughes and eventually committed suicide in 1962. Levertov, born of Welsh and Russian parents, spent World War

rate person in trying to be the perfect wife, mother, and homemaker.

Other writers soon embraced Friedan's idea. They wrote that women needed to pursue some of their own interests and pay some attention to their own emotional and intellectual needs. These ideas surfaced in political speeches, letters to newspapers, magazine articles, books, poems, essays, plays, and college textbooks.

However, not everyone was glad to see a woman's traditional role being so openly challenged. These people launched their own series of publications and vied for America's attention on the television news and in the print media.

The Writers

Gloria Steinem is a lecturer, writer, and editor of *Ms.* magazine. She was born in Toledo, Ohio, and is best known for her cofounding of *Ms.* magazine and her work with the National Organization for Women (NOW) and the National Women's Political Caucus. *Ms.* magazine is devoted to exploring issues from a female and feminist point of view. Steinem's essays tend to be political, pointing out instances of unfairness to women. She has said, "Feminism is the belief that women are full human beings; it's simple justice." Other women writing from a feminist point of view during this time were Kate Millett, Andrea Dworkin, Susan Faludi, Camille Paglia, and Erica Jong.

A Writer Who Helped Change The World

Sometimes writers act as social change agents, or they present new ideas and inspire people to rethink the status quo (how things are now). One female writer who acted as a change agent and helped shape American history was Ayn Rand, who published *The Fountainhead* in 1943. In it she introduced her philosophy, which she called objectivism. Objectivism is based on the ideas that the individual is the backbone of any society, that reason and reality are worth striving for, and that the government should impose few rules on how businesses are run.

Phyllis Schlafly told the other side of the story. Believing that women should retain their traditional roles within the home, Schlafly has published newsletters and given speeches at political meetings to deliver her message to the public.

Marge Piercy, a novelist from Michigan, writes from both a Jewish and feminist point of view. She has created Jewish characters, written historical novels, and has edited a poetry magazine. In the Hispanic community, some writers calling for women's rights are Sandra Maria Esteves, a poet, and Nicholasa Mohr, a novelist from New York City.

What Do We Learn From Fairy Tales?

Fairy tales are the favorite reading material of millions of American children. Aside from books, we meet and get to know these characters through movies and cartoons on television. Many of the stories are based on tales first written in Europe. The Brothers Grimm were writing in Germany in the early 1800s, while Hans Christian Andersen was writing in Denmark about the same time.

Fairy tales have plots, themes, characterization, and consequences, just as other forms of literature do. A close look at some of the more popular tales reveals that some of these messages may not be healthy ones for American children. For instance: In Disney's *The Little Mermaid* (based on the Hans Christian Andersen tale), Ariel gives up everything to be with Eric, the prince.

Ariel, a mermaid, sacrifices her entire identity, shedding her fins and growing lungs so she can live on land. She forsakes her family and friends in the sea. And remember, she does all this for a man she barely knows. What does Eric give up to win Ariel?

In *Beauty and the Beast,* a Disney film based on a Grimm tale, Belle is an outcast in her town. While she is beautiful, she is also bookish and independent, so the villagers are uncomfortable with her. The beast, on the other hand, appreciates her for her brains. At the end, however, she has been transformed into a fairy princess sort of heroine, all ball gown and elaborate hairdo.

Here is what one scholar said about the type of fairy tales that American children read:

The Contemporary Age

The Contemporary Age, for the purposes of this chapter, is defined as 1980 until the present. This period is characterized by the emergence of many voices, including many people of different cultures, whose writing has not been printed by the mainstream American press or read by many white Americans. The multicultural people represented here include Hispanic Americans, African Americans, Asian Americans, and Native Americans. Contemporary white women are also represented.

The Writers

Contemporary Hispanic Writers

In the 1980s, Arte Publico Press began publishing poetry by Evangelina Vigil of Texas and Chicago writers Ana Castillo and Sandra Cisneros. Arte Publico Press was founded to give Hispanic writers a chance to publish their works,

"What have the Grimm translations [into English] offered to North American children? Of the total of 210 stories in the complete edition, there are 40 heroines, not all of them passive and pretty. Very few translations offer more than 25 tales, and thus only a handful of heroines is usually included. Most of them run the gamut from mildly abused to severely persecuted. In fact, a dozen docile heroines are the overwhelming favorites, reappearing in book after book from the mid-nineteenth century to the present. Cinderella and Frau Holle succeed because of their excessive kindness and patience; Sleeping Beauty and Snow White are so passive that they have to be reawakened to life by a man; and the innocent heroines of "The Little Goose Girl" and "The Six Swans" are the victims of scheming and ambitious women." — from Kay Stone's article titled "Things Walt Disney Never Told Us," which appeared in *Women and Folklore,* edited by Claire R. Farrer and published in 1975.

Kay Stone identifies several types of women considered acceptable in fairy tales: beautiful, royal, white, kind, patient, and passive. She also shows how fairy stories have given us one of the most abused stereotypes in American culture, that of the wicked stepmother.

The next time you read a fairy tale or see a movie based on one, ask yourself: How does this story portray women and what messages am I getting about how to behave?

since many of them were still ignored by mainstream American publishers. Cisneros, possibly the most well-known Hispanic American female writer today, gained fame for her first novel, *The House on Mango Street.* She went on to write poetry and short stories. The U.S. government recognized her as a major new talent with two National Endowment for the Arts fellowships (which give an artist money to live on while she or he creates).

Other Hispanic American women writers of this time include Californian Helena Maria Viramontes, who wrote short stories, and New Mexico's Denise Chavez, a short story writer and playwright whose works includes the popular play *The Flying Tortilla Man.* Novelist Laura Esquivel is known among mainstream Americans for her book *Like Water for Chocolate,* which was written originally in Spanish and has been made into a movie. Teresa Palomo Acosta, a Texan, writes about Mexican Americans, cowboys, and the oral history of the area in which she grew up.

Contemporary African American Writers

Critics consider African American Toni Morrison one of the most important novelists of the twentieth century. Morrison published her first book, *The Bluest Eye,* in 1969 and received a Pulitzer Prize for fiction in 1988 for *Beloved.* In 1993 she became the first African American to be awarded the Nobel Prize for literature. Morrison's other works include *Sula, Song of Solomon, Tar Baby,* and *Jazz.* In her works she has explored how white (and black) perceptions of beauty have harmed black women. She also touches on the importance of ancestors and culture and writes about slavery, artistic expression, and rebirth.

Many other important African American women writers are publishing today. Alice Walker is an award-winning poet, novelist, essayist, biographer, short story writer, and lecturer. Her best-known work is *The Color Purple,* which was made into a movie. Jamaica Kincaid is probably best known for her autobiographical novel *Annie John.* Her later works discuss how white Europeans have exploited (used) the island nations in the Caribbean Sea. Poet Maya Angelou is famous for *I Know Why the Caged Bird Sings* and for the original poem she recited at the inaugural ceremony when Bill Clinton was sworn in as president of the United States in 1993. Angelou's themes include the search for identity, survival, courage, persistence, and the rebirth of innocence in the face of great obstacles. Poet Nikki Giovanni is known for her strong objections to racism and for her portrayals of the closeness of African American families.

One new genre to emerge in modern times is the African American romance. Kingston Publishers offers a line of books that center on romances between African Americans. The settings vary from modern times to the Civil War and the civil rights era of the early 1960s.

Contemporary Asian American Writers

Asian American writers working today include Maxine Hong Kingston, Amy Tan, and Jade Snow Wong. Kingston, the Chinese American daughter of immigrant parents, won the National Book Critics Circle Award in 1976 for her novel *The Woman Warrior.* In the work, which is actually an autobiography, Kingston describes how hard she worked to reconcile her Chinese heritage with American customs. Tan is best known for her novel *The Joy Luck Club,* which was also made into a movie, about the relationships of Chinese American mothers and daughters. Wong, who grew up in San Francisco's Chinatown, also writes autobiographical material about her life as a Chinese American growing up in a traditional Chinese household.

Contemporary Native American Writers

One of the most respected Native American woman writers today is Laguana Pueblo novelist and poet Leslie Marmon Silko. She is best known for her 1977 novel *Ceremony,* about the lives of World War II Native American veterans, and her 1991 novel *Almanac of the Dead,* in which she discusses how Native Americans were abused and oppressed by Europeans for over five hundred years. Chippewa poet and fiction writer Louise Erdrich has won many awards for her humorous portrayals of Chippewa life in North Dakota in such novels as *Love Medicine* and *The Bingo Palace.* Mary Crow Dog dictated her life story in the two books *Lakota Woman* and *Ohitika Woman.* In them she discusses her role in the American Indian Movement (AIM) and her life as a Sioux feminist living in a male-dominated white culture. Another Native American writer is simply called Starhawk. She writes in a genre called ecofeminism, which combines a concern with ecology and women's rights.

Contemporary Caucasian Writers

Among the white women writing in the United States today are mystery writer Marcia Muller, who was the first to introduce a professional female private investigator. Novelist Anne Rice is continuing the horror tradition with her series of novels about vampires, including the book *Interview with the Vampire,* which was made into a movie. Jean Auel has developed a wide readership for her

Maya Angelou's I Know Why the Caged Bird Sings.

novels about the Ice Age. Joyce Carol Oates is widely regarded as a major literary talent. She has written short stories, novels, and poems. Annie Dillard, who grew up near the Blue Ridge Mountains in Pennsylvania, wrote a book about the area and published it as *Pilgrim at Tinker Creek* in 1974. Barbara Tuchman, a historian, has concentrated on writing about domestic life in the Middle Ages. Author Tina Rosenberg has won a Pulitzer Prize for nonfiction, a National Book Award, and the Helen Bernstein Award for Excellence in Journalism for *The Haunted Land.* Playwright Wendy Wasserstein won a Pulitzer Prize for

Anne Rice is one of today's most popular authors.

drama for *The Heidi Chronicles,* a hit Broadway play.

Some of the best writers of children's books are women. They include fantasy writer Madeleine L'Engle, who is known for her young adult series that begins with the novel *A Wrinkle in Time.* Judy Blume is another popular young adult author. Critics and teachers alike give Blume high marks for her sensitive treatment of the teenage years. Younger children enjoy the exploits of Ramona and her friends in a series by Beverly Cleary. Lucille Clifton, a black woman born in New York State, writes about the strong women who head many black families.

Other Voices: Women Writers From Around the World

England

England has a rich literary tradition full of women writers. A few are profiled here.

Ann Radcliffe helped create the genre we know today as the romance. Her novels, written in the late 1700s, feature young girls, handsome young men, unlikely adventures, and a marriage at the end. Mary Wollstonecraft is famous for *A Vindication of the Rights of Women,* which was published in 1792. The classic of the women's rights movement of the 1800s, it explained the unjust treatment of women in law and by society. Wollstonecraft was the mother of another famous writer, Mary Wollstonecraft Shelley, who was married to the romantic poet Percy Bysshe Shelley. Mary Shelley founded the horror genre with the publication of her novel *Frankenstein* in 1818.

Jane Austen's novels of English country life and manners, written in the five-year period between 1811 and 1816, are still read and enjoyed today. Actress and screenwriter Emma Thompson received an Academy Award in 1996 for her film adaptation of Austen's novel *Sense and Sensibility.* Alicia Silverstone starred in *Clueless,* a modern film version of Austen's novel *Emma.* While Austen's work is considered classic (timeless), her imitators continue to use her style to create historical romance novels.

George Eliot (the pen name of Marian Evans) is considered one of England's greatest novelists. She wrote about people coping with change as England moved from a farming to an industrial society in the mid-1800s. Emily and Charlotte Brontë, writing in the mid-1800s, created another genre called the Gothic horror story. Emily's best known work is *Wuthering Heights* and Charlotte's is *Jane Eyre.* Both novels feature heroines lured away to distant castles where the lord of the manor has a dark secret.

Elizabeth Barrett Browning wrote in the mid-1800s, mostly about social causes. Today she is best known for her *Sonnets from the Portuguese,* a series of poems she wrote describing her deepening love for her husband, poet Robert Browning:

> How do I love thee? Let me count the ways.
>
> I love thee to the depth and breadth and height
>
> My soul can reach, when feeling out of sight
>
> For the ends of Being and ideal Grace . . .

Christina Rossetti published her first book of poems in 1862. She was the first woman to gain public acclaim for her long, narrative (storylike) poems. Some consider her England's finest woman poet.

Modern English women writers include the critic and essayist Virginia Woolf (1882–1941) and novelist Doris Lessing (b. 1919). Woolf is best known for her use of stream of consciousness technique, which brought the rhythm of poet-

Several of Jane Austen's novels have been adapted for the screen.

ry into prose writing. Some of her most famous novels are *Orlando* (which was made into a motion picture), *To the Lighthouse,* and *Mrs. Dalloway.* Lessing was born in Persia (now Iran) and grew up in Rhodesia (now called Rwanda). In her novels, Lessing explores the problems of black-white relationships, the idea of creativity, and the special concerns of women. Daphne du Maurier, with such novels as *Rebecca* and short stories like "The Birds," continued the Gothic horror tradition, and Mary Roberts Rinehart wrote novels that combined romance with mystery. Barbara Cartland, one of the bestselling

Women Detective Writers

Some of the bestselling writers of all time have been women who wrote detective fiction. England, for instance, has a long history of such writers. The "Golden Age" of detective fiction was between 1920 and 1945. Among the women writing at this time were:

- Dorothy Sayers, famous for amateur detective Lord Peter Wimsey and writer Harriet Vane

- Margery Allingham, famous for the mysterious aristocratic sleuth Peter Campion

- Josephine Tey, famous for police detective Alan Grant

- Agatha Christie, famous for Belgian private detective Hercule Poirot and sweet old Miss Marple

- Ngaio Marsh (a New Zealander originally), famous for police detective Roderick Alleyn and painter Agatha Troy

- Patricia Wentworth, famous for her elderly lady detective, Miss Silver.

Many critics feel that a second "Golden Age" is flourishing in England again. The modern mystery writers include:

- P. D. James, famous for police detective/poet Adam Dalgleish

- Anne Perry (who lives in Scotland), famous for Victorian-era police detectives William Monk and Thomas Pitt

- Elizabeth George (who lives in United States), famous for her aristocratic police detective who is also a member of British royalty

- Ruth Rendell, famous for her police detective Inspector Wexford, and for her nonseries suspense novels, which she writes under the name Barbara Vine.

authors of all time, is famous for her romances set in the early 1800s.

France

France has produced many women writers of note. Three are introduced here. George Sand was the name taken by Madame Amandine Lucile Aurore Dudevant, a novelist writing in the mid-1800s. She was a prolific writer and is considered one of the best novelists France has ever produced. She lived an unusual life, especially for her time. Although married, she took many lovers and frequently chose to live apart from her husband. Her novels depict life in the French countryside and are respected for their keen portrayal of human relationships.

Colette was a novelist who first published in 1900. Most of her novels dealt with women in love, their motives, and the moral consequences of their actions.

Simone de Beauvoir was writing in the 1940s and is best known for her book *The Second Sex.* In this work, Beauvoir criticizes Western culture as male-dominated and oppressive to women. *The Second Sex* served as a catalyst (start) for the modern women's movement in many countries, including the United States.

Asia

Indian women have been writing for centuries and even contributed to the sacred Hindu writings called the Veda. Among the more modern writers are Ruth Prawer Jhabvala and Anita Desai, both of whose works describe the tension that arises when Eastern (India) and Western (Europe) cultures clash. Novelists Kamala Markandaya and Nayantara Sahgal write about history, politics, and social change in India. Poet Kamala Das takes as a subject women's sexuality.

Anne Ranasinghe is a Sri Lankan poet who tries to reconcile her German ancestry with her Eastern heritage. (Sri Lanka is an island in the Indian Ocean off southeast India.) Chitra Fernando, another Sri Lakan writer, writes short stories, as does Yasmine Goonaratne, who published *Stories from Sri Lanka* in 1979.

In Japan, *Jogaku Zasshi, the Magazine of Women's Learning,* was published from 1885 to 1904. The magazine's goal was to encourage Japanese women to write and to publish. Next came *Nyonin Geijutsu,* which began publication in 1928. While this literary magazine was only published for five years, its purpose

Author George Sand

also was to suport the efforts of Japanese women writers. One of the first Japanese women to be published was Higuchi Ichiyo, who wrote in a realistic manner of the growth of a woman from adolescence to adulthood. Most Japanese literature of this time was written with a very formal, stylized technique. However, Ichiyo and her colleagues helped bring a more natural and modern voice to Japanese literature.

Alexandra David-Neel, a French woman, journeyed to Tibet around 1914. (Tibet is a historical region of central Asia between the Himalaya and Kunlun mountains and is a center of Lamist Buddhism.)

David-Neel was also ordained as a Buddhist lhama (priest). She wrote about her conversion to Buddhism, the beauty of Tibet, and the effect of the Sino (Chinese)-Japanese War on the area in 1937.

In China, Eileen Chang's *Rice Planting Song* was published in Taiwan in 1950. Her work foretold the harshness of life on mainland China under the communist leader Mao Tse-tung.

Middle East

Swiss writer Isabelle Eberhardt journeyed to Morocco in the late 1800s. When she found out how restricted women were in a Muslim society such as that in Morocco, she disguised herself as an Arab boy and wandered throughout North Africa. She later wrote about her adventures. American Elizabeth Warncock Fernea, the wife of an anthropologist working in the Middle East, observed the life and culture around her. Later, she wrote a book about her experiences called *Middle Eastern Women Speak,* that also describes the feelings of women in Iraq, Egypt, and Morocco. Nikki R. Keddie, an American scholar, has written about the revolution in Lebanon that began in 1973, the Iranian Revolution in 1979, and Shi'ism, a form of the Muslim religion. Egyptian Nawal El Saadawi is a medical doctor, novelist, and essayist who writes about the condition of women in the Middle East.

Africa

African writers include black and white women. Among the African writers of European descent are Isak Dinesen, which was the pen name of Danish baroness (noblewoman) Karen Blixen. She used a male name in publishing her stories because she felt a man's name gave her greater freedom as a writer. Her most famous book, *Out of Africa,* describes her adventures as a coffee planter in British East Africa (now Kenya). Dinesen's book was made into a movie starring Meryl Streep and Robert Redford.

Nadine Gordimer was born and raised in a white township outside of Johannesburg, South Africa, in 1923. At that time, South Africa was a strictly segregated society, with blacks and whites living in separate towns under a system called apartheid. For forty years, Gordimer used the short story format to speak out against racial oppression. Gordimer won a Nobel Prize for literature in 1991, a tribute to her life's work in helping to make the world aware of her country's segregationist policies.

The works of black African writers, including women, are gaining a wide readership. Pantheon Books has published an anthology (collection) of black African women authors called *Daughters of Africa, An International Anthology of Words and Writings by Women of African Descent from the Ancient Egyptians to the Present.* Among the more famous black African women writers is Obioma Nnaemeka, whose 1991 article "African Women Writers and Oral Tradition" discusses how women rebel against their traditional roles in African societies and how they try to cross cultural bound-

aries (from those of the European con-
querors to African tribal societies).

Australia

Australia's native people are called
Aborigines. The first white people to live
in Australia were British soldiers and
prisoners, since Australia was a penal
(prison) colony during the 1700s and
1800s. Gradually white society began to
expand from the ocean shores inward.
This background is the subject of much
Australian writing, both historic and modern. Daisy Bates wrote a moving book
in 1938 that she called *The Passing of
the Aborigines.* The book was based on her
thirty years of living with the Aborigines
in Nullarbor, a region of south-central
Australia. Catherine Langloh Parker collected the oral stories of the Aborigines into
a volume called *Aborigine Stories,* which
she published in 1896. Ada Cambridge,
Jessie Couvreur, and Rosa Praed wrote
about life on the Australian frontier.

Chile

Poet Gabriela Mistral published her
first work in 1914 and soon became a
well-known poet and diplomat to nations
such as Mexico, Spain, Italy, Brazil, and
the United States, and to the United
Nations. (A diplomat is a person who
represents his or her country to a foreign
government.) Mistral's later works included novels. She was awarded the Nobel
Prize for literature in 1945 in recognition of her work toward peace. The following excerpt from Mistral's poem

Danish-born author Isak Dinesen.

"Children's Rings" shows how she incorporates the theme of peace in her writings.

> Give me your hand and we shall dance
> Give me your hand and you will love me
> Together we will form a flower
> We'll be a flower and nothing more.
> We will sing the same song
> We will dance the same step
> We will wave like a grain stalk
> A stalk and nothing more.
> Your name is Rose and mine is Hope
> But you will soon forget your name
> Because we'll simply be a dance
> Upon the hill and nothing more.

Prominent novelist Isabel Allende
was born in Lima, Peru, but has lived
much of her adult life in Chile, where her

family held great political power. She worked for the United Nations and then as a newspaper columnist in Venezuela. Recently she has been working as a professor in the United States. Her novels, such as *The House of the Spirits* and *Of Love and Shadows,* focus on politics, language, and the racial tension produced by living in a dual culture (for instance, most of South America is ruled by people of European heritage while much of the native population is Indian).

Brazil

Clarice Lispector was born in the Ukraine but moved to Brazil when she was less than a year old. From about 1950 to 1975 she worked in Brazil as a lawyer, journalist, and editor. Her award-winning novels and short stories explore the female experience using tools such as monologues (long speeches made by one person) and stream of consciousness. Nelida Pinon, a journalist and university professor, is a novelist and short story writer who is known for experimenting with different styles and whose subject matter includes human relationships.

Argentina

Luisa Valenzuela is a journalist and a political activist who has worked with Amnesty International, a political organization concerned with people held prisoner because of their beliefs. She uses her novels and short stories to explore the relationship of gender, language, and

roles. Poet Maria Elena Walsh writes for children and adults. Her poetry is so lyrical that it has been set to music, becoming popular songs in Argentina. Her writing for children uses fantasy and humor, while her work for adults deals with human relationships.

Uruguay

Journalist and teacher Christina Peri Rossi has written award-winning short stories and novels, but she was forced to live in exile in Spain because the Uruguayan military government objected to her works. She has written about the social injustice in her country and about the need for free political expression.

Mexico

Rosario Castellanos was an upper-class woman who lived in the state of Chiapas along Mexico's border with Guatemala. She had served as the cultural director of the state of Chiapas and later as Mexico's ambassador to Israel. Her poems and short stories address the social and racial injustice suffered by the native people in Chiapas and the status of women in Mexican society.

Elena Garro was born in Puebla, Mexico, but lived in the United States, Spain, Mexico, and France. Her short stories, plays, and memoirs (life story), such as her award-winning *Recollection of Things to Come,* reflect on the passage of time and how it affects memory.

Canada

Novelist Carol Shields won the Pulitzer Prize for fiction in 1995 for *The Stone Diaries*. Shields, who was born in the United States, moved to Canada when she was 22 years old. Margaret Laurence, a novelist and short story writer, is known for her works set in Africa and her strong female characters who are the heads of their families. Margaret Atwood is a university professor who has written poems, novels, and children's books. Her most famous work is *The Handmaid's Tale*, a bleak picture of life in the future in which women have few rights. Alice Munro is a short story writer and novelist who explores the life of rural southwestern Ontario and the differences between country and city life in such works as *Dance of the Happy Shades* and *Something I've Been Meaning to Tell You.*

It is evident that no matter which country they're from, female writers, as a whole, will continue to be a strong force in the literary world. As new writers emerge, most will continue to use their talent as an outlet to make society aware of the constantly changing issues that women of the world must face.

19

Music

"Don't compromise yourself. You are all you've got."

—Janis Joplin, 1970s
rock 'n' roll star

Music and song are an important part of every human culture. They help people express feelings, such as joy at a wedding or sorrow at a funeral. Some music and song are part of rituals, such as religious services or royal coronations. Military music, especially that played by bands, may be used to evoke patriotic feelings. Songs, such as national anthems, become symbols of an idea or belief.

Women have always had an active role in singing, creating, and playing music. From the lullabies sung at the side of a baby cradle to the chants in convents, from the working songs of slaves to Broadway musicals, women have contributed much to the world's musical traditions.

This chapter describes some of those contributions. The first major section focuses on classical music and its singers, musicians, composers, conductors, teachers, and programs and schools. You will find information about female opera stars, as well as women who compose (write), perform, and conduct classical

Timeline: Women's Musical Contributions Through History

A.D. 800s Kasia of Byzantium (now Istanbul, Turkey) writes hymns that are still used today in the Byzantine (Eastern Orthodox) Church.

1100s Hildegard of Bingen, the abbess of a Roman Catholic convent in Germany, writes sacred music meant to be sung by the nuns under her care.

Mid-1600s Women singers become commonplace in operas and ballets in France.

1838 Jenny Lind, the "Swedish Nightingale," makes her operatic debut.

1896 Amy Marcy Cheney Beach becomes the first woman to have a symphony, *Gaelic Symphony,* performed in the United States.

1920s Bessie Smith, the greatest of the blues singers, creates a new type of sound called blues-jazz.

1931 Anne and Elisabeth Macnaghten and Iris Lemare found the Macnaghten-Lemare Concert Series to promote the work of other contemporary composers.

1939 Marian Anderson sings before the Lincoln Memorial after being barred from performing at Constitution Hall because she is black.

1960s Girl Groups are groomed and marketed through a one-stop production company in the Brill Building in New York City.

1971 Carole King's album *Tapestry* sells 14 million copies. It remains on the charts for 302 consecutive weeks.

1983 Ellen Taaffe Zwilich becomes the first woman to win a Pulitzer Prize for music. She is honored for her *Symphony No. 1.*

1987 Aretha Franklin, the "Queen of Soul," becomes the first woman inducted into the Rock and Roll Hall of Fame.

1996 Janet Jackson becomes the highest-paid female performer when Virgin Records offers her a reported $80 million to sign a new contract.

music. The second major section is on contemporary music, and it includes singers/musicians and composer/songwriters. Here you will find the women who have helped create and make popular music such as rock 'n' roll, jazz, country, and folk. There are also sections on some of the subgenres, such as gospel, rap, and salsa. Note: Broadway musicals are covered in Chapter 20: Dance and Theater.

History of Music

Ancient Civilizations to the Middle Ages

Dating from about 500 B.C. to A.D. 300, the music of the ancient Greeks and Romans is the earliest form of music from the Western world. Greek and Roman philosophers from this era believed that music originated with the gods, and that it reflected the laws of harmony that rule the universe. They also believed that music influenced humans' thoughts and actions.

As Western civilization developed, however, the musical form of the ancient Greeks and Romans was replaced by music from the Christian church. During the Middle Ages (500–1500) most professional musicians were employed by the church. Since the church objected to the paganism associated with the ancient Greek and Roman societies, it discouraged the performance of this type of music. As a result, a music form known as the chant developed in Europe. Chants are melodies unaccompanied by musical instruments that are usually based on sacred writings or prayers. From the fifth to the seventh centuries, these chants were used during specific times in church ceremonies. Not suprisingly, all but a few women were excluded from the musical aspect of the church—just as they were from other areas within it.

Beginning in the ninth century, however, musicians began to feel the need for a more elaborate musical form than the chant. Consequently, musicians began composing works that added as many as four voice parts that could be sung simultaneously with sections of the chants. These composers also began to reintroduce the use of musical instruments such as the lyre (a string instrument similar to the harp), the fiddle, the organ, and small bells and drums.

During the early fourteenth century, the French clergyman Philippe de Vitry introduced a major stylistic change in music. Called *ars nova,* or "new art," this style was characterized by the increasing attention given to secular (non-church) music. For the first time, major composers began writing both sacred and secular music.

The Baroque Era

The baroque period (c.1600–1750) of music began with Italy's first attempts at opera and ended with the death of composer Johann Sebastian Bach. The French term "Baroque" was given to a broad category of music. It includes opera, a drama in which all or part of the dialogue is sung, and which contains instrumental accompaniments. Composer Claudio Monteverdi greatly developed opera during the seventeenth century by using less intricate compositions than those used in ars nova. Opera is also the first genre to truly integrate various voices and instruments.

Additional musical genres originating during the baroque era include the cantata, the oratorio, and the sonata. Early cantatas were usually secular stories related by a solo singer through arias. However, as cantatas spread throughout Europe, they evolved into works that included several singers and sometimes a chorus. Oratorios are similar to cantatas except that they focus on a religious theme. This genre of music began in Italy, but became popular throughout Europe through the works of German-English composer George Frideric Handel, who composed the most famous oratorio, the *Messiah* (1741). The instrumental work known as the sonata had two forms in Italy, the first being a group of slow and fast dance movements, and the second being an abstract work in slow and fast sections. This second type of sonata became known as a "church sonata."

The Classical Era

The music of the classical period (c.1750–1825) emerged as the result of younger composers preferring a more spontaneous musical expression rather than the rigid music of the baroque period. Classical music is characterized by the balance between the content of the music and the form in which it is expressed. French, German, and Italian composers all made significant contributions to this period of music, although their styles took different forms. The French relied on nonmusical images, while the Germans played an important role in developing abstract forms such as the sonata and large instrumental genres, such as the concerto and symphony. Italian composers also contributed to new genres, especially the symphony.

Differentiated musical genres began to emerge during the classical period. As a result, chamber music became distinguished from symphonic music. Since about 1750, chamber music has been principally played by a string quartet (two violins, a viola, and a cello). Symphonic music, however, is a long and elaborate composition written for a large group of musicians who play together on various instruments including string, woodwind, brass and percussion. The most important composers of these genres of music were Franz Josef Hadyn, Wolfgang Amadeus Mozart, and Ludwig van Beethoven. These composers were part of a group that became known as the Viennese classical school.

Haydn's early symphonies and quartets became the first classical works of lasting value. His symphonies and string quartets greatly influenced the works of Mozart and Beethoven. Mozart is widely regarded as the greatest composer who ever lived. He began writing music at age five and by the time of his death thirty years later, had written over six hundred works. Mozart is best known for merging the styles of Italian and German composers and creating a style of music that summarized all the major developments of the classical period. He also composed operatic works that have never been surpassed. Although Beethoven began composing in the classical style, his later string quartet works began to fall into what would later become known as the romantic period in music.

The classical period is also characterized by two important developments. The first was the emergence and spread of public concerts, and the second was the liberation of musicians as independent artists. Female singers were taking advantage of these developments. It became commonplace after the classical period to see women performers.

The Romantic Period

Music of the romantic period (c.1820–1900) is characterized by the interest that composers took in setting romantic poems, novels, and dramas to music. Romantic music is different from its predecessors and successors in that it emphasizes colorful harmony and instrumentation, allows freedom and flexibility in rhythm and treatment of musical form, and contains long, expressive melodies.

Even though the Viennese classical style of music continued to be prevalent throughout Europe during the beginning of the romantic period, more adventurous composers began moving toward romantic elements rather than maintaining just classical ones. Some of these composers included German Johannes Brahms, whose works combined the best of both the classical and romantic schools, Polish composer and pianist Frederic Chopin, who is regarded by some as the greatest of all composers of piano music, and German composer Richard Wagner, who created an opera style known as music drama.

In this style all aspects of a work contributed to the central dramatic purpose. The compositions of this period along with those of the classical period became beautiful vehicles for female singers to display their talent.

The Modern Period

Although the music of the romantic period was characterized by individuality, this idea of personal expression in music has become more pronounced during the twentieth century. One example of this self-expression can be found in the musical genre of vaudeville, which became especially popular in the United States between the 1880s and the early 1930s. Vaudeville is a series of unrelated songs, dances, magic acts, and sketches performed on a stage. Famous performers during the vaudeville era included George M. Cohan, Harry Houdini, Eva Tanguay, W. C. Fields, and Fay Templeton. As radio, and later television, became popular after the 1930s, the number of vaudeville shows and entertainers began to decline.

Even though vaudeville eventually faded from the music scene, other genres began to emerge and continue to evolve during the twentieth century. These new musical genres, such as country, jazz, pop, blues, folk, rock 'n' roll, and rap, contain the notable features of twentieth-century music: originality, diversity, and rapid change. These new diverse forms have allowed women from all over the world to shine in all aspects and gen-

Words to Know

Alto: A low female voice that falls between a soprano and tenor.

Cabaret: Short programs of live entertainment presented in a restaurant.

Chamber music: Instrumental music played by two to ten players with one player for each part and all parts being equally important. After 1750, chamber music has typically been played by string quartets.

Classical instruments: Several types of instruments such as the harpsichord, piano, violin, cello, flute, and oboe used to make the music of the classical period.

Contralto: The lowest female singing voice, lower than a soprano and higher than a (male) tenor.

Gold record: Sales of one million recordings (songs) or 500,000 albums.

Harpischord: An instrument popular during the classical period of music. It resembles a piano, but has two keyboards and strings that are plucked by quills.

Mezzo-soprano: A woman's singing voice that is midway between soprano and contralto.

Oratorio: A large musical composition for voices and orchestra, telling a sacred story without the use of costumes or scenery.

Platinum record: Sales of two million recordings (songs) or one million albums.

Sacred music: Music, especially popular during the Middle Ages, that is based on scriptures or prayers and used during religious services.

Soprano: The highest female singing voice.

Stringed instruments: Musical instruments such as a guitar or violin that are played by plucking or striking tightly stretched strings.

Symphony: A long and elaborate musical composition in which several instruments play each part.

Quartet: A group of four musicians that perform a composition written for four voices or instruments.

Vaudeville: A series of unrelated songs, dances, magic acts, and sketches performed on a stage and popular during the early twentieth century.

res of music. Women such as Beverly Sills and Midori continue to bring classical music to audiences around the globe, while Janet Jackson, Alanis Morissette, and Tracy Chapman keep producing new styles of popular and folk music.

It is impossible to discuss all the women who have helped shape music over the centuries. Presented here are only some of those whose innovative work raised music—either classical or popular—to new levels.

Classical Singers

Classical music was really the first musical genre that allowed women to begin showing their talent, especially as singers. Compositions and operas from the great composers Mozart and Beethoven provided beautiful vehicles for European female singers to display their vocal ranges. In the United States, operettas, or "little operas," became the genre of choice for classical female singers. Operettas have many of the musical elements of an opera, but they deal with more popular subjects and contain spoken dialogue. Among the most famous are *Porgy and Bess*, the *Mikado*, and the *H.M.S. Pinafore*.

One of the earliest of the famous classical singers was Francesca Caccini, an Italian singer and composer who lived from about 1597 to 1640. Her first professional appearance was singing at the wedding of Henri IV, King of France, to Marie de' Medici. Caccini became a court singer in Florence, Italy, where she sang as she accompanied herself on the lute (a stringed instrument), guitar, and harpsichord (a keyboard instrument resembling a piano). Her opera, *La Liberazione di Ruggiero,* was played during the first opera season in Warsaw, Poland.

Sophie Arnould was a French soprano (the highest female singing voice) who lived from 1740 to 1802. She debuted with the Paris Opera in 1757 and was its lead singer for the next twenty years. She was an accomplished actress, a useful talent on the opera stage. Her wit made her a sought-after figure in Paris salons, the place where people such as writers, artists, and musicians meet for discussion and debate. As was true of many stars of her day, a nobleman she knew became her lover and financial protector. She had three children by him.

Italian soprano Brigitta Banti lived between 1756 and 1806. She began her career as a street singer but eventually went on to sing opera at the Paris Opera in France. She was immensely popular in Europe and became the principal soprano at the King's Theater in London, England, a job she kept until her retirement in 1802.

The Grisi sisters were famous Italian opera stars of the mid-1800s. Giudetta Grisi was a mezzo-soprano, and Giulia Grisi was a soprano. Giudetta retired in 1838, but Giulia played to audiences throughout Europe, Russia, and the United States until 1861.

Spanish mezzo-soprano Maria-Felicia Malibran lived from 1808 to 1836.

A poster advertising opera singer Jenny Lind in the starring role of La Somnambula.

During her short lifetime, her reputation rivaled that of many other divas (female opera singers) who lived much longer lives. She performed throughout Europe. Her sister, Pauline Viardot, lived from 1821 to 1910 and was also a famous mezzo-soprano.

Swedish soprano Jenny Lind remains one of the most famous voices of all time. She lived from 1820 to 1887 and began her career in vaudeville. After her operatic debut in 1838, she went on to perform with the Royal Opera in Stockholm, the Berlin Opera, Her Majesty's Theater in London, and many opera houses during a tour of the United States. After she retired from the stage, the "Swedish Nightingale" as she was called, taught singing at the Royal College of Music in London and helped her pianist-husband found London's Bach Choir.

Marietta Alboni lived in Italy from 1823 to 1894. This contralto made her debut in 1842 and was considered one of the best examples of classical Italian opera singers. She toured extensively throughout Europe and the United States.

German singer Lilli Lehmann was born in 1848 and performed on stage almost to the time of her death in 1929. Her soprano roles took her to the United States and to Covent Gardens in London. She premiered *The Ring,* Richard Wagner's famous three-part opera.

Australian soprano Nellie Melba lived from 1861 to 1931 and was famous for performing with opera companies in Paris, France; Brussels, Belgium; London; Milan, Italy; and New York City. Many of her recordings still exist and continue to be played on classical radio stations. The cracker called Melba Toast is named after her.

American singer Sissieretta Jones was born in 1869 in Virginia and died in 1933. Even though she had an opera-quality voice, she was performing at a time when opera careers were denied to African Americans. So Jones took her remarkable talent to music halls and theaters. This talent made her the toast of Europe, where she performed for royalty. At home in the United States, she was invited to perform for four different presidents. She was known as Black Patti, and she eventually formed a touring group called Black Patti's Troubadours. Her nickname was the result of a racist compliment she had been given by music critics who compared her style favorably with one of the best divas of the day, an Italian-American named Adelina Patti. Throughout her career, Jones refused to travel south of Louisville, Kentucky, saying that she had no interest in touring the segregated southern states.

American soprano Mary Garden was born in 1874 and studied singing in the United States and France. She is best known for her interpretations of the songs of the French composer Debussy. During her career, she premiered a number of new roles and was first the leading soprano and then the director of the Chicago Grand Opera. She died in 1967.

Lotte Lehmann was a German American soprano who lived from 1888 to 1976. She studied in Germany and then joined the Hamburg Opera. She performed in Austria, England, and the United States. Lehmann is best remembered for her roles in the powerful operas of Wagner and for her interpretations of the songs of Beethoven and German folk music (called lieder).

Norwegian soprano Kirsten Malfrid Flagstad lived from 1895 to 1962 and was famous for her singing roles in Wagner's operas as well. She performed in Norway until her 1935 debut with the Metropolitan Opera in New York City. She

later sang in England. After retiring from the stage, she directed the Norway State Opera from 1958 to 1960.

English soprano Joan Cross was born in 1900 and has become famous for working for many different opera companies. During her career, she also opened an opera school and produced several operas in England, Norway, the Netherlands, and Canada.

Maria Callas, considered by many the greatest dramatic soprano of modern time, was born in New York City in 1923 but moved to Greece in 1937. She became a Greek citizen in 1966. After making her operatic debut in 1947 in Verona, Italy, she had numerous engagements throughout Europe. Callas was famous for her ability to interpret her songs in a way that provoked great emotions in her audience. This ability led to her nickname, "La Divina" (the Divine One). She retired from the stage in 1965. In 1971 and 1972, she gave a legendary series of classes at the Juilliard School of Music, followed by recital tours in 1973 and 1974. Callas did in 1977.

Spanish soprano Victoria de Los Angeles was born in 1923 and studied music in Barcelona, Spain. She made her operatic debut in 1945 and has sung with the Metropolitan Opera. Her international engagements have taken her to Italy, Germany, and Argentina. She is known for the passion she brings to her interpretations.

Joan Sutherland is an Australian soprano who was born in 1926. She stud-

Marian Anderson

Marian Anderson, the great American contralto, was born in 1902 in Philadelphia, Pennsylvania. At its peak, her voice had a range of over three octaves. She is known for her performances of operatic, classical, and spiritual songs.

Anderson began singing in her neighborhood church at an early age to raise money for singing lessons. Her studies took her to New York City, where she won a prize that launched her professional singing career. She then toured Europe and finally made her American debut in 1936. Three years later, a storm erupted around Anderson after she was denied permission to perform at Constitution Hall in Washington, D.C. The Daughters of the American Revolution objected to Anderson's appearance at the hall because she was an African American. First Lady Eleanor Roosevelt supported Anderson, however, and arranged an alternate concert site in front of the Lincoln Memorial.

Anderson went on to sing at the White House in 1955. The same year, she made her official operatic debut at age 53 when she became the first African American singer to appear with the Metropolitan Opera, America's premier opera company. Throughout her career, Anderson refused to compromise her principles and always included black spirituals in her concerts.

In addition to her singing career, Anderson was interested in social rights. She supported the Civil Rights movement and became a delegate to the United Nations in 1958, representing the United States.

In 1991, Anderson was the subject of an hour-long PBS documentary. Typically modest, the singer was quoted as saying, "I hadn't set out to change the world in any way. Whatever I am, it is a culmination [end result] of the goodwill of people who, regardless of anything else, saw me as I am, and not as somebody else."

ied in Australia and England. After joining the opera company at Covent Garden in London, Sutherland went on to become an international star. Her repertoire, or songs she was prepared to perform, included Italian operas and the songs of the German-born composer, George Frideric Handel. She and her husband, pianist Richard Bonynge, have formed their own opera company in Australia but make Switzerland their home.

Leontyne Price, an internationally famous African American soprano, was born in Mississippi in 1927. She was the first black singer to reach international diva status and has helped open the operatic stage to younger African American performers. Her career began in the 1950s, and has since included world tours and releases of numerous critically acclaimed recordings. Through the mid-1990s, Price had earned 13 Grammy awards. She has been honored with a Lifetime Achievement Award from the National Academy of Recording Arts and Sciences, the group that bestows the Grammys.

Beverly Sills was born Belle Silverstein in 1929 in New York. This famous American soprano first performed at age three, singing for a radio program. She made her professional opera debut in 1947. In 1955 she joined the New York City Opera Company, where she sang leading roles for several years. She gained national fame in 1966 in the role of Cleopatra in Handel's opera *Giulo Cesare* (Julius Caesar). A series of international engagements followed, and she returned to the United States in 1975 to make her debut at the Metropolitan Opera. For ten years, beginning in 1979, she was director of the New York City Opera. In 1994 she was named the first woman chairperson of the Lincoln Center, the prestigious New York City arts complex.

Kathleen Battle is an African American soprano known equally for her world-class operatic voice and her temperamental ways. Her recordings have ranged from opera to blues and gospel songs. One of her earliest performances was at the famed Tanglewood in Massachusetts, where she sang with the Boston Symphony Orchestra. Critics applauded her voice, and her operatic career was launched. However, she is said to be a perfectionist, and her demanding ways have alienated more than one opera house. In 1994, she walked

American opera singer Leontyne Price in costume for her title role in Aida.

out of a performance four days before it was scheduled to begin. In 1995, she had been contracted to perform with the Metropolitan Opera in New York City, but her contract was terminated because she was difficult to work with.

Barbara Hendricks performs at Notre Dame Cathedral in Paris in honor of the late French president Francois Mitterrand.

New Zealand opera star Kiri Te Kanawa was born in 1944 and is of mixed European and Maori (New Zealand native) ancestry. She has performed throughout Europe and with the Metropolitan Opera in New York City. Kanawa has also published a book of the Maori stories and legends that she remembers from her childhood.

African American soprano Barbara Hendricks was born in Arkansas in 1948. She studied at the Juilliard School of Music and made her opera debut with the San Francisco Opera in 1975. Her credits include performing with the Metropoli-

tan Opera in New York City and the Berlin Opera in Germany. She has won numerous awards, released more than fifty recordings, and in 1988 appeared in the film *La Boheme* (which is based on Giacomo Puccini's opera). Hendricks has also served as a Goodwill Ambassador for the United Nations High Commission for Refugees, allowing her to visit many refugee camps in Africa and Asia.

Cecilia Bartoli, an Italian opera singer performing during the mid-1990s, has sold more than one million records in the United States. The recordings capture some of the glory of her famous voice, which has won her major performances, including those at the Metropolitan Opera House and Carnegie Hall. Bartoli has also won Grammy awards for her recordings. Other modern opera stars include Monserrat Caballe of Spain and Edita Gruberova of the Czech Republic.

Classical Musicians

Besides becoming singers of classical music, women also became instrumental performers. They proved that they were able to play classical instruments just as well as men.

Fanny Cacilie Mendelssohn-Bartholdy was a German pianist and composer who lived between 1805 and 1847. She was the sister of composer Felix Mendelssohn and was considered a child prodigy at the piano. Her compositions are for piano and voice. Some of her works, however, were mistakenly attributed to her more famous brother.

Clara Wieck Schumann was a German pianist, composer, teacher, and wife of composer Robert Schumann. She lived from 1819 to 1896, and was an extraordinary pianist. She toured throughout Europe and had gained an international reputation by the time she was sixteen years old. She married in 1840. After the birth of her eight children, Schumann resumed her concert career with the encouragement of composers such as Brahms and Chopin.

Teresa Carreno was a Venezuelan pianist who lived between 1853 and 1917. She spent most of her creative life in Germany. Carreno popularized some of the newer composers of her time, including Edvard Grieg and Edward MacDowell. While she is best remembered as a piano virtuoso (a musical performer of great ability or technique), she also performed in opera and as a conductor.

English pianist Myra Hess lived from 1890 to 1965. After winning a scholarship to the Royal Academy of Music in London, she made her professional debut in 1907. She is remembered for her interpretations of the piano music of Beethoven and Robert Schumann. During World War II (1939–45), Hess gave lunchtime concerts at the National Gallery in London because all the concert halls were closed. She organized other musicians and singers and was later given public recognition for her help in maintaining wartime morale.

Romanian pianist Clara Haskil lived between 1895 and 1960. She was born in Bucharest but gained her musical knowledge from study in France and Austria. An international performer, she was best known for her interpretation of the music of Mozart.

English violinist Anne Macnaghten was born in 1908 and became equally famous for her concert performances and her promotion of English concert music. She founded and performed with an all-female string quartet (foursome) in the 1930s. Her work was celebrated with the founding of the Macnaghten-Lemare Concert Series, which promoted her work and that of other contemporary English composers. The series has since been renamed the New Macnaghten Concerts and is a favorite place for launching new talent.

Australian pianist Eileen Joyce was born in 1912 in Tasmania, the island off the southeast coast of Australia. She studied music in Australia, Germany, and London. Joyce played with the London Philharmonic Orchestra during World War II, and later with major orchestras throughout Europe. She was known for her willingness to include modern music in her concerts instead of relying on the standard classical compositions most orchestras play.

American violinist Doriot Anthony Dwyer became the first woman to chair a major orchestra in 1952, when she was appointed the first-chair flutist with the Boston Symphony Orchestra. Dwyer has performed as a soloist and given many concerts in addition to her symphony performances.

French organist and composer Jeanne Demesieux lived from 1921 to 1968. She studied at several schools, including the Paris Conservatoire, from which she was awarded prizes for her playing. She made her public debut in 1946 and then toured Europe and the United States. Her compositions include six works for the organ.

English cellist Jacqueline DuPre was born in 1945 and studied at the Violoncello School and the Guildhall School of Music. In 1961, she made her debut in London, and went on to perform many duets with her husband, Daniel Barenboim. A special piece for cello and orchestra was written for her and she gave its first performance in 1968. She has since retired but continues to teach master classes (a class taught by an acknowledged leader in an art).

German violinist Anne-Sophie Mutter was born in 1963 and at age six was a noted prodigy. By the age of fifteen, she was playing with the major orchestras of Europe and making recordings. Mutter went on to become a major world talent as an adult.

Canadian cellist Ofra Harnoy was born in 1965 and has devoted her life to encouraging a broader audience for classical music. She now lives in suburban Toronto, Canada, the city that boasts billboards featuring Harnoy in decidedly nonclassical poses. She looks like a punk rocker, an image designed to coax younger listeners into investigating her music. An internationally acclaimed performer, Harnoy has played in Asia, the Middle East, and North America. She has won four Juno awards (Canada's equivalent of the American Grammy award) for best instrumental artist.

Midori is the stage name of a Japanese violinist who was born Midori Goto in Osaka, Japan, in 1971. Midori was a child prodigy who studied with Dorothy Delay at the Juilliard School of Music. She gave her first public performance at age six. Midori gained public acclaim at the age of fourteen with a performance at Tanglewood. As an adult, she has played with the best orchestras in the world, often performing the most demanding violin compositions. Today Midori continues with a demanding concert schedule (ninety performances each year) and a recording contract with the Masterworks series.

Classical Composers

One of the earliest known female composers was Kasia, who lived during the ninth century in Byzantium (now Istanbul, Turkey). She was a poet, hymn writer, and founder of a convent. Some of her hymns are still in use in the Byzantine (Eastern Orthodox) Church.

French composer Elisabeth-Claude Jacquet de la Guerre lived from about 1666 to 1729. A child prodigy, she began her career playing the harpsichord (a keyboard instrument resembling a piano). She became a court musician, earning an international reputation for her technical skill. Her compositions include works for the harpsichord and violin, as well as operas and choral pieces (songs performed by choirs).

Austrian Maria Theresa von Paradis was born in 1759 and died in 1824. She was a composer, pianist, organist, and singer. Von Paradis was blind from an early age, a disability that seems not to have interfered with her career. The first stage of her career saw her as a concert pianist and then a singer. Later, a special device was invented so she could write down her music. As a result of this invention, she entered the second stage of her

Violinist Midori

career as a composer. Her works include piano sonatas (a musical composition for one to four instruments, one of which is usually a keyboard instrument) and songs. She founded an institute for musical education in 1808 in Austria.

Norwegian composer Agathe Backer-Brondahl lived between 1847 and 1907. She was also a pianist and undertook several concert tours. She is best remembered for her songs, of which she wrote almost two hundred. They have become standard pieces in Norwegian classical singing.

Amy Marcy Cheney Beach was born in New Hampshire in 1867. She became the first woman to have a symphonic musical work performed in the United States. This momentous event took place in 1896, when the Boston Symphony performed her *Gaelic Symphony*. Beach had a long and distinguished musical career. She debuted as a concert pianist in 1883, but her real love was composing.

In 1892, Beach's *Festival Jubilate* was performed by a special orchestra of 120 musicians. The piece was written to celebrate the opening of the Women's Building at the World Columbian Exposition in Chicago. The same year, the oldest choral group in the United States performed her *Mass in E-Flat* and was accompanied by the Boston Symphony. The New York Philharmonic Society performed her concert aria (a solo vocal piece accompanied by instruments) *Eilende Wolken,* also in 1892. Beach toured Europe and in 1926 founded the Association of American Women Composers. At the time of her death in 1944, she had written 150 works, including songs and pieces for piano, opera, choral groups, and chamber music (music intended to be performed in a private room).

Germaine Tailleferre is a French composer best known for her modern scores. She was born in 1892 and became associated with a group of six French composers who moved away from the legacy of romantic music left by a previous generation of composers. She has written music for orchestra, musicals, and ballets.

Lili Boulanger, a French composer, lived between 1893 and 1918. During her brief life, she became the first woman to win the Prix de Rome, a prize given for the best musical composition, in 1913. Her piece was a cantata (a musical piece with solos for singing voices) titled *Faust et Helene*. During World War I (1914–18), she took time out from composing to nurse the wounded. Her works include choral pieces, orchestral works, and instrumental pieces.

South African composer Rainier Priaulx was born in 1903 and has written several works for string quartets. Priaulx has incorporated African native melodies into her music, which includes works for piano, voice, and dance.

English composer Elizabeth Poston was born in 1905. She gained fame when her music became part of the score for the film *Howard's End* (1992). Poston also published several books of holiday and folk songs.

English composer Elisabeth (Macnaghten) Lutyens was born in 1906 and studied music in Paris and London. She cofounded the Macnaghten-Lemare Concert Series, which promote the music of English pastoral (rustic) composers such as Benjamin Britten. Her interest in alternative music styles has persisted, and her technique is considered groundbreaking and influential for a later generation of composers. She has written more than 150 compositions, focusing mostly on chamber and stage works for musical theater.

Australian American composer Peggy Glanville-Hicks was born in 1912.

She studied music in Australia, England, and Austria. Her love is modern music and she has championed its inclusion in traditional orchestra repertoires. She has written operas, film scores, ballet music, songs, and instrumental music.

Rosemary Brown was born in England in 1917 and is a most unusual composer. Brown, who has little formal musical education, has produced more than four hundred works in the style of major composers such as Frederic Chopin, Franz Liszt, and Johann Sebastian Bach. She claims that the inspiration for her works came directly from the dead composers themselves and that she received their messages during trances.

Ruth Gipps is an English composer and conductor who was born in 1921. Early in her career, she was a concert pianist and played cello in orchestras. In 1950, she became choirmaster of the Birmingham Choir in England and then began to conduct in earnest. Her compositions include five symphonies and works for piano, violin, viola, horn, and choral pieces.

Swiss composer Tona Scherchen-Hsiao was born in 1938 to a Swiss-Chinese couple. She studied Western music in Switzerland and Chinese music and native instruments in China. She has also lectured and conducted in addition to writing prize-winning music for orchestras. In addition, Scherchen-Hsaio has experimented with using electronically produced music in her compositions.

Ellen Taaffe Zwilich was the first woman to win a Pulitzer Prize for Music.

 ## Window on the World: Greece

Eleni Karaindrou is a Greek composer best known for her musical scores of films and plays. She was born in the mountains of Greece and studied at the Hellenikon Odion, a famous Greek music school. She founded the Laboratory for Traditional Instruments and actively campaigns to preserve and publicize her country's musical heritage.

By the mid-1990s, Karaindrou had scored eighteen films, thirteen plays, and ten television series. One of her best-known movie scores was for *Ulysses' Gaze,* which won a Grand Jury Prize at the 1995 Cannes Film Festival in France.

She was honored in 1983 for her her *Symphony No. 1.* Zwilich was born in Florida in 1939. In 1975, she became the first woman to graduate from the Juilliard School with a doctorate in composition. In addition to composing, Zwilich is an accomplished musician who plays the violin, trumpet, and piano. She performed professionally as a violinist with the American Symphony Orchestra. She is the recipient of numerous composition awards, and among her works are three symphonies and eight concertos. Zwilich's compositions have been played by every major orchestra in the United States, and she is also well known abroad.

Shulamit Ran, who was born in Israel in 1947, first came to the United States in 1963 after winning a scholarship to the Mannes School of Music in New York City. The same year, Ran performed her own piano composition, titled *Capriccio,* with the New York Philharmonic Orchestra. In 1991 Ran became the first woman appointed as a composer-in-residence by a major U.S. orchestra. The honor was bestowed by the Chicago Symphony Orchestra, and Ran was expected to compose a full-length work as well as be responsible for the orchestra's educational programs. Ran also won a Pulitzer Prize for music for her *Symphony,* which premiered in 1990 with the Philadelphia Orchestra.

Classical Conductors

Many professionals in the music field consider conducting the last great challenge for women in classical music. Conductors lead an orchestra or group of musical performers. There have been women conductors, but they have been few and far between and tended to be regarded as oddities during their time.

Nadia Boulanger, a Frenchwoman who lived from 1887 to 1979, was one of the first well-known women conductors. She was also a teacher and a composer, although her written works do not rival that of her sister, Lili Boulanger. Nadia Boulanger won the second Prix de Rome

with her cantata *La Sirene* in 1908 but soon left composing in favor of teaching. She taught at the American Conservatory in Fontainebleau, France, and at the Juilliard School and several colleges in the United States.

In 1937, Boulanger became the first woman to conduct a symphony orchestra, in London. She followed that by becoming the first woman to regularly conduct the Boston Symphony Orchestra in 1938 and the New York Philharmonic in 1939. One of her greatest contributions was to help create a renewed interest in early musical forms such as madrigals. (A madrigal is an unaccompanied vocal composition for two or three voices in simple harmony.)

Sarah Caldwell was born in 1928 and was known as a child prodigy in mathematics and music. She gave concerts at age ten and had her own radio show when she was sixteen years old. Caldwell became a noted opera conductor and producer and founded the Opera Company of Boston in 1957. In the mid-1970s, she gained recognition as the first woman to conduct the Metropolitan Opera in New York City. Caldwell got the job only after Beverly Sills, a famous opera star, convinced the management to hire her. Once Caldwell broke the ice, other women began to conduct on a fairly regular basis. They include Judith Somogi, Eve Queler, Karen Keitner, and Laurie Ann Hunter.

Chinese conductor Zeng Xiaoying was born in 1929. Her early work focused on composing folk songs and operettas. She turned to conducting classes and orchestras and earned a scholarship to study in Moscow, Russia. After returning to China, Xiaoying became the principal conductor of the Central Opera Theater in Beijing in 1977.

We need only look to Simone Young as proof of the truth that conducting is the last barrier to fall to women. This woman, who is conducting today, has been "the first" in a number of areas. Young, who was born in Australia in 1961, specializes in conducting music for operas. She was the first to conduct at the Berlin Staatsoper in Germany in 1992. She was also the first woman to conduct at the Vienna Staatsoper in Austria, the Bayerische Staatsoper in Munich, Germany, and the Bastille Opera in Paris. In 1996, she made her American debut and became one of the few women to conduct the Metropolitan Opera (The Met) in New York City. She obtained a contract to work with the Met until 1998.

Young's many talents are being recognized, and she is scheduled at the major opera houses in Europe and the United States through 1999. Her repertoire includes more than sixty scores. Her talent with languages is especially valuable to someone involved in opera (many of which are written in French, German, and Italian). Young speaks those languages as well as Russian.

Classical Teachers

Wanda Landowska was a Polish teacher and player of the harpsichord (a forerunner of the piano). She revived interest in this instrument by founding a school in Paris around 1918. Landowska later added a concert hall where harpsichord pieces were performed. She continued to teach almost to her death in 1959.

Nadia Boulanger was one of the most famous teachers of musical composition in the twentieth century. She taught at schools and colleges in France and the United States, and she served as director of the American Conservatory in Fontainebleau, France. Among her pupils was the American composer Aaron Copland.

Dorothy DeLay is famous as the teacher of violin child prodigies at the Juilliard School of Music in New York City. She was born in Kansas in 1917 and earned several degrees in music. Delay has taught at many schools and has offered master classes in the United States, Europe, Asia, Africa, and the Middle East. An award-winning teacher and essayist, Delay has also conducted workshops at the music festivals in Aspen, Colorado.

Contemporary Singers and Musicians

By the late 1800s, many creative people working in the world of arts and literature had begun to rebel against what they saw as the rigid formulas or recipes in which their work was produced. Writers such as James Joyce, Mark Twain, and Gertrude Stein began to write novels that used dialect and followed their characters' thought processes. Artists such as Vincent van Gogh, Pablo Picasso, and Mary Cassatt experimented with portraying the world in abstract shapes instead of realistically. They also learned to paint light sources in new ways. Musicians were also flexing their creative muscles. They experimented with atonality (off-key sounds), incorporated new and native instruments into their compositions, and wrote songs with themes about social justice and the rights of workers, blacks, and women. They wrote in a variety of genres, ranging from folk music to rock 'n' roll to rap.

Folk

Folk music and songs are usually old, are rarely written down, and may be anonymous (by an unknown writer). They are the songs and tunes that grow up around a culture as it develops. American folk music is a blend of the songs of many of the early immigrants, including the English, Irish, and French. The songs also show the influence of African slave chants, New England whaling songs, French Cajun holiday music, and Native American songs.

Lucy McKim Garrison was the first woman to collect and document slave songs, a task she carried out between 1861 and 1867. Garrison was born in Pennsylvania in 1842 and died in 1877. During the U.S. Civil War (1861–65), Union (Northern) forces captured the Sea Islands off the North Carolina coast. Garrison's father

was a soldier stationed there. She lived on the Sea Islands with him, and spent her time listening to, writing down, and learning the history of the slave songs she was hearing. She published *Slave Songs of the United States* in 1867.

Elizabeth Cotten was born in 1892 in North Carolina. Some of her early exposure to folk music came when she worked as a maid for the family of Pete Seeger, considered by many to be the father of modern American folk music. She began performing at age sixty, singing "Freight Train" while accompanying herself on guitar. She had written the song when she was twelve years old, and it became an instant hit. It is now a standard in many folk singers' repertoires. She recorded several records before her death in 1987.

Odetta Holmes was born in 1930 in Alabama and is known simply by the stage name "Odetta." She played a major role in the folk music revival of the 1960s. Her folksy blues songs are accompanied by an acoustic guitar (a guitar that does not feature electronically modified sound). Odetta has played throughout the United States and Canada, including performances at the prestigious Newport Folk Festival in Rhode Island and the New Orleans Jazz Festival. She has also performed in musical theater and in films.

Judy Collins was born in 1939 in Seattle, Washington. She is known worldwide for her soprano renditions of folk and popular songs. Her biggest hit was the song "Both Sides Now" (written by Joni Mitchell), but by the mid-1990s, she had

Window on the World: Ireland

Women of Ireland often produce music influenced by traditional Celtic (Irish folk) music. Folk music is the common music of people passed down from person to person.

Mary Black is a native of Dublin, Ireland, whose music is a blend of pop, jazz, and traditional Celtic music. She is one of the artists featured on the best-selling album ever produced in Ireland: *A Woman's Heart, Volume 1*. This record and *Volume 2* include songs by Black and other famous Irish women singers, such as Maura O'Connell, Eleanor McEvoy, Sharon Shannon, and Frances Black.

One of the most visible native Irish singers carrying on the Celtic tradition is Dolores O'Riordan, the lead singer of the immensely popular rock group the Cranberries. The group's first album, *Everybody Else Is Doing It, So Why Can't We?*, sold two million copies after its release in 1993. They produced a second album, *No Need to Argue*, in 1994. O'Riordan, who was 23 when *No Need to Argue* came out, weaves Irish poetry, melodies, and bits of song into her own compositions. She is a social critic, one whose songs have described the political violence in Ire-land, drug use among teens, and the war in Bosnia. The group's third album is titled *To the Faithful Departed.*

Sinead O'Connor's name has become synonymous with good music and controversy. Born in Dublin in 1966, she released her first album in 1987 and won critical acclaim for her alternative pop/folk/rock style. But she lost the respect of many older fans when she tore up a picture of the pope, the leader of the Roman Catholic Church, on national television, argued publicly with her mother, and made an angry attack on Frank Sinatra. (O'Connor has since apologized for her attack on the pope.) In an interview she has claimed that her anger stems from the influence the Roman Catholic Church has on Irish social policy, especially the country's strict laws against divorce, birth control, and abortion, which she claims are "anti-woman."

Women of Irish ancestry who are integrating Celtic music into their own works include Englishwoman Emma Christian, American Connie Dover, Australian Maireid Sullivan, and Canadian Loreena McKennitt.

Window on the World: Japan

Both Japanese vocalists and singers from other countries perform with the chorus called Tokyo International Singers. Since it was founded in 1980, the group has given more than fifty concerts each year. It performs great choral works during the year and lighter music at its summer concerts.

Through Tokyo International Singers, Japanese members are provided with the opportunity to perform choral works not usually done in Japan. They also get the chance to work with foreign conductors. Through their performances, the members of the group have a chance to meet, share interests, and form friendships with other members from Europe, North America, Africa, and elsewhere in Asia through their love of music.

Among the Japanese singers associated with Tokyo International Singers is soprano Michiko Yuri. Yuri was born in Nagoya and graduated from the Tokyo National University of Fine Arts and Music. She has performed operatic roles, held recitals, and conducted the Mine no Kai women's choir. Alto singer Namiko Tanaka graduated from the same university. She has performed in numerous oratorio solos and concerts, as well as in operas in Europe and the United States.

Pianist Akemi Watanabe is the principal accompanist for Tokyo International Singers. She has studied at the Toho Music University and the Vienna Academy in Austria. Her repertoire ranges from jazz to folk and classical.

---

also released twenty-three albums, many of which have gone gold or platinum. By the late 1960s, Collins was a major figure in American folk music. Like many other folk musicians, she mixed politics with music. She was an anti-Vietnam War protester and a civil rights activist. Her albums moved from traditional folk ballads (romantic or sentimental songs) to include new antiwar songs and civil rights anthems, along with folk tunes from various foreign countries. Among her later works are *Voices,* a multimedia project, and a 1995 book titled *Shameless,*

a novel she wrote to help her cope with the 1992 death of her son.

Helen Reddy was born in Australia in 1941 and is best known for her rousing rendition of "I Am Woman," a song she wrote with Ray Burton. When it was released in 1972, it sold more than one million copies, 80 percent of which were purchased by women. Reddy won a Grammy award for the song in 1973, and in her acceptance speech she thanked God "because She makes everything possible." The song became the anthem of the feminist movement of the 1970s. Although Reddy produced a string of hits throughout the 1970s, she has recently concentrated on social issues such as feminism and environmentalism and occasionally performs at clubs and conventions.

Singer-songwriter Buffy Sainte-Marie was born on a Cree Indian reservation in Western Canada in about 1942. She was adopted by a white family and only rediscovered her Native American heritage as a teenager. The discovery affected her dramatically as a person and as a singer. Sainte-Marie was interested in music from an early age, and she began to include Native American rhythms and instruments in her act. She went to New York City in the early 1960s and soon became a regular on the folk music scene there. By 1965 she was playing Carnegie Hall and doing concert tours in the United States, Canada, and Mexico. When the folk music revival faded in the 1970s, Sainte-Marie broadened her musical style. She released albums in which her songs were backed by string ensembles, country musicians, and hard rock bands. She won a Grammy award for her song, "Up Where We Belong."

Joni Mitchell was born in Canada in 1943 and, according to the *New Rolling Stone Encyclopedia of Rock & Roll,* "is one of the most respected singer/songwriters in rock [and] one of its most daring and uncompromising innovators." Mitchell's popularity peaked during the folk music revival of the 1970s. However, she has obtained current popularity with her combination of folk music and jazz works.

Singer Helen Reddy

Many of Mitchell's albums have gone platinum or gold. In her current style, she has collaborated on composing with jazz great Charles Mingus. Her other collaborators have ranged from country singer Willie Nelson to rocker Tom Petty and punk rocker Billy Idol. Mitchell has won numerous awards. Her creativity extends to coproducing her albums, as well as to painting (she designed her early album covers) and photography.

Suzanne Vega was born in 1959 in California and grew up in a neighborhood called Spanish Harlem in New York. She is best known as one of the catalysts of a folk music revival in the mid-1980s.

Joan Baez

In the 1990s, Joan Baez is almost as well-known for her political activism as for her folk singing. But in the 1960s, she was dubbed the "Queen of Folk Music," and music critics praised her crystal-clear soprano. Over the years Baez has given unflagging support to such political causes as the Civil Rights movement, the Farm Workers' movement, the anti-Vietnam War effort, and the freeing of political prisoners.

Baez was born in New York City in 1941, the daughter of a Mexican physicist and a Scottish American English teacher. She was raised as a Quaker, a religion that believes strongly in nonviolence. She began playing the guitar and singing in high school. After the family moved to Boston, Massachusetts, Baez began to play in the many folk music coffeehouses there.

Baez's professional debut came in 1959, when she appeared at the well-known Newport Jazz Festival in Rhode Island. She released her first album, titled *Joan Baez,* in 1960. By 1962, she was famous enough that *Time* magazine did a cover story on her.

Baez's specialty was interpreting the songs brought to America by immigrants over hundreds of years. She sang the Irish lament "Danny Boy," the Appalachian "River in the Pines," the Scottish "Barbara Allen," and American classics such as Stephen Foster's "I Dream of Jeannie With the Light Brown Hair."

Baez's politics intertwined with her music by the mid-1960s. She did a concert tour through the southern states, playing only at black colleges as a protest against

A singer-songwriter, Vega pioneered a folk genre known as technofolk rock. The style combines folk, rock, and computer-generated electronic dance music. Her breakthrough song, "Luka," a ballad about an abused child, came in 1987. She also scored the film *Pretty in Pink* (1986).

Tracy Chapman, an African American born in Cleveland, is a singer-songwriter. She broke into the recording industry in the mid-1980s and released *Tracy Chap-*man in 1988. The album became a number one international hit, with sales of $3 million in the United States and $6.5 million overseas. Chapman also earned two Grammy awards in 1988, one for best new artist. By the mid-1990s, she had released another two albums, both of which were praised by critics.

One of the newest talents on the folk music scene is singer/guitarist Mae Moore from Vancouver, Canada. Her

racial discrimination. She joined marches led by Martin Luther King Jr., the prominent leader of the Civil Rights movement. Soon she was protesting the involvement of American soldiers in the war in Vietnam. Her version of "We Shall Overcome" became the rallying cry for both the Civil Rights and anti-war movements. Baez founded the Institute for the Study of Non-Violence in California in 1965.

As rock 'n' roll captured the interest of young Americans, Baez drifted from folk music to try out other styles. She recorded country, rock, and Spanish-language songs. Her career hit another high note in 1975 with the release of the album *Diamonds and Rust*. In 1979, she cofounded Humanitas, the International Human Rights Committee, which was dedicated to nonviolence and an end to war. In 1985, she sang at a Live Aid concert to fight world hunger. Twice she sang at benefits to raise money for Amnesty International, a group dedicated to freeing political prisoners.

Baez made a musical comeback in the 1990s, becoming popular with a new generation of fans. She released her *Play Me Backwards* album in 1992 and received critical acclaim for it. By 1994, she had released a total of thirty albums, eight of which became gold records.

Baez's political activism has continued during the revival of her musical career. In 1993, she left a concert tour to play and sing in Sarajevo at the height of the war in Bosnia. In addition to her music awards, she has won numerous awards for her human rights work.

debut album, *Bohemia,* was released in 1992, and she followed up with an equally acclaimed release, *Dragonfly,* in 1995. Moore blends folk with jazz, rap, storytelling, and poetry to produce a unique brand of music.

Jazz, Blues, Rhythm and Blues

Jazz is an American music form that developed in the early part of the twentieth century. It evolved from African rhythms and slave chants and eventually spread from its African American roots to a worldwide audience. Blues is a type of popular music evolved from southern African American songs. It is usually distinguished by its slow tempo (beat) and woeful lyrics. Blues laid a foundation for the development of rock 'n' roll, rhythm and blues, and country music. Rhythm and blues evolved after World War II (1939–45). A combina-

African American singer Bessie Smith

tion of jazz and blues music, it retains an emphasis on vocals while also adding a strong simple rhythm.

It is interesting to note that most of the famous jazz, blues, and rythm and blues female (and male) singers are African American. This is not surprising, considering the source of the music. Jazz blends African rhythms with American pop songs. The blues was born during a time of segregation in the Deep South. Rhythm and blues was the black culture's blending of familiar blues sounds with the new sounds of rock 'n' roll.

The "mother of the blues," "Ma" Rainey was born in 1886 and died in 1939. She released a number of blues and pop recordings with some of the most famous backup musicians—guitarists, trumpeters, and piano players—of her era. She took her act on tour, and some of the famous names of the next generation got their start in "Ma" Rainey's show.

In 1889, American jazz singer Ida Cox was born in Georgia. Like most jazz singers, this African American star honed her skills in the local church choir. Her career included singing the blues and jazz in nightclubs and then touring with her band. She died in 1967, shortly after making her final recordings with a backup band made up of some of the nation's top jazz players.

Alberta Hunter was born in Tennessee in 1895 and died in 1984. This African American jazz singer, composer, and actress played in nightclubs, released recordings, and entertained the troops during World War II. Her international tour sites ranged from London to Turkey and Denmark.

Bessie Smith, whose style influenced the next several generations of blues singers, was born in Tennessee in about 1894 and lived until 1937. She was the first singer to blend folk-style music with jazz to create her own particular brand of music, called blues-jazz. During her short life, she toured with "Ma" Rainey's traveling show and became a recording sensation in New York City. Her debut song, "Downhearted Blues," sold two million copies and she became known as the "Empress of the Blues." Smith, with her rich contralto voice, was backed up by the best known jazz musicians of the day, including Louis Armstrong and Benny Goodman. She died prematurely at age 39 when her tour bus crashed in Mississippi. Some believe that racism helped kill Smith, because she was denied entry into an all-white hospital close to the crash site and had to be rushed to a black hospital some distance away. Smith was inducted into the Rock and Roll Hall of Fame in 1989.

Lil Armstrong was an African American jazz singer and pianist who was born in Memphis, Tennessee, in 1900. She worked with several groups before forming the first of several jazz bands in 1920. She was briefly married to Louis Armstrong, the legendary trumpet player, and made several recordings with him. She died in 1971 after a career that included playing both European and U.S. jazz clubs.

African American jazz singer Ethel Waters was born in 1900 in Pennsylvania. She had her early musical exposure through her church and went on to become a well-known performer and recording artist in the United States. Waters also appeared in films, music theaters, and cabarets (nightclubs).

African American singer Eleanora "Billie" Holiday was a legend during her lifetime (1915–1959). She was born in Baltimore, Maryland, and began singing professionally in 1931. She was soon recording with Benny Goodman, Count Basie, and Artie Shaw, three of the biggest band leaders of the 1930s. Holiday also had a solo career, singing in nightclubs, and making several films. Her career took her on tours of the United States and Europe, but she could not shake her unhappy childhood. She died a heroin addict, at age forty-four, ending a thirty-year music career.

Ella Fitzgerald was one of the most famous of the female jazz singers and was popularly known as the best of a talented group of jazz singers in the big band era (1920–50). The African American singer was born in Virginia in 1918, but was brought up in an orphanage in New York. She won a talent contest at age sixteen, and went on to become a cabaret (nightclub) singer famous for her "scat singing" technique. (Scat singing is where improvised syllables are sung to a melody.) Her tours took her throughout the United States, Europe, and Japan. Fitzgerald's recordings were done with the best jazz musicians of the day, including Duke Ellington, and all the famous songwriters such as Cole Porter and George Gershwin. Her singing earned her thirteen Grammy awards during her career, which continued until her death in 1996. She was also honored with a Lifetime Achievement award from the National Academy of Recording Arts and Sciences, the group that bestows the Grammys.

African American singer Sarah Vaughan was born in 1924 in New Jersey, and attended the Arts High School in

Billie Holiday

Newark. She had her start singing in a church choir. In 1943, Vaughan went on to win a talent contest at the Apollo Theater in Harlem (a famous black neighborhood of New York City). She sang "Body and Soul," accompanying herself on the piano.

She was "discovered" during the week-long engagement that followed. Over the next nearly fifty years, her jazz singing earned her the nickname "The Divine" Sarah Vaughan. She won many awards for her singing and recordings.

Cleo Laine was born Clementina Dinah Laine in 1927 in England. This famous jazz and pop singer, is best known for her cabaret performances. She has also performed opera and in concerts and on television. Laine holds the record for the highest note ever recorded by a human voice.

Ruth Brown was born in Virginia in 1928 and launched her singing career after winning an amateur night contest at the Apollo Theater in Harlem. Her career spans more than five decades, and she was still performing in the mid-1990s. Early on, Brown worked in nightclubs and television, and released several recordings. In 1988, in the latter part of her career, she was the subject of a PBS documentary titled *That Rhythm, Those Blues.* The next year, she won a Tony (theater) Award for her performance in the musical *Black and Blue* and a Keeping the Blues Alive Award. In 1990, her album *Blues on Broadway* earned a Grammy award for best jazz vocal performance by a female. In 1993, she was inducted into the Rock and Roll Hall of Fame. Brown has also received numerous awards from African American organizations for being a good role model.

Nina Simone was born in 1935 in North Carolina and has had a very successful career as a singer and a pianist. As an African American, she combines jazz, African folk, blues, gospel, and pop music into her performances. She studied at the Juilliard School of Music in New York City and hoped to become the first black classical pianist. Simone has always felt that racism kept her from achieving her dream. She became active in the Civil Rights movement and later, the militant Black Panther Party. Her politics alienated her more moderate listeners, and Simone's nightclub career faltered. Simone staged a comeback in 1993 with the release of her album *Single Woman.*

The four members of the Shirelles, a popular African American quartet, were born in New Jersey in the early 1940s. The singers (Shirley Alston, Addie Harris, Doris Kenner, and Beverly Lee) formed their group while in high school. They released their first professional recording in 1958, and the song "I Met Him on a Sunday" was an instant hit. It was written by the team of Carole King and Gerry Goffin, who would continue to write songs that the Shirelles would turn into hits. The quartet's style of rhythm and blues earned them three gold records and numerous music awards.

Aretha Franklin, "Lady Soul" or the "Queen of Soul," is one of the best rhythm and blues singers of all time. This African American singer was born in Tennessee in 1942 and started singing in the choir at her father's Baptist church in Detroit, Michigan. She began to sing professionally at age eighteen but did not release her first recording, "Never Loved a Man," until 1966. After that, it was a string of hits in genres ranging from rhythm and blues to jazz and gospel music. During her career, she has recorded more than forty albums and played to audiences throughout the United States and Europe. Franklin has won numer-

Window on the World: Africa

Tanzanian singer Said Tatu was born in 1949 and has become famous under the stage name "Shakila." Her repertoire includes French, patriotic, and native songs. She has toured extensively throughout Africa.

Sade, a Nigerian singer and songwriter, was born Helen Folsade Adu in 1959, and has become popular for her jazz and soul music. By 1983, she had moved to London, England, and formed her own jazz group, which she called Sade (pronounced Shar-day). One of her best known hits, "Smooth Operator," sold millions of copies worldwide.

ous music awards, including, by the mid-1990s, fifteen Grammys. She has also been honored with a prestigious Living Legend Award from the National Academy of Recording Arts and Sciences, the group that bestows the Grammys. In 1987, Franklin became the first women to be inducted into the Rock and Roll Hall of Fame.

Anita Baker was born in 1958 in Ohio but grew up in Detroit, where she still makes her home. This African American singer-songwriter-producer released her first solo album, *The Songstress,* in 1983. The record sold 300,000 copies and remained on the black music charts for more than a year. The album launched her into recording, performing, and making concert tours. Baker released *Giving You the Best That I Got* in 1988, an album that sold more than three million copies. In 1989, she performed at the inauguration of President George Bush and at the Montreux Jazz Festival in Switzerland. By the mid-1990s, she had won seven Grammy awards in the jazz, rhythm and blues, and soul categories.

Another generation of singers was born in the early 1970s in New York City. They are SWV or Sisters with Voices, a rhythm and blues trio that includes Cheryl Gamble, Tamara Johnson, and Leanne Lyons. This African American trio formed in 1990, signed with RCA records, and produced the hit song "Right Here." The song broke into the Top 100 on Billboard's singles charts and made the Top 20 in the rhythm and blues category. The group then produced a follow-up hit, "I'm So Into You," and their songs have continued to appear regularly at the top of the rhythm and blues chart. SWV's debut album, *It's About Time,* appeared in 1992, and they have since become regulars on the rhythm and blues concert circuit. In 1993, they were headliners at the Budweiser Superfest, the United States's longest-running rhythm and blues festival.

One of the newest faces on the jazz scene is Cassandra Wilson, who has gained a large following for her unorthodox style of jazz singing. Wilson, an African American, was born in Mississippi and traveled to New York City in 1982 to launch her career. In 1988, her song "Blue Skies" made it to the pop charts. However, Wilson has resisted being pigeonholed as a pop singer. She blends the soulfulness of rhythm and blues with a unique type of phrasing and improvisation, both standard elements of jazz. Her first album, *Blue Light 'Til Dawn,* appeared in 1993, and she released *New Moon Daughter* in 1996. This album mixes jazz improvisation, classic Southern blues, avant-garde (new) vocal techniques, and rural folk music sounds.

Country

Country music is based on traditional folk melodies of the British immigrants who came to America. Country music originated in the rural communities of the Appalachian Mountains and continues the British tradition of using string instruments, especially the fiddle. Bluegrass is an early type of country music that gained its own identity in the mid-1940s. It is a combination of country, jazz, blues, gospel, and Celtic folk music.

One of the most enduring country singers was Patsy Cline. She was born in Virginia in 1932, and entered the country music industry at a time when it was still dominated by male singers, but she helped pave the way for other women singers. Cline's career began when she won an amateur contest at age four and sang in the church choir. In 1948, she traveled to Nashville, Tennessee, the home of country music, to appear on radio. Cline began recording in the late 1950s and

soon became famous for her country style of singing, which added pop sounds and was backed by light jazz orchestrations. She died in a plane crash in 1963, but remains a major influence for many young female country and western singers.

Dottie West was born in Tennessee in 1942, and in 1964 she became the first female vocalist to win a country music Grammy award. Her song was "Here Comes My Baby." West's biggest hit was the 1974 release "Country Sunshine." She wrote more than four hundred songs before she was killed in a 1991 automobile accident.

Loretta Lynn was one of the first of the female country singers to hit the big time. She was born Loretta Webb in 1935 in Kentucky. When she was fourteen years old, she married Oliver "Moonshine" Lynn and the two endured a stormy marriage. After the birth of her four daughters, Lynn formed a band and released "Honky Tonk Girl" in 1960. The song was an instant hit, and Lynn has never looked back. Lynn's socially conscious songs are unusual in a musical genre that focuses on traditional relationships. She has protested the Vietnam War (1954–75), discrimination against African and Native Americans, and the submissive role that women have played in romantic relationships. She now lives in Tennessee, where she spends her time managing her huge music empire. Her autobiography, *Coal Miner's Daughter,* was made into a hit Hollywood film in 1980. Alana Nash, who wrote a biography of Lynn, calls her, "one of the most important stylists—and arguably the most suc-

k.d. lang

cessful traditional female star—in the history of country music."

Tammy Wynette, considered one of the major voices in country and western (male or female), was born in 1942 in Mississippi. Her recording career began when she worked to pay her child's medical bills. The result was a hit song titled "Apartment No. 9," which appeared in 1966. Wynette became famous for her traditional country themes of the wronged woman who remains strong in spite of abuse. She had a number of hits and sang duets with her husband, George Jones, with whom she had an abusive relationship. Her first *Greatest Hits* album remained at the top of the bestseller charts for more than a year in 1969 and earned her more than $1 million. Two other *Greatest Hits* albums and other works have followed.

Dolly Parton was born in 1946 in the Tennessee foothills and was performing by age ten. By the mid-1960s, she had become a professional singer with two recordings to her credit. After several years as part of a duet, she launched a solo singing career. Parton has become one of the best loved of the country stars to play at the Grand Ole Opry in Nashville. She is famous for her big hair, large bosom, and flair for comedy. She has toured, performed on radio and television, and appeared in Hollywood films, including *9 to 5* (1980), *Steel Magnolias* (1989), and *Straight Talk* (1992).

Among a newer generation of country singers is Kathy Mattea, who was born in West Virginia in 1959. By 1996, she had won two Grammy awards. Mattea first gained a national audience in the 1980s. She has performed at the White House and was named the Country Music Association's Female Vocalist of the Year in 1989 and 1990. Her style is a blend of country, bluegrass, folk, and blues.

Patty Loveless, born in 1958 in the Kentucky hills, moved into the front ranks of country performers in 1995 with her hit song "How Can I Help You Say Goodbye." The song was inspired by the illness and death of her grandmother, who had raised Loveless in Louisville, Kentucky. The song has become a standard at funerals and grief therapy workshops.

k.d. lang, born in 1961 in Alberta, Canada, has brought a new energy to country music. Early in her career in the 1980s, her concerts were flashy stage productions with lang wearing gaudy costumes and sporting a decidedly "uncountry" cropped haircut. Since then she has toned down her style. Her music, however, has remained a blend of country, punk rock, and folk. The *Nashville Banner* has called her "one of the most exciting new artists to come around in a while." lang was named "Canada's most promising female vocalist" by many critics and won a Juno Award (the Canadian equivalent of the Grammy) for best country singer in 1987.

Alison Krauss was born in 1971 in Illinois. Krauss, a bluegrass fiddler and singer, began playing the violin when she was five years old and was winning contests by the time she was eleven. She was fifteen when she recorded her first album. In 1989, she rereleased some of those songs on a hit album called *Two Highways,* which was backed up by her band Union Station. At only twenty-two years old, Krauss had recorded five albums, won two Grammy awards, sold more than five hundred thousand records, been inducted into the Grand Ole Opry, and recorded with some of country and western's top stars.

Gospel

Gospel music is an American music form developed by African Americans from the southern United States. It combines elements of jazz, folk music, and spirituals and is most often associated with African American Baptist churches, which have choirs and where music is a large part of each service.

Mahalia Jackson is one of the best-known of the early female gospel singers. Today, both the world press and critics call her America's greatest gospel singer. She was born in New Orleans in about 1911 and died in 1972. In between, she began singing in her church choir and then graduated to the choir of the Greater Salem Baptist Church in Chicago, Illinois. Then in 1932 she began singing with the Johnson Gospel Singers. This led to a recording career. After touring Europe in the early 1950s, she returned to the United States and became active in the Civil Rights movement. One of her best-remembered performances came in 1968 after the funeral of Martin Luther King Jr., the assassinated leader of the movement. Jackson moved the mourners to further tears with her rendition of "Precious Lord, Take My Hand," a gospel favorite.

Singer-songwriter Amy Grant was born in 1961 in Georgia and has become one of the first Christian singers to attract the interest of mainstream pop music fans. Although she was known to gospel fans in the early 1980s, her crossover album, *Unguarded,* didn't appear until 1985. Her 1991 release, *Heart in Motion,* brought criticism from some traditional gospel music fans who thought Grant was straying from the Christian message. Grant, however, believes that her music and lifestyle do convey her Christian val-

Gospel singer Mahalia Jackson

1920s. Although popular music was available on records to be played on the phonograph invented in the late 1800s, few people had access to such a device. Increasing availability and declining prices of radios during the 1920s allowed people all over the United States to be exposed to the subgenres of popular music such as jazz, the blues, and "swing."

One of the first prominent popular singers was Lotte Lenya, an Austrian American cabaret singer, who lived from 1898 to 1981. She is best known for her interpretations of the songs of Kurt Weill and Bertolt Brecht, a German song-writing team that produced *The Three Penny Opera* and other popular musical theater. Lenya's recordings continue to sell well because her voice and style capture the musical mood of Berlin of the 1920s and 1930s, a desperate economic time in which Adolf Hitler and the Nazis rose to power in Germany.

Edith Piaf was a French singer who lived between 1915 and 1963. Her small stature and plaintive voice earned her the nickname "La Mome Piaf" ("kid sparrow"). Piaf started as a street singer but eventually moved into the cabaret shows and nightclubs popular in Paris. She made several films and toured both Europe and the United States. Since her death, she has become a cult figure whose followers are drawn to the images her songs paint of smoke-filled bars and lost love.

Vera Lynn, born in England in 1917, was called the (Armed) "Forces Sweetheart" during World War II. Her song-

ues. She has won four Grammy awards, as well as five Dove awards from the Gospel Music Association.

Popular Music

Popular music is music that is in the mainstream of a society. American pop can be heard on the radio, at movies and on television, at concerts, in nightclubs, and at musical theaters. These are the songs whose popularity is measured on the pop charts—such as Billboard's and Rolling Stone's—by the number of records sold. Pop music first reached a wide audience with the invention of the radio during the

and-dance routine took her to the United States, Europe, South Africa, and Australia. She was the first English singer to reach the top of the American hit music list. Her most famous song was "Auf Wiederseh'n" (German for "goodbye"), which sold twelve million copies.

Judy Garland was born Frances Gumm in Grand Rapids, Michigan, in 1922. She appeared in numerous Hollywood films, including the 1939 classic *Wizard of Oz,* in which she played Dorothy. Garland was performing at a time when the Hollywood studios had almost total control over their stars' lives. She became hooked on the diet pills the studio gave her to control her weight and the sleeping pills she took to offset the effects of the diet pills. She also became addicted to alcohol and struggled with depression. As her career began to slide in the early 1950s, Garland fought back. She undertook a concert tour and then starred in the highly acclaimed 1954 movie *A Star Is Born.* She died of an overdose of sleeping pills in 1969 while on a concert tour attempting a comeback.

Petula Clark was born Sally Olwen in 1934 in England and has remained popular since the 1950s. She broke into the entertainment business with a radio show titled "Pet's Parlor," which she hosted when she was eleven years old. Her career spans radio, film, television, live concerts, and recording. As a singer, she has ten gold records and won two Grammys—for the songs "Downtown" and "I Know a Place."

Barbra Streisand performing during her 1994 tour.

Connie Francis was born in 1938 in New Jersey and had a string of hits before the British group, the Beatles, caught the attention of American teenagers in 1964. Francis had more than fifty U.S. chart singles and was popular in Europe and Asia, where the words of her songs were dubbed into the native language.

American singer, actress, and producer Barbra Streisand is one of the most famous and richest performers of all time. She was born in Brooklyn, New York, in 1942 and first performed as a nightclub singer. Streisand went on to act in films and on stage (often in romantic comedy

Mariah Carey is part of a new generation of successful female singers.

ney Houston, went on to sell fourteen million copies. Since the start of her career, Houston has become well known for her string of hit albums, her numerous Grammy awards, her music videos, and her film performances in movies such as *The Bodyguard* (1992) and *Waiting to Exhale* (1995).

Mariah Carey was born in New York around 1970 and has earned respect as a singer and as a songwriter. Her debut album, *Mariah Carey,* appeared in 1990. Soon her seven-octave vocal range caught the attention of the pop world and her record sold seven million copies worldwide. Carey cowrote and arranged the songs on her debut album, which earned her a Grammy award in 1991 for best new artist. Her later albums also went gold, and in 1993 she released *Music Box,* which sold eight million copies. Carey's fourth album, titled *Daydreams,* was released in 1996.

roles). Her most memorable stage role was in *Funny Girl* in 1964, a part she later recreated for Hollywood. By 1996, she had won eight Grammy awards for her recordings and an Oscar for her performance in *Funny Girl.* Streisand has also been honored with a prestigious Living Legend award from the National Academy of Recording Arts and Sciences, the group that bestows the Grammys.

Whitney Houston, born in 1963 in New Jersey, made Billboard chart history when her first album became the first by a woman to enter the chart at the number-one position. That album, *Whit-*

Rock 'n' Roll

One of the most popular forms of music in the twentieth century is rock 'n roll. It developed in the United States during the 1950s as a combination of rhythm and blues, country, and gospel music.

Women in Rock: A Mixed Welcome

Rock 'n' roll gained momentum as an art form in the 1960s with the British Invasion, when British groups such as the Beatles and the Rolling Stones grabbed and held young Americans' attention. Soon American-brand rock 'n' roll groups gained popularity, but few of them had women members. Occasionally, a group such as the Jefferson Airplane might front a female lead singer like Grace Slick. For the most part, however, rock music was performed by male artists.

This male dominance of rock can be seen as late as 1996, when American culture has supposedly overcome its bias against women working in previously male areas. For instance the Rock and Roll Hall of Fame and Museum, which opened in Cleveland, Ohio, in 1995 is the creation of a group of music industry professionals who formed the Rock and Roll Hall of Fame Foundation. Since 1986, the group has been inducting rock 'n' roll stars into its Hall of Fame and Museum. To be eligible, the musician or band must have released a record at least 25 years prior to the year of induction. A committee of 29 musical historians and critics nominates 15 people or groups each year, and a voting body of 600 music industry figures makes the final selection.

As of 1996, only ten women singers, songwriters, or groups have been inducted into the Rock and Roll Hall of Fame (it has honored a total of 135 people or groups). Only 59 compositions by female composers made the Hall of Fame's recently published list of the 500 most influential songs. Many of those 59 songs, however, were recorded by male-female duets or mixed-sex bands. Stephen Holden, writing in the *New York Times* in 1996, explains what he believes to be the reason for this oversight:

This sexual bias is a residue [leftover] of cultural tensions that date back to rock's earliest days. The 1950's pop-music culture in which rock erupted was so polite and squeaky clean it often seemed like a holdover from World War II, when the record industry catered to the dreams of women whose husbands and boyfriends were overseas.

Holden is saying that early rock 'n roll was a rebellious male reaction to the popular music of the 1940s and 1950s. Young male rock stars infused the genre with a confrontational, nonconformist attitude that essentially challenged any established order or rules. Today, any rock songs that seem to support society or the family or other traditions are seen as sellouts. Unfortunately, some of these male rockers associate female rock singers and songwriters with this nonconfrontational approach, and many continue to exclude the women from this still-male genre.

Despite the lack of encouragement, women have written, sung, and played rock music. Some of the more important contributors are included here, but for a more complete list, visit your local library or consult the *New Rolling Stone Encyclopedia of Rock & Roll*.

Tina Turner, an African American singer, dancer, and actress, was born in 1939 in Tennessee. She began singing at the Sanctified Church in Knoxville, where she was also introduced to a Baptist tradition called the "Holy Dance." This exposure helped her refine both her singing and dancing skills. She first gained fame as part of a duo with her husband,

Window on the World: India

Lata Mangeshkar, a popular music vocalist famous for her roles in Indian movies, is the bestselling musical artist in the world. Sales of her recordings have outpaced even giants such as the Beatles. Counted among he rfans are people in the huge Indian communities in Indonesia who purchase the recordings to remind them of their home. Mangeshkar is also hugely popular because she sings in Hindi, one of the major languages in India. Because Hindi and Arabic share the same language base, which means that many of Mangeshkar's songs can be understood by Arabic speakers, she is also very popular in North Africa, which has a predominantly Arabic population.

Mangeshkar was born in 1928 and gained fame as a background singer in the Indian film industry. Bombay, India, is the world's movie capital, producing more films each year than Hollywood. Indian films tend to be light entertainment, and many focus on romance. A typical Indian movie has eight to ten musical numbers. When the heroine opens her mouth to sing, she may be lip syncing to a recording by a back-up singer like Mangeshkar. She is in the *Guinness Book of Records* as the world's most recorded artist, with more than thirty thousand songs and two thousand films to her credit.

Ike Turner. Their debut song together, "A Fool in Love," became a hit on both pop and rhythm and blues charts in 1960. Turner went solo in 1975 with the album *Acid Queen* (she had played the Acid Queen in the rock opera *Tommy*). In 1978, her career took off (perhaps coincidentally, she had divorced her abusive husband the same year). She released several albums that went platinum and appeared in movies, including *Mad Max: Beyond the THunderdome.* By the mid-1990s, Turner had won seven Grammy awards. Tina (and Ike) Turner were inducted into the Rock and Roll Hall of Fame in 1991.

A movie based on the Turners' troubled marriage, titled *What's Love Got to Do With It,* was released in 1993.

One of the most famous rock 'n' roll singers of all time was Janis Joplin. She was born in Texas in 1943 and counted both country and jazz music as her early influences. In 1962, she joined Big Brother and the Holding Company, a California rock 'n' roll band, and gained national fame with her performance at the Monterey Festival in 1967. The band's album *Cheap Thrills* sold one million copies in 1968, largely based on the appeal of Joplin's raw, ragged singing.

She went solo in 1969, and in 1970 founded a new band. After producing a record titled *Pearl* in 1970, she died from a drug overdose. Joplin was inducted into the Rock and Roll Hall of Fame in 1995.

Grace Slick's is considered one of the greatest female voices in rock 'n' roll. She was born in 1943 in Chicago. She married filmmaker Jerry Slick in 1961 and performed with him in a band called the Great Society. Five years later she became the lead singer of the immensely popular band the Jefferson Airplane. She also enjoyed a solo career before returning to a slightly altered band that was renamed the Jefferson Starship, which was again renamed the Starship.

Bonnie Raitt was born in 1949 in California and launched her career in 1971 with the album *Bonnie Raitt.* This singer, songwriter, and guitarist is difficult to classify. Her style ranges from country and bluegrass to rock and rhythm and blues. She had her first commercial success in 1989, with the release of *Nick of Time.* It sold four million copies and won three Grammy awards (she had a total of seven by 1996). Raitt is an unusual performer in many ways. She had a long wait between her debut album and national fame (18 years), she is one of only a few women to play bottleneck guitar (a blues technique), and she is a Quaker, which is a religious group devoted to nonviolence. Her social conscience led to the founding of M.U.S.E. (Musicians United for Safe Energy). She also cofounded the Rhythm and Blues Foundation, with the purpose of raising money to care for blues

Madonna giving one of her electrifying performances.

pioneers left poverty-stricken in their old age. In addition, Raitt turns over all royalties from sales of the guitar named after her to a fund to teach girls to play guitar.

Madonna, perhaps the most extravagantlyu promoted female performer of the twentieth century, was born Madonna Louise Veronica Ciccone in 1958 in Michigan. She is a singer, actress, dancer, and songwriter. Her first album was released in 1983, and she had her first top ten hit, "Borderline," in 1984. Madonna has dominated the pop music scene since 1985 with her catchy songs and music videos. Her albums routinely go double and triple platinum. In 1992, she formed

Melissa Etheridge

her own production company, Maverick, which promotes female songwriters, singers, and musicians. Controversy has also surrounded Madonna, both for her sexy image and her antitraditional social messages. She has performed in a number of Hollywood films, including *Desperately Seeking Susan* (1985) and *A League of Their Own* (1992). Although her film work has met with mixed reviews from movie critics, she was chosen to play the title role in the 1996 film version of *Evita,* based on the life of former first lady of Argentina, Eva Peron.

In 1994 Sheryl Crow won two Grammy awards for her album *All I Wanna Do,* one for best record of the year and the other for best vocalist of the year. Crow, who was born in 1962 in Missouri, began her career as a backup singer for Michael Jackson and Don Henley (formerly of the Eagles). She went solo in 1993 with an album titled *Tuesday Night Music Club.* Both this album and her later performance at the Woodstock '94 music festival earned Crow critical acclaim and a legion of fans.

Melissa Etheridge, born in Kansas about 1962, is a singer, guitarist, and songwriter. Her style is hard, soulful rock. Etheridge studied at the Berklee School of Music in Boston, Massachusetts, and plays the piano, clarinet, drums, and saxophone. She was discovered by a talent agent in 1987 and wrote the music for the film *Weeds* (1987). Her debut album, *Melissa Etheridge,* appeared the same year and went gold. Etheridge's fans like her songs about a gutsy sort of bravery in the face of pain and disappointment. She won a Grammy award in 1993 for her song, "Ain't It Heavy." Her album *Yes I Am* appeared in 1994, and soon went triple platinum.

Janet Jackson was born in 1966 in Indiana, the youngest child in the famous musical family that includes Michael Jackson and the other four members of the musical group the Jackson Five. Her earliest work was as a television actress, starring in *Good Times, Diff'rent Strokes,* and *Fame.* She has been a concert performer and recording artist since adolescence. Jackson released *Control* in 1986, which hit the top of the Billboard

Alanis Morissette

Alanis Morissette was just twenty-one when she won four Grammy awards in 1996 for her album *Jagged Little Pill.* Later that year she broke Whitney Houston's record for selling the most albums in one year. "You Oughta Know," a song from *Jagged Little Pill,* became her first U.S. hit. The song and the entire album touched a nerve in her native Canada and in the United States. Morissette's raw and often raucous songs describe the uncertainty that young women feel and their vulnerability to hurt.

Morissette was born in Ottawa in 1975. She began writing songs and poems while in elementary school, and in 1984 joined the cast of the children's television program *You Can't Do That on Television* on Nickelodeon. She released her first album when she was nine years old, financing it with money from her television job.

Morissette's first adult album, titled *Alanis* and released in the early 1990s, won her a Juno Award (the Canadian version of the Grammy). The album featured dance-pop tunes, a style which Morissette has since abandoned. She moved to Los Angeles and met Glen Ballard, who helped her produce *Jagged Little Pill.* Morissette wrote, sang, and recorded each song on the album in a single day, an amazing creative feat.

By late 1996, Morissette was working on another album and playing to sold-out crowds in the United States and Canada.

charts and went platinum. In 1989, she released *Rhythm Nation 1814,* which also went platinum. This album is filled with songs on social themes such as homelessness, illiteracy, and prejudice. In 1994, Jackson won an MTV Video Music Award for best female video for the song "If," off her 1993 album, *janet.*

Grunge

In the late 1980s a new sound erupted from the Seattle, Washington, music scene that recalled the heavy rock of the 1970s. Called "grunge," this genre was dominated by such all-male bands as Nirvana and Pearl Jam until the mid-1990s, when the "Riot Grrrrl" groups came into their own. The most famous of these girl grunge groups is Hole, fronted by the flamboyant Courtney Love. Hole's 1994 album, *Live Through This*, was very well received by critics and fans alike—it went gold—but Love's contentious attitude and her and her bandmembers' highly publicized problems with drugs have alienated some fans. Nonetheless, Hole, Garbage, L7, and the other grrrrl groups mark a new generation of women rockers who are just as good as men at the rock 'n' roll game.

Motown

Motown was the brainchild of African American jazz enthusiast Berry Gordy Jr. In the 1960s, this Detroit-based musical production company became one of the largest and most successful houses, black or white, in America. Their product was a sound called Motown, a blend of rock 'n' roll, rhythm and blues, and classical instrumentation. Their look was a glamorous one, with the singers groomed to resemble and act like movie stars. The singers were black, young, and mostly urban born.

The most famous group of female singers to emerge from Motown was the Supremes. Later known as Diana Ross and the Supremes, the others in the threesome were Florence Ballard and Mary Wilson. The group began its rise to stardom in the early 1960s and, in addition to recording, performed on television, in Las Vegas nightclubs, on world concert tours, and with the Detroit Symphony Orchestra. By the time the original group disbanded in 1967, they had twelve number one hits on Billboard's pop charts. The Supremes are third on the all-time list of hits, behind the Beatles and Elvis Presley. The original Supremes were inducted into the Rock and Roll Hall of Fame in 1988.

Martha and the Vandellas were formed in 1962 with lead singer Martha Reeves and backup singers Annette Beard and Rosalind Ashford. They offered an alternative to the Supremes' sophisticated sound. The Vandellas were noted for their earthy, driving dance songs, which included "Dancing in the Street" and "Heat Wave." In the 1970s, Reeves began a solo career, where her efforts have met with critical but not commercial success. Martha and the Vandellas were inducted into the Rock and Roll Hall of Fame in 1995.

Mary Wells, who was born in Detroit, Michigan, in 1943 and died in 1992, was Motown's first big star. Her greatest hits were songs done with fellow Motown singer and songwriter Smoky Robinson, including "My Guy" in 1964. She also performed duets with Marvin Gaye and was an opening act for the Beatles. Wells left Motown in 1965, alleging that the company had not treated her fairly. Although she did have several minor rhythm and blues hits after leaving Motown, her career never recovered.

The Marvelettes were formed in 1960 with Gladys Horton, Katherine Anderson, Georgia Dobbins, Juanita Cowart, and Wanda Young. Their debut song, "Please Mr. Postman" was theirs and Motown's biggest hit. The song stayed on the pop charts for almost six months. The group also recorded several Smoky Robinson songs in the mid-1960s before disbanding.

The Girl Group Phenomenon

Amazons, Bluestockings, and Crones: A Feminist Dictionary and a Woman's Companion to Words and Ideas, published in 1992, offers this description of a unique period in rock 'n' roll history:

"Until the present, rock and roll had the most influential presence of women in its history during the period 1958–1965. Those were the years of the Girl Groups: young, all-female, and often black groups of singers who were brought together and produced by white, male producers, although Motown also had a few girl groups. They sang songs by contracted songwriters, about love and romance, "the boy." Their names, which were often also produced for them, reflect the yielding, diminutive, but sexy image these groups were meant to convey: the Chantels, the Shirelles."

These girl groups were produced in the Brill Building in New York City. The building housed a complete production set-up from songwriters to studio musicians, costumers, hair stylists, sound recording facilities, and advertising copywriters. The idea was to bring in young talent and package them with a certain look and sound for a targeted adolescent audience. The Brill Building and the Girl Group phenomenon remain one of the best examples of high-powered commercial packaging of artists.

Rap

Rap music began its rise to popularity in the United States in the mid-1980s. It is typically performed by African American artists and features spoken lyrics that reflect the current and social issues of life in American's large cities. Although rap started as a male dominated music form, some women have managed to break the sex barrier.

According to the *All Music Guide,* Queen Latifah "almost singlehandedly opened the doors for female rappers in the 90s." Latifah was born in New Jersey and released her first album, *All Hail the Queen,* in 1989. *Nature of a Sista* followed in 1991. Afrocentric ideas (the philosophy that emphasizes the role black civilization has played in culture and history) play heavily in Latifah's songs.

Salsa

Salsa is a form of Latin American dance music that has just recently become popular in the United States. Salsa mixes elements of jazz and rock 'n' roll with Afro-Caribbean rhythms and Cuban big-band dance melodies.

Many regard Celia Cruz as the undisputed "Queen of Salsa." She was born in 1929 in Havana, Cuba, and has entertained professionally for more than forty years. One of her greatest contributions is attracting a non-Hispanic audience to salsa music. She spent the first part of her career in Cuba, performing in night clubs and on radio. She came to the United States when Fidel Castro took power in Cuba in 1959. In the States, she has recorded and appeared in concert halls, on television, and in film. By 1996, her work had won her two Grammy awards and two gold records.

Gloria Estefan was born in 1957 in Havana. She is an accomplished singer, dancer, and producer. She first performed with the band the Miami Sound Machine but has since gone solo. Estefan and her band were originally popular in the Latin music market, but attracted a mainstream following with *Eyes of Innocence,* their 1984 album. (Estefan's husband, Emilio, produced the album.) Their first all-English album, *Primitive Love,* released in 1985, went double platinum. She has since had a string of platinum albums.

The singer Selena is perhaps better known in death than she was in life. Born Selena Quintanilla in Texas, the singer was killed at age 23. Before her death, she was well known in the Hispanic community for mixing salsa and pop sounds and for her electrifying stage performances. After she was gunned down in 1995 by her former manager at a Texas hotel, Selena became known throughout the United States. Five of her albums crossed over to land on Billboard's Top 20 chart. She won a Grammy Award in 1993.

Contemporary Composers and Songwriters

Mary Lou Williams is an African American pianist and composer of jazz music. Williams has been playing in blues clubs since the 1940s. Her music has been played by the New York Philharmonic Orchestra and used by Alvin Ailey in his modern dance productions. She has also written music for ballets and religious hymns.

Carole King is best known for writing a string of hit songs, but she has also recorded several albums. She was born in 1942 in New York, and began her songwriting career in 1959 with her ex-husband, Gerry Goffin. Together they wrote songs such as "Will You Still Love Me Tomorrow," "Up on the Roof," "Natural Woman," and "Hie-de-ho" for such diverse artists as the Shirelles, the Drifters, Aretha Franklin, and Blood, Sweat, and Tears. In 1971, King won a Grammy award for album of the year for *Tapestry* (the album was a phenomenon, selling more than fourteen million copies). This autobiographical album is credited with helping launch the introspective singer/songwriter acts that became popular in the 1970s. King was inducted into the Rock and Roll Hall of Fame in 1990.

Nanci Griffith is one of the most prolific and respected songwriters working today. She has produced songs in a variety of genres, including folk and country. Stars such as Kathy Mattea, Emmylou Harris, and Suzy Bogguss have recorded her songs. Griffith, who was born in Texas in 1955, also performs and has produced 11 albums of her own in her 16-year career.

Kate Bush, who was born in 1958 in England, is best known for her bestselling hit "Wuthering Heights," which made the top of the charts in England. Bush, a noted singer, has a four-octave range. She wrote the songs for her first album, *The Kick Inside,* which was released when she was only nineteen years old. Bush has continued to write and record.

Suzanne Ciani, who specializes in modern music with an electronic flavor, began writing music for commercials in the mid-1970s. Since then, she has scored the film *The Incredible Shrinking Woman* (1981) and a documentary on Mother Theresa of Calcutta. She composes primarily for the electronic keyboard and the synthesizer.

Among the innovative composers working today is Marnie Jones, who has released several recordings of harp music backed by less traditional instruments such as Indian drums and synthesizers. Liz Story is known for her improvisational (unrehearsed) piano numbers. Carla Bley has written a jazz opera titled *Escalator Over the Hill.* Chris Williamson is known as one of the founders of women's music, a genre of songs about women's issues and their view of life.

Although women have made great strides in all aspects of the music industry during the twentieth century, they still remain underrepresented in the areas of classical conducting and composition. Female performers have seemed to have found a niche, however, in the subgenres of popular music such as rock 'n' roll, country, blues, and grunge. As modern music continues to evolve and diversify, it is certain that women will continue to play an important role in whatever directions the industry will take.

20

Dance and Theater

"No one can arrive from being talented alone. God gives talent, work transforms talent into genius."

—Anna Pavlova, Russian prima ballerina

Women dancing, acting, performing—it seems that history is full of stories about women on the stage. But it has been only comparatively recently that women were encouraged to perform publicly. In public performances prior to 1650, the roles of women were danced and acted by men who wore women's clothing and either used masks or makeup to hide their masculine appearance. It was considered indelicate for a woman to want to take center stage and bask in the public's attention.

When women first began to dance and act in public, they were considered loose women rather than artists. These female performers were fair game for their male admirers, no matter how dishonorable the intentions of those admirers. Their performances were referred to as "leg shows," and it became fashionable for a wealthy young man to have an opera dancer as a lover.

It took almost a century before female performing artists began to command and receive respect from the public. Stars such as Belgian ballerina Marie Anne de Cupis de Camargo, English actress Fanny Kemble, and Italian actress Eleanora Duse were so

Timeline: Women in Dance and Theater

1726 Belgian ballerina Marie Anne de Cupis de Camargo raises the hem of her skirts so her audiences can see and appreciate her intricate (fancy) footwork.

1878 Italian actress Eleanora Duse pioneers a more natural way of acting by not wearing makeup, choosing simple costumes, and making less exaggerated hand gestures.

1906 Anna Pavlova is named prima ballerina (female star of a ballet company) of the Russian Imperial Ballet.

1927 The musical *Show Boat* opens on Broadway, becoming the first musical to focus on a serious theme. The plot revolves around an interracial marriage in the South during the 1880s. Norma Terris plays the lead role of Magnolia.

1932 Martha Graham, the modern dance pioneer, opens her own dance company in New York City.

1943 *Oklahoma!* premieres on Broadway and forever changes how dance is used in musicals. Instead of being an entertaining interruption to the main action, dance is incorporated in the story-telling process. Joan Roberts plays Laurey, the leading lady.

1949 Maria Tallchief, an Osage Indian, becomes America's prima ballerina with her performance in *The Firebird,* choreographed by her husband, George Ballanchine.

1962 At age 53, prima ballerina assoluta (absolute first ballerina) Margot Fonteyn begins her legendary partnership with danseur (male ballet dancer) Rudolf Nureyev.

1963 Katherine Dunham choreographs the opera *Aida,* becoming the first African American to create dance for America's premier company, the Metropolitan Opera.

talented that their performances, rather than their personal lives, became the topic of conversation and critics' reviews. In some cases, however, women are still struggling to educate the public about a woman's place in the performing arts. Women continue to demand that, when their talent merits it, they be considered artists rather than mere entertainers.

Before looking at the modern era, where women took to the stage more freely, let us look at some of the origins of dance and theater. These origins can be traced back to the folk dances and ritual performances that were a part of daily life in every human culture. All peoples—whether they were Native Americans living on the plains, Tatar tribes spread across the steppes (plains) of Asia, or South American mountain dwellers near Lake Titicaca—have some sort of performing arts in their histories.

(Note: In this chapter, the word "theater" is spelled "er" rather than "re," even when referring to British theaters.)

Folk and Ritual Performance

Folk dance is the name given to patterns of steps that can be learned and repeated and are used during ceremonies and festivals. Folk dancing dates back to the beginning of time, when people were moved to celebrate the birth of a child, a marriage, or the harvesting of crops. Sometimes dances became part of a ritual and, as a result, the same steps were passed on from generation to generation. The ritual might revolve around a funeral, a coronation (crowning), or a battle. Often, props and other accessories were needed to complete the dance. These include masks, staffs, spears, shakers and other musical instruments, sand or grain, and food offerings. These folk dancers were the earliest actors, people doing a performance in front of a live audience.

Examples of American folk dance include square dances (a dance where four sets of couples form squares), clogging (a dance where the performer wears shoes having a wooden sole), and the Virginia Reel (a dance where two lines of couples face each other and perform various steps). Other folk dances that have become popular in other cultures are the Hungarian *czardas,* the Bohemian (Czech Republic) polka, the Israeli *hora,* the Irish jig, and Brazilian samba. Examples of ritual dances include those done by Native Americans praying for rain, African tribesmen preparing for a hunt, and Aztec (Mexican) priests preparing a sacrifice to ensure their god remained happy with them. The Scots sword dance was also a ritual performed to celebrate a victory in battle.

Many folk and ritual dances revolve around young people and courtship. In some cultures, such as those in Eastern Europe and the Middle East, women and men perform in separate line or circle dances. Each group watches the other, and the best dancer is sought after as a mate. Sometimes the dance calls for the males to swoop in among the females and race off after having chosen a partner. This dance movement mirrors the ancient custom of the bridegroom abducting the bride. In other dances, male and female dancers pair off and perform an elaborate set of steps together. Examples of courtship dances are the *El Jarabe Tapito* (Mexican Hat Dance) and the Spanish *fandango.*

Some of these early ritual courtship dances evolved into the court dances that were so common starting with the Middle Ages (about 500–1500) on. The dances ranged from the minuet (a slow stately dance) to the waltz (a ballroom dance) to the quadrille (a square dance of French origin), and each had an intricate series

Window on the World: Mexican Dance

Amalia Hernandez is the founder, director, and choreographer of the Ballet Folklorico de Mexico. Hernandez has approached dance from both scientific and anthropological points of view. She is intensely interested in Mexican culture (anthropology), especially ancient culture dating to Pre-Columbian Mexico (the time before the landing of the Europeans in the late 1400s). Her goal has been to recreate a sense of the life and movement of these prehistoric peoples.

To do this, she has spent years traveling through Mexico to collect field samples that reveal different aspects of the ancient Mexican culture. Like a person working a puzzle, Hernandez has pieced together these hints of history into a vivid recreation of the past.

Although the Ballet Folklorico de Mexico also performs more modern dances, it focuses on those from the folk cultures of Mexico. Hernandez includes a selection of folk dances from the different regions of the country. These dances, which tend to be highly stylized, are performed to folk music.

Since its formation in the early 1960s, the Ballet Folklorico de Mexico performs regularly at the Palace of Fine Arts in Mexico City and also tours throughout Mexico and in foreign countries.

of controlled movements and steps. The dances gave a young couple a chance to talk at a time when girls were rigidly chaperoned. Some regard modern dances such as the twist, disco, and today's rock dances as the modern equivalent of the Medieval courtship dance.

Since the turn of the century in 1900, scholars and amateur researchers have taken an interest in learning more about folk art, music, and dance. They see these art forms as a unique part of American heritage. Field research, interviews, documentation, and library work are some of the tools that have been used to reveal

and document this part of American culture. One of the more influential folklorists has been Fora Elizabeth Burchenal, who was born in Indiana in 1876. Before her death in 1959, Burchenal had founded the American Folk Dance Society (1916). In her job as inspector of athletics for the New York Department of Education, she made folk dancing a part of the physical education curriculum. Today the American Folk Dance Society is part of the National Committee of Folk Arts.

Folk dancing is equally popular in other countries. Among the famous troupes, or groups of dancers, performing in the 1990s are the Ballet Folklorico de Mexico (see box), the Philippine dance company called Bayanihan, and the Moiseyev Dance Company of Russia.

Women in Dance

Ballet

Ballet is a classical form of dancing that emphasizes upright postures, specific foot positions, graceful use of the arms and head, and the appearance of weightlessness. Ballet has its foundations in the ritualistic and highly stylized, or carefully planned, dances of the Middle Ages and Renaissance. The first *ballet de corps* (ballet company) was formed in France in the 1660s for King Louis XVI (the Sun King). At first the female roles were played by men wearing masks, but by 1700 women ballet dancers (called ballerinas) had starring roles in most companies.

Early ballerinas wore long dresses to preserve their modesty since no woman showed her legs or even her ankles in public. As ballet became more athletic, however, costumers began to respond to the need for greater freedom of movement. Belgian ballerina Marie Anne de Cupis de Camargo caused a commotion in 1726 when she appeared in a ballet dress with a skirt raised a few inches above her ankles. Her other costume innovations included taking the heels off her shoes and wearing close fitting leggings (the forerunners of tights). Soon the skirts grew even shorter and the bodices smaller. The abbreviated costumes gave the dancers more freedom and allowed the audience to see the dancers' intricate arm and leg movements more clearly.

From the beginning, ballet was a dance form intended to tell a story. Performers used music, dance, mime (acting without speech), gestures, costumes, and scenery to help convey the story. Among the most famous of the classical style ballets are *Sleeping Beauty, Swan Lake, Giselle,* and *Coppelia.* Later ballets include *Rodeo* by Agnes De Mille and *The Four Temperaments* by George Ballanchine.

This section offers a look at some of the most famous of the ballerinas, as well as those who work behind the scenes. The names included here tend to be women working during the 1900s. For a collection of earlier ballerinas and choreographers, a good source is your local library or a book titled *The International Dictionary of Women's Biography,* compiled and edited by Jennifer S. Uglow.

Ballerinas

Anna Pavlova (c. 1882–1931) was born in Russia. She and her family were peasants, poor farmers whose life was a day-to-day struggle. During her childhood, Pavlova suffered from two almost always fatal diseases, diphtheria and scarlet fever. She survived, and her physical strength helped her reach the top of the Russian ballet world. At age ten, she entered the Imperial Ballet School and then made her ballet debut with the Imperial Ballet in 1899 at the age of seventeen.

By 1906, she had been made prima ballerina of the Russian Imperial Ballet, a position she kept until 1912. That year, she resigned to lead her own ballet company on a worldwide tour. During her trip, Pavlova learned many of the dances of the peoples she was visiting, and she began to incorporate these folk dance steps into her own routines. Today Pavlova's name is synonymous with the role of the *Dying Swan,* a four-minute solo created especially for her by the famous choreographer Michel Fokine. She is considered one of a handful of premier ballet dancers of the twentieth century.

Alicia Markova was born in England in 1910. (Her original name was Alice Marks.) Even as a child, her dance talent was apparent. By age ten, she had made her debut at a London theater. Later, she became the first prima ballerina of the Vic-Wells Ballet company in 1933. She also danced with Ballet Russe de Monte Carlo and the American Ballet Theater. In 1950 she cofounded the London Festival Ballet. After an illustrious career, she retired in 1963 and began to teach and produce ballets.

Tamara Toumanova is a French-Russian ballerina who was born in China in 1919. Her career is unusual since it includes not only traditional ballet performances that are done in theaters but also musicals done on Broadway, such as *Stars in Your Eyes,* and films created in Hollywood. She began her career with the Ballet Russe de Monte Carlo in 1932. She has also appeared with the major ballet companies in Europe and the United States. Toumanova's films include Alfred Hitchcock's *Torn Curtain* (1966) and a turn with Gene Kelly in *Invitation to the Dance* (1956).

Maria Tallchief was born in 1925 on an Osage Indian reservation in Oklahoma. She was the first American dancer to gain an international reputation as a prima ballerina. After high school, she joined the Ballet Russe (an American-based company founded by a Russian choreographer) and later became a member of the New York City Ballet. In 1947, she had the distinction of being the first American ballerina to dance with the Paris Opera in more than one hundred years. Tallchief was such a respected dancer that many choreographers began to create dances especially for her. The most famous of these was George Ballanchine's (her choreographer-husband) version of *The Firebird,* which he choreographed for her in 1949.

Russian ballerina Maya Plisetskaya was born in 1925 and is famous for the high and graceful leaps she made as a star with the Bolshoi Ballet in the 1940s. She has performed around the world, and in 1994, she opened the First International Maya Dance Competition, which was designed to reward and encourage talented young dancers. In 1995, at age seventy, Plisetskaya performed a thirty-five minute solo work created especially for her. The piece was called *Kurozuka* and was danced to traditional Japanese music. Plisetskaya was working with the Bavarian State Ballet School in Germany in 1996.

Prima ballerina Anna Pavlova

Encore: Margot Fonteyn

Prima ballerina assoluta Margot Fonteyn was born in 1919 in Surrey, England. She made her debut with the Sadler-Wells Ballet (now the Royal Ballet) in London in 1934. Fonteyn's great artistic talent (many consider her the most gifted ballerina of the twentieth century) was soon recognized. Choreographers began to create works especially for her. She joined the Royal Ballet in London and was quickly named its prima ballerina. She held this position until she assumed guest star status in 1959. During her career, Fonteyn also danced guest roles with the best known companies, including the Paris Opera, La Scala in Milan, Italy, and theaters in the United States.

In 1962, at age 53, Fonteyn embarked on one of the most inspirational dance partnerships ever witnessed in the ballet world. Fonteyn met and was soon partnered with the young Russian danseur Rudolf Nureyev. Their performances included *Swan Lake, Romeo and Juliet,* and Marguerite and Armand in *Camille*. The pair became a worldwide sensation and played to sold-out theaters wherever they toured. John Percival, the *New York Times* ballet critic, wrote: "They were a partnership the like of which we have never seen before and will never see again." Fonteyn was named *prima ballerina assoluta* (absolute first ballerina) by the Royal Ballet in 1979.

Fonteyn also created a series for the British Broadcasting Company that helped make ballet understandable to a huge audience of young people. Her program, called "Magic of Dance," aired in 1980 and is credited with popularizing this dance form in England and other countries. Fonteyn, the first prima ballerina of international stature to come out of England, died in 1991.

Natalia Makarova was born in Russia in 1940. This ballerina and actress received her training at the Vaganova Ballet School, which groomed talent for the Kirov Ballet, to which she was accepted in 1959. She performed to great acclaim before audiences in Russia, England, and the United States. Makarova also toured with the International Festival of Ballet in 1964, an experience that prompted her to give up her Russian citizenship and remain in Europe. She eventually joined the American Ballet Theater and then formed her own troupe, which she called Makarova and Company. In 1983, she won a Tony Award for her performance in *On Your Toes,* a Broadway musical about a ballerina.

American Suzanne Farrell was born in Ohio in 1945. She studied at the School of American Ballet before joining the New York City Ballet in 1961. She left the company briefly before returning in 1975. Farrell is considered a major interpreter of the works of the famous choreographer George Ballanchine. He, in turn, composed works especially for her, including the role of Dulcinea in *Don Quixote.*

Gelsey Kirkland, who was born in 1953, joined the New York City Ballet when she was just fifteen years old. By the age of nineteen, she had become one of the principal dancers in the company. Kirkland later moved to the American Ballet Company. Among her partners were the great male ballet dancers from Russia, Rudolf Nureyev and Mikail Baryshnikov.

Choreographers

Bronislava Nijinska was born in Russia in 1891. She was trained as a ballerina and performed with several Russian companies before opening her own school in Kiev, Ukraine, during World War I (1914–18). Nijinska became the principal choreographer for the Diaghilev Ballet, where she created many famous ballets, including *Les Biches* in 1924. Before her death in 1972, Nijinska had choreographed dances for ballet troupes in Argentina, France, Brazil, the United States, and England.

Ninette de Valois was born Edris Stannus in Ireland in 1898. De Valois, a dancer and choreographer, is also the founder of the Royal Ballet, which is based in London, England. She began her dance career with the British National Opera in 1918 and later danced with French and Russian companies. In 1926 she opened the Academy of Choreographic Art in London. In 1931 she and Lillian Baylis cofounded the Vic-Wells Ballet, which would later be known as the Sadler-Wells Theater Ballet. De Valois also opened ballet schools in Turkey, Iran, and Canada. In 1956 she created the British National Ballet, which she used as a base for choreographing, teaching, and lecturing.

American Ruth Page was born in 1899 in Indiana. She began her career as a ballet dancer with the dance company of ballerina Anna Pavlova. By the time of her death in 1991, she had choreographed more than one hundred ballets. Page is known for being the first choreographer to use American themes in her ballets and the works she did for opera. Her series of *American Dances* premiered in Moscow, Russia, in 1930.

Agnes de Mille was born in about 1908 in New York. She is famous as the founder of the American style of ballet dancing that energized the traditional movements of ballet into an athletic dance form. Many dance critics believe that de Mille forever changed American musical theater when she choreographed *Oklahoma!* She not only combined ballet, folk dance, and modern dance into a single form, she made the dancing seem like a natural part of the stage action.

De Mille came to dancing after graduating from college, and by 1939, she had been offered a position with the forerunner of the American Ballet Theater as a choreographer, director, and dancer. Her better known works are *Rodeo* (1942), *Oklahoma!* (1943), *Carousel* (1945), *Brigadoon* (1947), *Gentlemen Prefer Blondes* (1949), and *Paint Your Wagon* (1951). She founded the Heritage Dance Theater in 1973, which features folk and historical dances. In 1992 she premiered a new work titled *The Other.* She died in 1993.

Birgit Ragnhild Cullberg is a Swedish dancer and choreographer who was born in 1908. She founded the Svenska Dansteater in 1946, and began choreographing for the Royal Swedish Ballet in 1952. She also worked as a guest choreographer for the American Ballet Theater and the New York City Ballet. Since 1967 she has directed her own troupe, the Cullberg Ballet, which is based at the Swedish National Theater.

Wendy Toye was born in 1917 in London, England. This choreographer, director, dancer, and actress began her dance career in 1930 and by 1948 had formed her own dance company called Ballet-Hoo de Wendy Toye. She is best known for her choreography for the musicals *Show Boat, Annie Get Your Gun,* and *Peter Pan.*

Modern Dance

American modern dance dates back to about 1900, when dancers such as Isadora Duncan, Loie Fuller, and Ruth St. Denis became annoyed at the restrictions of classical ballet training and performances. Back then, and even today, dancers began their education with a firm grounding in ballet steps and movements. This includes ballet's five foot positions and a series of turns and leaps. The modern dance founders, however, wanted a dance that would more accurately reflect how people actually moved. Their desire was not to create the effect of grace and weightlessness, which are the goals of ballet. They wanted to use the body to make social comments, to explore movement, and to create visual works of art. Unlike ballet, many of their dances were abstract (they did not tell stories) or they showed social protests.

Dancers

Doris Humphrey was born in 1895 in Illinois. She studied and then taught at the Denishawn School in Los Angeles, California, in order to support her family. (The Denishawn School was a famous modern dance academy opened by choreographers Ruth St. Denis and her husband Ted Shawn.) It was at the school that Humphrey first explored her genius as a choreographer. Her vision was to train dancers and create steps for them so that they could provoke a definite reaction from their audiences. She cofounded her own school in 1926 and devoted herself to creating dances with abstract and psychological themes.

One of Humphrey's early works was titled *The Shakers* (1929). The Shakers were an American religious group led by women who gained equality by renouncing their sexuality. Humphrey's dance was a social comment on their sacrifice. Her work included movements from Shaker dances and captured the fervor and spiritual nature of the Shakers. Her later works also emphasized social themes, questioning and commenting on culture and human behavior. Humphrey continued to perform in her own and others' works until she was handicapped by arthritis in 1944. She, thereafter, devoted herself to choreography and hosted workshops at several prestigious schools. She died in 1958.

African American dancer Judith Jamison was born in 1944 in Pennsylvania. Although she studied many forms of dance as a child, she has made her reputation as a modern dancer. Jamison attended the Philadelphia Dance Academy, where she studied formal ballet. In 1964, she made her professional debut in *The Four Marys,* a new ballet by Agnes de Mille. (De Mille had been teaching a master class at the Philadelphia Dance Academy when Jamison caught her eye and was invited to perform in the ballet.) Jamison later became a principal dancer with the Martha Graham Company before moving to the Alvin Ailey Troupe, one of the premier African American companies in the United States.

In 1971, Jamison performed *Cry,* a dance choreographed for her by Ailey. This solo dance was dedicated to black women. The following year Jamison attended the First World Festival of Negro Arts in Dakar, Senegal. She was the first woman elected to the board of the National Endowment for the Arts. (The board decides which people and groups receive money.) In 1996, Jamison was serving as the artistic director of the Alvin Ailey American Dance Theater.

Choreographers

Loie Fuller was born in 1862 in Illinois. Fuller is respected for the technical advances she brought to dance. Although she was not a trained dancer herself, she had a keen sense of theater and performance. She may have developed this sense through her earlier career with vaudeville (an early form of American musical theater that was a collection of separate acts with no connecting theme), the circus, and acting. At any rate, Fuller used new techniques to light the stage and the dancers and also experimented with fabrics to create different moods. She even performed some of her own works, including a stint at the Metropolitan Opera House in New York City. There her costume shocked the audience as much as her dances did. She wore no corset (a tight undergarment worn in the 1800s) and no shoes, and she danced in filmy garments which swirled as she turned. In 1925, she appeared at the New York Hippodrome, where she danced to celebrate womanhood and the power of modern machinery. She died in 1928.

Isadora Duncan, born in 1878 in California, is considered one of the forerunners of modern dance. Although trained in ballet, she resisted the for-

Encore: Martha Graham

Martha Graham is known for almost single-handedly creating modern dance, along with one of its best known techniques called "The Graham." This technique focuses on the body's solar plexus as the dancer's source of energy and emotion. (The solar plexus is a bundle of nerves located behind the stomach. Graham saw this as the seat of human feeling.) In 1916, Graham began studying with Ruth St. Denis, the famous dancer and teacher, at the School of Dancing and Related Arts in Los Angeles.

Graham was born in 1894 in Pennsylvania and made her debut as a dancer in 1920 with the Denishawn dance company. The performance was *Xochitl,* a ballet based on the Aztec (Mexican) religion. For the next five years, she performed both independently and with other companies and began to choreograph dances. In 1930 she founded her own dance company (and more than three-quarters of her dancers went on to found their own companies or become choreographers). Graham liked creating dances that featured heroines from history. Her subjects included the American poet Emily Dickinson; the French patriot St. Joan of Arc; and the tragic Mary, Queen of Scots.

Graham was awarded a Guggenheim Fellowship in 1932, becoming the first dancer to receive this grant of money that made further study possible. She was soon devoting all her time to choreographing. Among her most famous works are *Revolt,* the first dance of social protest in the United States, and *Appalachian Spring,* danced to the composition of the same name by Aaron Copland.

In 1976, Graham was awarded the Medal of Freedom, one of the highest honors bestowed by the American government. Then, in 1981, received the Samuel H. Scripps American Dance Festival Award, the largest grant ever given to anyone in the field of dance. The award citation credited Graham with "creating a dance technique that has become the basis of the education of hundreds of thousands of dancers around the world and establishing a new form for dance and twentieth-century theater." By the time of her death in 1991, Graham had produced 180 original works.

mality of the dance form. Duncan preferred to move in an unstructured way, interpreting the music as she danced. Her costuming was equally unconventional.

She did not wear tights or shoes, preferring loose fitting tunics (a short pleated and belted dress) and bare feet. She made her debut in San Francisco, California, in

1890 but later went to Europe, since her style of dance was not popular in the United States. In Europe her free-form style was received enthusiastically, and she returned to the United States a star. While in Europe, though, she had opened dance schools in France, Germany, and Russia, and she later opened one in the United States. Duncan died in 1927, leaving a profound influence on the next generation of modern dance choreographers. Her life was the subject of a Hollywood movie, *Isadora,* which appeared in 1971.

Ruth St. Denis was born in 1879 in New Jersey. This dancer, choreographer, teacher, and lecturer is considered a pioneer in modern dance. Her first dance was performed in 1906. It was titled *Radha* and was based on Hindu (Indian) dance movements. She continued to experiment with religious themes in her music. In 1915 St. Denis cofounded the Denishawn School in Los Angeles, California, with her husband, choreographer Ted Shawn. It was the first major dance school to open in the United States. The school closed in 1932 at the height of the Great Depression. St. Denis later cofounded Natya: The Authentic School of Oriental Dancing in New York City. Throughout her long career as a choreographer (she died in 1968), she continued to borrow exotic and spiritual themes from other cultures and based her dances on myths, especially those from the Orient (eastern Asia).

Anna Sokolow was born in Connecticut in 1915. She studied with Martha Graham and eventually began a dance career with Graham's troupe. Her great interest, however, was choreography, which she first took up in 1934 with her own dance troupe. She is known for setting her works to jazz music and for exploring social issues through dance.

Born in 1919 in Trinidad, an island in the Caribbean Sea, Pearl Primus is best known for her dances based on the rituals of African and other black cultures. Primus's choreography, like that of Katherine Dunham (see box), was heavily influenced by her background in anthropology, which is the study of human cultures. Primus studied at Columbia University in New York City and eventually earned a doctorate (the highest degree) in the subject. In 1943, she gave her first performance as a professional dancer in a work called *African Ceremonial,* which she had choreographed. She went on to perform dances of West Indian, African, and African American origin. Primus furthered her interest in African culture and was named first director of Liberia's Performing Arts Center (in Africa) in 1959. She also was named director of the Art Center of Black African Culture in Nigeria, Africa. The dancer later opened the Primus-Borde School of Primal Dance with her husband, dancer Percival Borde. In 1996, she was involved with the Pearl Primus Dance Language Institute in New Rochelle, New York.

Yvonne Rainer was born in 1934 in California. A student of Martha Graham, she began her career as a choreographer in 1961. In 1962, she was a

Encore: Katherine Dunham

Prominent choreographer Katherine Dunham was born in 1909 in Illinois. Of Madagascan, African, French-Canadian, and Native American heritage, she was born at a time when racism and segregation were common. Dunahm persevered, however, and managed to attend the University of Chicago, where she studied dance.

By 1931, Dunham had formed her own dance company. Her first lead role came in the West Indian ballet *La Guiablesse* in 1933. Dunham had a lifelong interest in anthropology, and she earned first a master's and then a doctoral degree in the subject. She did field work (research done in places other than in a library) in the Caribbean. As her dance company toured the world, her interest in folk dance continued, and she began to incorporate many native dance steps into her works. One such dance was *L' Ag' Ya*, which opened in 1944. Dunham based her choreography on a fighting dance she had observed in a fishing village on the Caribbean island of Martinique.

Dunham's goal was to acknowledge and celebrate the contributions of black cultures in dance. In the 1940s, she did choreography for Broadway and Hollywood. Two of her best known works during this time were *Cabin in the Sky* and *Stormy*

founding member of the Judson Dance Theater, which produced experimental dances. Rainer is known for writing dances that are performed to popular music. She began to work in film in the 1970s when she wrote, choreographed, and produced short works that explored how human emotions can be linked to events in society.

Choreographer Trisha Brown was born in 1936 in Washington State. She is known for challenging the notion that female dancers must be delicate and light. Her style of choreography includes using unusual movements such as running, blocking (as in football defense), and dodging. She formed her own dance company in 1970. Brown continues to emphasize natural movements and unusual props such as ropes, pulleys, and building structures in her choreography.

Modern dancer and choreographer Twyla Tharp was born in 1941 in Indiana. She studied at the American Ballet Theater School and went on to perform with the Paul Taylor Dance Company. Tharp began her own dance troupe in 1965 and concentrated on works without music and performed in nontheater settings. In the 1970s, she began to choreograph works danced to both classical and popular music, including jazz. She is also known for the rapid, jerky movements of her dancers. Tharp has

Weather. In 1940, she formed the Tropical Revue, the first all-black dance troupe. Five years later, she opened the Dunham School of Dance in New York City. The group toured extensively.

During the 1963–64 season, Dunham choreographed the Metropolitan Opera's production of *Aida,* a famous tragedy about an African princess. Dunham became the first African American to choreograph for the Metropolitan Opera. She also established schools for the performing arts in Haiti and Illinois. Her influence continues to be felt among another generation of modern dance choreographers.

choreographed for Hollywood films as well, including *Amadeus* and *Hair.* She is unique in that she is able to move back and forth between the worlds of modern dance and ballet. She has choreographed for both the Joffrey Ballet and the American Ballet Theater. In 1988 Tharp became a full-time artistic associate and resident choreographer of the American Ballet Theater.

Teachers

Martha Hill was born in 1900 in Ohio. During her long life (she died in 1991), she taught numerous young people who went on to become star dancers, choreographers, and directors. Among her students were Martha Graham and Doris Humphrey. In 1932, Hill founded the dance program at Bennington College in Vermont and the program at the Juilliard School in New York City in 1952. She also helped her most gifted dancers by finding teaching positions for them at Bennington and by establishing residencies for them to teach at the American Dance Festival, which is held each summer in Connecticut.

Hill began teaching in 1920 at the Kellogg School of Physical Education in Battle Creek, Michigan. She also taught at several other schools before starting the graduate program in dance at New York University. Hill believed in teaching her students about music and other forms of dance such as the ritual steps of Native American dances, ballet, modern dance, folk dance, and country dance. Hill's varied course offerings encouraged her students to explore beyond the European roots of ballet. Her legacy is a modern dance style that combines all types of dance with tumbling, running, and other athletic movements.

Women in Theater

The art of entertaining has a long tradition. Modern musicals have their origins in the works of traveling troubadours, or entertainers, of the Middle Ages, who journeyed from town to town telling stories through song and music. This form of storytelling was eventually formalized into an art form called opera, which developed in Italy around 1600. The American influence of jazz music and modern dance helped bridge the gap from grand opera to musicals.

Serious theater, or drama, can take the form of tragedies or comedies. Tragedies typically explore some serious flaw within the character of the hero or heroine and often end unhappily. Comedies, especially the early ones, revolve around misunderstandings between a couple who was romantically involved. The comedy ends happily, with the lovers reunited and usually looking forward to marriage.

From the mid-1500s until the late 1800s, the theater was very stylized. That is, actors used exaggerated gestures and speaking voices to create their characters and sense of the story. In the 1900s, however, actors and other people involved with theater, such as costumers and playwrights, began to use a more natural, realistic style. Gone were the elaborate gestures, speaking voices, costumes, scenery, and props.

Let us look first at some of the great serious actresses who played to audiences in the United States and throughout Europe. From there we will examine some of the actresses and entertainers who helped make Broadway one of the premier theater capitals of the world.

Drama

Modern drama (both comedy and tragedy) can trace its origins to classical Greece (five hundred years before the birth of Christ), when theater was an important part of life. Theater again became important during the Middle Ages, when church plays and religious festivals were common. These religious plays (called miracle or mystery plays) were used to explain and teach people about religion at a time when very few people could read. Such plays eventually evolved into the entertainment that became common at royal courts.

With the financial support of the nobility, playwrights such as William Shakespeare and Christopher Marlowe and, later, actors and theater owners, could devote themselves to art. The result was the creation of a new art form, the multi-act play that used a company of actors to tell a story in a theater. This art form also relied on costumes, scenery, and props to help create atmosphere. Today, national, regional, and local theater companies perform throughout the United States.

Some of England's most famous theaters continue to offer their patrons a mix of drama, opera, ballet, and musicals. They include Covent Garden, Drury Lane, the Victoria (Old Vic) Theater, the Sadler-Wells Theater, the Prince of Wales Theater, the Royal National Theater, and the Gaiety Theater. The English theater district is called the West End. The other famous European theaters include La Scala in Milan, Italy; the Comedie Francaise in Paris, France; the Schiller Theater in Berlin, Germany; and the Norske Teatret in Oslo, Norway.

Canada has also gained a reputation for its Shaw Festival, held at Niagara-on-the-Lake, Ontario, and its Stratford Festival, held in Stratford, Ontario. The Shaw Festival concentrates on works by George Bernard Shaw and other playwrights of his era, while the Stratford Festival offers plays by Shakespeare and his contemporaries. A playwright or actor who becomes associated with one of these theaters is said to have "made it" (succeeded professionally) in the world of theater and dance.

America's premier theater district is Broadway, which is in the borough of Manhattan in New York City. Broadway theaters stage musicals, dramas, operas, ballets, and other dance programs. Off-Broadway refers to the theater district that developed in the surrounding areas of Broadway. Since only a handful of plays and musicals could be produced each year for the Broadway stage, the Off-Broadway area was a place where less famous artists could more than likely have their work produced.

Today, most major U.S. cities have at least one theater for the performing arts. Many cities also have outdoor theaters, which are the sites of musical concerts as well as dance and theater performances. Regional theater has also done much to open the theater business to new talent, including writers and actors. Among the more famous regional theaters in the United States are the Steppenwolf Theater in Chicago, Illinois; the Alley Theater in Houston, Texas; and the Magic Theater in San Francisco, California.

This section looks at some of the most famous actresses in the Western world (Europe and the Americas). Although there have been literally thousands of actresses who performed over the last two hundred years, the women discussed here have all made a special contribution to furthering their art form. They have either introduced new techniques, become the first woman to accomplish a formerly male task, or been named the best in their fields during their lifetimes. For more information about women performers, visit your local library.

The Legends

Eleanor "Nell" Gwyn was born in England in 1650. When Gwyn was about ten years old, the English king returned to the throne (the country had been ruled by a nonroyal government that took power in a rebellion in 1649). The new king, Charles II, loved the pleasures of life. One of these pleasures was theater. Gwyn became one of the first nationally known actresses in England. She performed with the king's theater and was the leading comedienne, singer, and dancer of her time. She caught the eye of Charles and they began a romance that continued for twenty years. Gwyn continued to act and entertain and was granted a pension (retirement money) by King James II, who succeeded his father to the throne.

Mrs. Siddons, the "Tragic Muse," was born Sarah Kemble in England in 1755. She acted with her father's traveling troupe of performers and married a fellow actor, William Siddons. Her talent caught the attention of the foremost actor of the day, David Garrick, who also managed the Drury Lane Theater in London. Garrick hired Siddons to play opposite him, and together they dominated the London stage. She soon gained fame for her performance as Lady Macbeth in the Shakespearean tragedy *Macbeth.* Siddons eventually left Drury Lane to move to the Covent Garden theater, where her actor-brother, John Kemble, worked. Kemble, known as "Glorious John," and Siddons enticed the theatergoing crowds to Covent Garden. She retired from the stage in 1812 and died in 1831.

Fanny Kemble was Sarah Siddons and John Kemble's niece, and she carried on the family reputation for excellence. In 1829, a last-minute casting change put Fanny Kemble in the role of Juliet in the Shakespearean tragedy *Romeo and Juliet.* Kemble's performance made her an overnight sensation. She continued to captivate London audiences until 1832, when she toured the United States and played at the Park Theater in New York City. Kemble eventually married a southern plantation owner, but the slave system there horrified her enough that she returned to England. There she wrote a book called *Journal of a Resident on a Georgia Plantation.* When the book appeared in 1863 (at the height of the American Civil War) it caused many English people to rethink their support for the Southern Confederacy. Eventually the English parliament decided not to equip the Confederacy, a move that helped ensure that the South lost the Civil War. Aside from this political episode, Fanny Kemble remained the one true Juliet to theater audiences in Europe and the United States. She is also credited with making Shakespeare popular with a large theatergoing audience.

Sarah Bernhardt, or "The Divine Sarah" as she became known, was born Henriette Rosine Bernard in 1844 in France. She began to train for an acting career at the age of thirteen and first appeared at the Comedie Francaise, the leading theater in Paris, in 1862. After a bumpy start, she became a star performer by 1869, known for her beauty, speaking voice, and ability to project the heart of the character she was playing. In

1879, she took the London stage by storm and then did the same in the United States in 1880 with the traveling troupe she had founded. Bernhardt was known for her elaborate acting style, which included colorful costumes and highly exaggerated gestures. In 1893, she became director of the Théâtre de la Renaissance in France and renamed it Théâtre Sarah Bernhardt. She continued to perform on stage almost up to her death in 1923. Her most famous roles were that of Marguerite in *La dame aux camelias* (known to U.S. audiences as *Camille*) and as Phaedre in the play of the same name. She was also famous for her rivalry with fellow actress Eleanora Duse.

Ellen Terry was born in England in 1848. She is most closely associated with the Lyceum Theater, where first she starred and then became the manager after a successful career on the London stage. She played all the major Shakespearean heroines, as well as in the plays of George Bernard Shaw. In 1903, she managed productions of William Shakespeare's and Henrik Ibsen's plays.

Lillie Langtry was born on the Isle of Jersey in the English Channel in 1852. Langtry is remembered as much for her breathtaking beauty as for her acting talent. She began acting in 1881 after separating from her husband. Her London debut was in the role of Kate Hardcastle in the Oliver Goldsmith play *She Stoops to Conquer*. Langtry had a comedic flair but did drama equally well. One critic called her "the finest Cleopatra of our time" (the play the critic was reviewing

Sarah Bernhardt in costume as Lady Macbeth.

was was Shaw's *Caesar and Cleopatra*). Langtry's beauty and talent won her acclaim in both England and the United States. She had a gift for making headlines and made a fortune of $2 million with her acting. She died in 1929.

Encore: Diahann Carroll

Diahann Carroll, the multitalented African American performer, was born in New York City in 1935. At age ten, she won a Metropolitan Opera scholarship and began formal singing lessons. In college, she appeared at the Latin Quarter Club in New York City and launched her professional singing career.

Carroll appeared in *House of Flowers* in 1954. She played Ottilie, an innocent girl who remains virtuous in spite of temptation and is united with her true love at the musical's end. She next appeared in *Carmen Jones,* an all-black version of the opera *Car-*

men. Carroll then worked in television until 1961, when she returned to New York to appear in the Richard Rodgers's musical *No Strings.* Her part was that of a high-fashion model with a love interest. In the play, Carroll made musical history by being half of Broadway's first interracial kiss. She won a Tony Award for this role in 1962.

In the late 1960s, Carroll returned to television to star in *Julia.* It was the first television series to star an African American woman. Carroll also made films in Hollywood, including *Porgy and Bess* (1959), *Goodbye Again* (1961), *Paris Blues* (1961),

---

Italian actress Eleanora Duse was born in 1858 and, like Sarah Siddons, came from a family of actors. She first gained a national reputation in 1878, and then an international reputation the following year for her work in French tragedies. She toured Russia, South America, the United States, Italy (where she formed her own troupe), Africa, and England. It was on the London stage in 1893 that Duse's rivalry with Sarah Bernhardt came to a head. Both played Magda in the play titled *Heimat* by the German playwright Hermann Suderman. Theater critics debated who performed better, some liking Bernhardt's emotionally extravagant style, while others preferred Duse's more natural mannerisms. Duse relied

on facial expressions and graceful gestures to create her characters. Unlike the other actresses of her time, Duse wore no stage makeup. She died in 1924.

Edith Evans was born in England in 1888. She began her career by starring in amateur (nonprofessional) productions but by 1917 had begun to work with Ellen Terry, the famous actress-manager. The critics loved Evans, who was a character actress and changed her appearance for each role she played. One of her most famous performances was as Lady Bracknell in *The Importance of Being Earnest.* Evans appeared with the Royal Shakespeare Company, made movies and television shows, and performed for royalty. She received best actress awards

Claudine (1974), *Sister, Sister* (1982), and *The Five Heartbeats* (1991). Carroll also played recurring roles in long-running television series during the 1980s, including *Dynasty, A Different World,* and *Lonesome Dove.*

Carroll's later stage career has included a nonmusical performance as the mother in *I Know Why the Caged Bird Sings.* This 1978 play, based on the life of poet Maya Angelou, was made into a video starring Carroll in 1994. The next year, Carroll revived the role of Norma Desmond, the aging Broadway star, in the Andrew Lloyd Webber musical *Sunset Boulevard.*

from the New York Film Critics, the British Academy, and the Berlin Film Festival for work in the movie *The Whisperers* (1966).

English actress Margaret Rutherford was born in 1892. She played character roles such as Miss Prism in *The Importance of Being Earnest* (1952), Mrs. Danvers in *Rebecca* (1940), and Madame Arcati in *Blithe Spirit* (1945). Each of these roles called for entirely different mannerisms, posture, speaking voice, and appearance. Rutherford was a genius at creating such clearly defined characters. She revived her best stage roles in the films of these plays and received an Academy Award for *The VIPs,* a movie made in 1963.

Born in England in 1912, Wendy Hiller built her stage career around the plays of George Bernard Shaw. She won critical acclaim for her work as Eliza in *Pygmalion* (the play was later made into a hit Broadway musical called *My Fair Lady*), as Joan of Arc in *St. Joan,* and as Major Barbara in the play of the same title. She appeared in both London and New York. Her later roles were character parts, which she performed for both theater audiences and for film.

Actresses on Broadway

Some of the leading ladies on Broadway have included Helen Hayes, Jessica Tandy, Julie Harris, Maggie Smith,

Vanessa Redgrave, Colleen Dewhurst, and Jean and Maureen Stapleton.

During her lifetime, Helen Hayes was known as the "first lady of American theater." She was born in Washington, D.C., in 1900 and died in 1993. As a girl she played stage roles such as Pollyanna. Her adult roles included Cleopatra, Queen Victoria, Portia, and Amanda Wingfield in *The Glass Menagerie.* She won Tony Awards in 1947 and 1958. Also in 1958, the Fulton Theater in New York City was renamed in her honor. Hayes worked in film as well, and won an Academy Award in 1970 for her role in *Airport.*

Julie Harris, who was still active in the mid-1990s, was Hayes's successor to the title of "first lady of American theater." Harris has won more awards than any other living actress and has earned them for her work on the stage, in film, and in television. One of her most moving roles was that of Emily Dickinson in *The Belle of Amherst,* a one-woman play that included the reading of some of this poet's verse. In 1995, she appeared in *The Glass Menagerie,* playing the mother, Amanda.

Other respected Hollywood actresses who began their careers on Broadway include the dancer Eleanor Powell and movie stars Katharine Hepburn, Lauren Bacall, Carol Burnett, and Glenn Close. Close's many talents include Shakespearean drama (she played the mother in the 1990 film version of *Hamlet*), singing, comedy, and dramatic performances in *Barnum* and *Sunset Boule-* *vard.* She won a 1995 Tony Award and an Outer Critics Circle Award for her work as Norma Desmond, the lead character in *Sunset Boulevard.*

Katharine Hepburn, another Broadway legend, first starred in *The Warrior's Husband.* After becoming a film star in Hollywood, Hepburn did subsequent work in the theater, appearing in several Shakespearean plays, *Jane Eyre, The Philadelphia Story* (she also starred in a highly successful film version), and *Coco,* a play about the life of designer Coco Chanel in 1969.

Diahann Carroll, appearing in *No Strings* in 1961, participated in the first interracial kiss on Broadway. Carroll, an African American, played a model who fell in love with the leading man, a white singer. In the mid-1990s, Carroll was playing Norma Desmond in *Sunset Boulevard* (see box).

Other Broadway leading ladies of the 1990s include Zoe Caldwell, winner of three Tony Awards, and Mercedes Ruehl, who took the 1991 best actress in a play Tony Award for her work in *Lost in Yonkers.*

Vaudeville

Vaudeville is a form of musical theater that was popular in the United States from after the Civil War (about 1870) until the 1930s. Vaudeville theaters around the country used the same basic formula. They offered a lineup of separate acts. No story or theme linked the acts. The acts could be skits, comedy routines, jug-

A photo of some Ziegfeld Follies' girls in costume.

gling, animal acts, or singing and dancing. Many stars who became famous in other musical forms had their start in vaudeville theaters. The most famous of the vaudeville theaters, and the goal of all entertainers, was Tony Pastor's Music Hall in New York City.

Ziegfeld Follies

The Ziegfeld Follies were a series of musical revues produced by Florenz Ziegfeld. "The Follies," as they were called, were staged on Broadway from 1896 until 1932. Their consistent theme was to glorify the American woman. The Follies were a starting point for some of the best theater talent of the twentieth century. The best composers, lyricists, actresses, singers, dancers, and technicians were involved in these annual shows, which were known for their elaborate sets, huge casts, revealing costumes, and memorable tunes. Many Follies songs became popular with the general public, and many are still sung today, including "Shine On Harvest Moon" and "By the Light of the Silvery Moon."

Musicals

Modern audiences enjoy musicals in much the same way that earlier audiences enjoyed opera. The two art forms have much in common. Both use music and song to paint characters and develop a plot. Musicals, however, unlike opera, are sung in the audience's own language. In the United States, musicals are written and performed in English, while operas tend to be sung in the language of the composer—and most are done in Italian, French, or German.

Musicals became popular in the United States in the early 1900s. The first musicals were more of a musical revue, that is, a series of songs and dances with no connecting plot. Several artists are credited with creating the musical as we know it today: a story told in two or three acts, complete with songs, dance routines, and elaborate costumes and stage sets. In the 1930s, Jerome Kern, Irving Berlin, George Gershwin, George M. Cohan, Richard Rodgers, and Oscar Hammerstein began creating stories told in song.

Two significant events in the development of musicals included the 1927 opening of *Show Boat* and the 1943 production of *Oklahoma! Show Boat* is the story of an interracial marriage in the 1880s, and it marked the first time that a musical focused on a serious theme. *Oklahoma!* was the first musical to use dancing as an important tool in telling a story, not just as an entertaining interruption. Agnes De Mille did the choreography for *Oklahoma!* and used it as an opportunity to introduce her famous mix of ballet, modern dance, and acrobatics.

Today, the creation of musicals is a field still mostly populated by men. The creative geniuses at work at the end of the twentieth century include Andrew Lloyd Webber, Tim Rice, and the former Alan Menken/Howard Ashman partnership. However, Elaine Stritch, whose company focuses on revues of Stephen Sondheim songs, is one of the few women to make a major name as a creator of musicals. Her show *Sondheim: A Celebration at Carnegie Hall* appeared on television in 1993. Stritch is also known as an actress, and she has performed on Broadway for more than forty years. In 1995, she appeared in *Show Boat* as Parthy.

Musicals are a favorite way for young performers to launch their careers on Broadway, since most musicals have an ensemble (a large cast), which calls for dozens of singers and dancers to perform supporting roles. Over the years, thousands of young women whose names have never made the music history books have sung, danced, and performed in Broadway musicals. Many of the women introduced in this section had their start in one of these ensemble casts and later made their reputation as stars and leading ladies.

Singers

Lillian Russell launched her career in 1883 on the vaudeville stage of Tony Pastor's Music Hall in New York. She went on to perform in the Ziegfeld Follies and then starred in her own company called Opera Comique Co. Before 1900, Russell was acknowledged as the queen of comic opera, the art form that evolved into the present-day musical.

Fanny Brice performed in the early 1900s in vaudeville, radio, and, most sig-

Lillian Russell

nificantly, nine of the Ziegfeld Follies. She is famous for her renditions of songs that have become part of the American repertoire, including "My Man" and "Second Hand Rose." Brice's life was the subject of a 1964 Broadway musical called *Funny Girl.* The film version, released in 1963, starred Barbra Streisand and helped to make her a star.

English actress-singer Gertrude Lawrence was equally famous for her Broadway musicals and her West End theater performances in London, England. She made her reputation performing in a musical revue that became popular in London and then opened in New York. While Lawrence had limited singing talent, she was an immense hit with both audiences and composers. George Gershwin wrote two musicals for her, *Oh, Kay!* (1926) and *Lady in the Dark* (1941). At her urging, Richard Rodgers and Oscar Hammerstein wrote *The King and I* for her. Lawrence also appeared in nonmusicals and was especially popular in comic plays. Lawrence's life was captured in a 1968 Hollywood film, *Star,* with Julie Andrews in the lead role.

In 1935, Ethel Waters became the first African American to star in a racially mixed cast on Broadway. The play was *At Home Abroad.* Waters first appeared in black vaudeville in 1917 and began a career in musicals in 1927. She was known for her rhythm and blues sound, and for being an actress as well as a singer. Her work in the 1940 musical *Cabin in the Sky* won her national acclaim and helped renew interest in black theater. *Cabin in the Sky* also starred the famous black dancer Katherine Dunham.

Pearl Bailey is a performer known throughout the world for her role in the 1967 Broadway production of *Hello, Dolly!* Her other Broadway musicals included *St. Louis Woman* in 1946, *Arms and the Girl* and *Bless You All,* both in 1950, and *House of Flowers* in 1954.

Carol Channing won Broadway fame in the musical *Gentlemen Prefer Blondes,* which premiered in 1949. She appeared in another big hit, *Hello, Dolly!,* in 1964. Channing is best remembered, however, for her performance in *Mame.* (Rosalind Russell recreated the Mame role, minus the singing, for the Hollywood movie *Auntie Mame* in 1958, and in 1974 Lucille Ball played Mame in the film titled *Mame.*) Channing's fans praise her squeaky voice, large eyes, unmistakable platinum blonde hair, and flair for comedy.

Julie Andrews played Eliza Doolittle in *My Fair Lady,* Queen Guinevere in *Camelot,* and leads in *The Boyfriend* and *Victor/Victoria* before recreating some of the roles for the Hollywood film industry. Her Hollywood musicals included *Mary Poppins* (1964) and *The Sound of Music* (1965). Another actress to remake some of her Broadway roles into Hollywood films was Debbie Reynolds, who starred in *The Unsinkable Molly Brown* (1964).

Many other stars had a series of hit musicals. Mary Martin played Maria in *The Sound of Music* and then performed in *I Do, I Do* in 1966 before becoming forever associated with the role of Peter Pan. Patti LuPone played the title role in *Evita* and Norma Desmond in *Sunset Boulevard.* Ethel Merman, the "Queen of Broadway," was acknowledged as the best interpreter of Irving Berlin songs. Her musicals included *Call Me Madam, Annie Get Your Gun,* and *Panama Hattie* (see box).

Sometimes Broadway musicals take an ethnic theme. For instance, *The Flower*

Encore: Ethel Merman

Ethel Merman, called the "Queen of Broadway," was born in 1908 in New York. She began her singing career in cabarets and appeared in vaudeville shows. Her Broadway debut came in 1930, when she starred as Kate Fothergill in the Gershwin musical *Girl Crazy.* Her huge voice and arrogant manner soon made the show's songs famous, including "I Got Rhythm."

Merman's next hit was *George White's Scandals,* which opened on Broadway in 1931. The famous Merman song associated with this musical is "Life Is Just a Bowl of Cherries," which challenged the audience to make the best of their economic woes during the Great Depression (1929–40). *Take a Chance* followed in 1932, with the songs "Eadie Was a Lady" and "Rise 'n' Shine," which both proved to be showstoppers. (The audience halted the performance with their prolonged clapping.)

Merman's long working relationship with Cole Porter began in 1934, when she opened his show *Anything Goes.* The hit songs from this show were "Blow, Gabriel, Blow," "I Get a Kick Out of You," and "You're the Top." Merman recreated her role as nightclub singer Reno Sweeney for a 1936 Hollywood movie version of *Anything Goes.* Another Porter musical followed called *Red, Hot and Blue!* The songs remembered from this musical are "It's De-Lovely" and "Ridin' High." In 1939 came *Stars in Your Eyes* and another Porter musical, *Du Barry Was a Lady.* Merman quickly made hits of "Do I Love You?" and "Friendship."

Panama Hattie (1940) marked Merman's fourth Cole Porter outing. Her work in the role of Panama Hattie, a nightclub owner, made the show her longest running Porter musical. Another Porter hit, *Something for the Boys,* came in 1943 and was her first wartime musical. (The United States entered World War II in 1941.)

One of Merman's greatest hits, *Annie Get Your Gun,* opened in 1946. This Irving Berlin musical featured Merman making hits out of songs like "There's No Business Like Show Business" and "They Say It's Wonderful." After a four-year run, she opened a new musical titled *Call Me Madam,* also by Irving Berlin. Merman made a Hollywood version of *Call Me Madam* in 1953. *Happy Hunting* followed in 1956, and *Gypsy* in 1959. Merman played the mother in *Gypsy,* a point in her career where she gave up leading lady roles for character roles. At most performances, the audiences stopped the show with wild applause when she sang "Rose's Turn," a bittersweet anthem to motherhood.

In 1966, Merman revived *Annie Get Your Gun* at the Lincoln Center in New York City. She then starred briefly as a replacement lead in *Hello, Dolly!* Merman died in 1984.

Drum Song opened on Broadway in 1958 with an all-Asian cast. Among the singers were Juanita Hall, Pat Suzuki, and Myoshi Yumeki. An all-black cast performed *Carmen Jones,* a version of the opera *Carmen.*

Among a younger generation of stars appearing in musicals are Liza Minnelli, Bernadette Peters, and Sarah Brightman. Minnelli, who is the daughter of singer-actress Judy Garland, has appeared in Broadway musicals, Hollywood films, and on television. Peters is one of the foremost interpreters of Stephen Sondheim's songs. Brightman is best known for appearing in Andrew Lloyd Webber's productions, including *Cats, Phantom of the Opera,* and *Aspects of Love.* In the mid-1990s, the most coveted roles for female stars included Eva Peron in *Evita,* Christine in *Phantom of the Opera,* Kim in *Miss Saigon,* and Cosette in *Les Miserables.*

Dancers

In the earlier generations of Broadway dancers, a young woman usually started out as a dancer in a large chorus line. With enough talent and luck, she might be singled out and eventually become a star. Some of the more famous dancers were Marilyn Miller, Adele Astaire, Ginger Rogers, and Eleanor Powell. Miller became famous for her dancing in *Sally* (1920) and *Sunny* (1925), roles written especially for her. She went to Broadway based on the success of her Hollywood role in *Sugar Babies.* Astaire and her husband, Fred, were the most famous dancing couple of the 1930s. Ginger Rogers, who replaced Adele Astaire as Fred's performing partner, combined beauty, grace, and athleticism. Critics have called Eleanor Powell's "the hottest tap shoes ever." She appeared in several Ziegfeld Follies and then on Broadway. When talking movies appeared, she went to Hollywood to begin a successful film career.

The next generation of dancers included Gwen Verdon and Carol Haney, who were Broadway dancing sensations in the 1950s and 1960s. Cyd Charisse, who trained as a ballerina, was known for her strength and grace. She appeared in *Smoke Gets in Your Eyes.*

Shirley MacLaine, who is better known today as an Oscar winning actress and author, got her start on the Broadway stage in 1954 when the lead in the musical *Pajama Game* broke her ankle and MacLaine, the understudy, was called in to take her place. She became an overnight sensation. MacLaine went on to star in more than two dozen films and often returned to the Broadway stage.

Paula Abdul was one of the best-known modern dancers working in the mid-1990s. Abdul, who was born in 1962 in North Hollywood, California, is also a choreographer and singer. She studied tap and jazz dancing as a child and performed with musical theater groups. Abdul's dancing ability and exotic good looks (she is of Brazilian, Syrian, and Jewish French-Canadian ancestry) won her a place with the Laker Girls, the

Lengendary dancers Ginger Rogers and Fred Astaire.

cheerleading squad for the Los Angeles Lakers basketball team, in 1980. She was soon choreographing the cheerleading acts, and her dance-influenced numbers were quickly being copied by other squads. Today Abdul is one of the most sought-after choreographers in Hollywood. Her work has included choreography for film, music videos, and stage numbers.

Lyricists and Choreographers

Marguerite Monnot is the lyricist wrote the songs for the French musical *Irma La Douce,* which premiered in 1960. Monnot is also famous as the author of many of the songs sung by Edith Piaf.

Carole Bayer Sager often collaborated with composer Marvin Hamlisch. Some of her songs included "Georgy" (1970) and "They're Playing Our Song" (1979). Marilyn Bergman also collaborated with Hamlisch but much more often with her husband, composer Alan Bergman. Their songs include those from the Broadway musicals *Something More* (1964) and *Ballroom* (1978). The Bergmans' songs also included those from the remake of the film *Sabrina,* which was released in 1996.

Betty Comden and Adolph Green were songwriting partners who worked together from the 1940s to the 1980s. They each began their Hollywood careers by performing in nightclubs, and they continued to perform through 1958, when they did a special revue called *A Party With Betty Comden and Adolph Green.*

They are best known, however, for the string of hit songs they produced together. Among their works are the musicals *On the Town* (1944), *Billion Dollar Baby* (1945), *Peter Pan* (1954), *Applause* (1970), and *A Doll's Life* (1982).

In 1984, Arlene Phillips choreographed *Starlight Express,* a musical by Andrew Lloyd Webber. Phillips, an innovative choreographer, put her dancers on roller skates so they could move like the vehicles they were portraying.

Teachers and Other Support People

As with the world of dance, most theater people in supporting roles began their careers as actors. After acting for a time, they discovered that their interests or talents led them to teaching students, managing theater companies, directing theater troupes, producing stage plays, and making technical improvements in staging, costumes, makeup, and lighting.

French actress Madeleine Bejart managed her family's company of touring actors during the mid-1600s. She later merged her troupe with one managed by Marie Champmesle, and their joint venture was called the Comedie Francaise. Today, this theater is the oldest operating theater in Europe.

Lilian Baylis was an English actress who founded the Victoria Theater (Old Vic) and Sadler-Wells theater companies. Baylis took over management of the Victoria Theater in 1920 and soon made it a leading venue for opera, ballet, and theater. After performing all of Shakespeare's plays at the Old Vic, she rebuilt and opened the old Sadler-Wells Theater in 1923. Opera and ballet were the focus of this theater.

In 1853, Laura Keene became one of the first female theater managers in the United States. She took over the management of the Charles Street Theater in Baltimore, Maryland. Keene also opened her own theater in New York City in 1855, where she was both the manager and the leading lady. Keene contributed several innovations to theater management. Instead of producing many different plays, she kept popular plays on the bill for a longer time, thus creating the "long run" for plays. She also made the afternoon matinee a standard feature.

Eva Le Gallienne was an English actress who left the stage to direct and manage her own theater in 1926. For five years she ran the Civic Repertory Company, until it was forced to close at the height of the Great Depression in 1931. She returned to acting but later opened a second venture, the American Repertory Company, which also failed. She acted until her death in 1991.

African American Theater

Until the mid-1960s, many black and white Americans did not mix freely in society or business. In the South, there were even laws that prohibited black and white people from eating at the same restaurants, using the same drinking fountain, sleeping at the same hotels, living in the same neighborhoods, or attending the same schools. This practice of keeping the races separate was called segregation. Sometimes segregation was enforced by law, while other times it was enforced by custom.

Segregation meant that many of the most talented African American actors, singers, dancers, and musicians could not attend the best drama or arts schools, nor could they perform in the premier theaters. They were not welcome to join the best dance troupes or the well-known acting companies. African Americans responded by creating their own schools, theaters, and companies. One of the prestigious places for black entertainers to play was Harlem, a culturally and artistially rich black neighborhood of New York City. Other entertainers took to the road in traveling revues. Some performed in nightclubs and vaudeville theaters in cities with large black populations such as New Orleans, Louisiana; Detroit, Michigan; and New York City.

Among the famous African American entertainers who performed under the restrictions of segregation were Jackie "Moms" Mabley, Florence Mills, and Josephine Baker. Two of the most prominent of the black entertainers were able to break into the white world of Broadway, however. They were Ethel Waters and Pearl Bailey (discussed above, under "Singers").

Jackie "Moms" Mabley was born in 1894 in North Carolina. She was a dancer, singer, and comedienne who performed in black vaudeville theaters and night-

Although Josephine Baker never became a star in the United States, she was very popular in Europe.

clubs for more than fifty years. By the time she moved to Cleveland, Ohio, at age fourteen, Mabley had two children (both were the results of rape). Despite her early tragedies, Mabley decided on a career in entertainment. First she created a singing and dancing routine. Then she switched to comedy and became a hit when she was discovered by a national audience in the mid-1960s. She appeared on television and made recordings before her death in 1975.

Florence Mills was born in 1896 in Washington, D.C. She was the leading black musical comedy singer and dancer from about 1920 to her death in 1927. Mills was known for dressing in male attire to create roles and for singing and dancing to both folk and popular music. In 1913, she began working in a cabaret in Chicago, Illinois. She gained attention with her debut in *Shuffle Along* in 1921 and solidified her reputation with her dancing in the *Plantation Revue* in 1922, before touring London the next year. The Plantation was a famous black nightclub in the 1920s. In 1924, Mills returned to New York City to star in a musical called *Dixie to Broadway* and then went back to London for a tour with the musical *Blackbirds* in 1926. Mills died in 1927 while undergoing a common operation to remove her appendix.

Dancer and entertainer Josephine Baker was born in 1906 in Missouri but lived much of her life in Paris, France, where the audiences were more colorblind than they were in America. In France, Baker was a star, idolized for her elegant good looks and artistic talent. When she visited America, however, Baker was seen as an upstart black performer. As a result of this attitude, she spent most of her career dancing, singing, and acting with the Folies-Bergeres, the premier music hall in Paris. She also toured Europe and made recordings.

The black theater tradition continued to flourish even after segregation officially ended. For instance, *The Wiz* (1975) and *Your Arms Too Short to Box With God* (1976) were popular musicals that starred all-black casts and drew huge audiences of both black and white people.

Direction of Women in the Performing Arts

The state of live dance and theater in mid-1990s America is influenced by three social trends. First, we are in an era in which there is a loud public outcry against using tax dollars to provide government support for the arts. Second, since the 1980s we have seen a decrease in the number of tax dollars and financial grants made by the U.S. government to colleges and universities. When the dollars dry up, school administrators tend to look at the arts as a first place to cut programming. Third, the price of theater tickets continues to rise, which puts live performances out of reach for many people.

The response to these trends has been that more people are receiving their dance and theater entertainment through television. The British Broadcasting Company in England and National Public Television in the United States have produced highly acclaimed series on dance, opera, and theater. Regional and amateur theater and dance troupes are also gaining larger audiences, who enjoy both their quality and their more affordable ticket prices. Broadway is experiencing a resurgence not so much by introducing new plays and musicals, but by resurrecting proven hits and playing them for a new generation of theatergoers. These revivals have included *Carousel, Show Boat, Guys and Dolls, State Fair, Victor/Victoria,* and *Hello, Dolly!* Incidentally, this trend is mirrored in Hollywood, which has seen many remakes of the classic movies of the 1940s and 1950s.

What do these trends mean for female performers? On a national level, it means fewer starring roles for women. It also means that only proven stars get the choice roles. On the local level, it means more opportunity for women to pursue their dream of acting or dancing and singing. When a woman works at a theater near her home and for a troupe with a limited touring schedule, her own schedule is more flexible. She can more easily combine other activities (such as family life) with her artistic career. The trends also seem to suggest more opportunity for women working in nontraditional roles in the theater. Women who may have had no opportunity to open a Broadway play can turn to smaller, regional theaters as a showcase. Among the more famous of the regional playwrights are Wendy Wasserstein, who opened *The Sisters Rosenzweig* in Seattle, Washington, and Eileen Atkins, whose *Vita and Virginia* opened Off-Broadway.

Whatever the trends and their social significance, young women (and men) will continue to flock to New York City, looking for their big break in a Broadway production. Dancers will still move across the country to receive tutoring from the best instructors at the Juilliard School and Martha Graham's school. Apparently the attraction of seeing one's name in lights has not dimmed, even though the opportunities for success may be more limited.

21

Film and Television

"The gigantic silver screen . . . glows, and on it women may be seen to be astonishing in their beauty. . . . They talk, and everyone listens. They cry, and everyone feels sad. They laugh, and everyone perks up. . . . Most important of all, men worship them."

—Jeanine Basinger,
A Woman's View:
How Hollywood Spoke to
Women, 1930–1960

During the golden age of movies (1930s to 1950s), women were the major stars of the silver screen, and men were of secondary importance. Actresses were considered goddesses by their adoring fans, and the major moviemaking studios saw to it that this image of their stars was spread far and wide.

Hollywood, California, was the center of this magical world. Hollywood provided the women of the world with a romantic fantasy, where catching the handsome hero was the beautiful heroine's sole reason for being, and where it was presumed that once he was caught, they would both live happily ever after.

Self-sacrifice, the giving up of something precious, has long been a major theme in the movies. Women played characters who started out yearning for a career, but ninety-nine times out of a hundred they sacrificed their career for love—the reason being that Hollywood was not interested in stories about women pursuing a career unless that career took second place to a man's love.

Timeline: Women in Film and Television

1896 May Irwin and John Rice perform the first screen kiss in *The Widow Jones.*

1919 Mary Pickford and three men set up United Artists movie studio. She takes an active part in its management.

1920 Famous Players-Lasky Productions (later Paramount Pictures) signs Lois Weber to direct several films, and she becomes one of the highest-paid directors of her time.

1928 Janet Gaynor wins the first Best Actress Academy Award for the silent film *Sunrise.*

1932 *Grand Hotel,* starring Greta Garbo, is the first blockbuster movie.

1935 Shirley Temple, age six, receives a special award from the Academy of Arts and Sciences for "her outstanding contributions to screen entertainment during the year 1934."

1939 *The Women* is released. It contains the largest all-female cast of all time (135 speaking roles for women).

1940 Hattie McDaniel is the first African American to receive an Academy Award. She is chosen best supporting actress for her role in *Gone With the Wind.*

1952 Marilyn Monroe becomes a major film star for her portrayal of Lorelei Lee in *Gentlemen Prefer Blondes.*

1964 *Bewitched* begins its seven-year run on television. Many believe the show reflected society's about-to-be challenged notion that women should stay

Many of the women who made it to the top in Hollywood's Golden Age were tough women. Stars like Joan Crawford, Bette Davis, and Katharine Hepburn were adored by their mostly female audiences but derided by their peers as sexless, boisterous, and too career-minded.

The hold that the major stars had on their audiences lasted until the big motion picture studio system began to fall apart in the 1950s, although that influence still lingers today. Women all over the world copied the stars' hair styles and clothing fashions and looked to them as role models

It is a fairly recent phenomenon that men have dominated the movies. In the 1920s, 1930s, and into the 1940s, when the men went off to war, women usually appeared ahead of men on movie posters and in the credits. The men came home from war, and during the 1950s, war movies with huge male casts became popular. Women began to share movie billing with men, and women's dominance on the movie screen began to fade.

at home no matter how "powerful" they were.

1972 Cicely Tyson plays the first great African American heroine to be shown on the movie screen in *Sounder*.

1973 Julia Phillips is the first woman to receive an Academy Award for best picture as coproducer of *The Sting*.

1974 Tatum O'Neal, age nine, receives the Academy Award for best supporting actress for her performance in *Paper Moon*. She is the youngest person to receive a regular Academy Award.

1981 Katharine Hepburn wins her fourth Academy Award, for *On Golden Pond,* making her the actress to win the most awards.

1985 *The Golden Girls* premieres, making it the first successful modern sitcom in which all of the central characters are women.

1992 Julie Dash is the first African American woman writer-director to have a feature-length film (*Daughters of the Dust*) open nationwide.

1993 Mary Tyler Moore becomes the actress to win the most awards in television history after receiving her sixth Emmy.

1995 Kate Mulgrew takes the captain's seat on *Star Trek: Voyager,* becoming the first female captain on a spinoff of the original 1960s television series.

While women stars once dominated the screen, few have made it to the ranks of director or producer. The 1920s and 1930s were the heyday for women screenwriters, however. Some women, such as Judith Crist, Pauline Kael, and Janet Maslin, have become respected movie critics. Other women, such as Edith Head, have succeeded as costume designers. Some, such as Joan Didion, have succeeded as writers.

This chapter looks at the movie styles of each decade and what roles women played in the movies. Some of the major stars are profiled. The last part of the chapter looks at women actors on television.

History of Film

America has dominated the commercial film industry for much of the twentieth century. At first, a few powerful companies called movie studios (Paramount, MGM, United Artists) controlled the industry. Their early leading ladies were not given star billing for fear they would ask for more money. Later, the studios changed tactics and made women stars by orchestrating publicity stunts. One of the first such stunts happened when a movie studio arranged for a false story to appear in the newspapers that Florence Lawrence had been killed in a street-car accident. Public interest was aroused by the supposed tragedy. Lawrence's studio then placed an advertisement in the papers denouncing the "black lie" and announcing Lawrence's next film. Within a year, Lawrence's name was appearing on movie posters in large letters.

Stars of the Silent Screen

After World War I (1914–18), Hollywood, California, became the undisputed movie capital of the world. At first, permanent acting companies headed by a few major stars appeared in one silent film after another. Two such stars of the silent screen were Theda Bara and Mary Pickford.

Theda Bara and Mary Pickford

Theda Bara was born Theodosia Goodman in Cincinnati, Ohio, in 1890. The movie studio for which she worked gave her the name Theda Bara, which is an anagram (mixed-up word) for "arab death." The studio devised a mysterious background for her, centering around her upbringing as the daughter of an Arab sheik and a princess.

Mary Pickford was born Gladys Smith in 1893 in Toronto, Canada. She made her first stage appearance when she was five years old. She soon went to Hollywood and began appearing in movies. By 1913 she was known around the world as "America's Sweetheart" and in America as "Little Mary."

The two women starred in totally different types of pictures. Bara, chosen to play the part of a vampire in *A Fool There Was* (1915), went on to play the same type of role in some forty films. Her role was that of a deadly woman whose charms led to the destruction of the men she entrapped. The kind of woman she portrayed came to be known as either a "vamp" or a "femme fatale" (deadly woman). In later years stars such as Lana Turner, Marlene Dietrich, Ida Lupino, Barbara Stanwyck, and more recently, Kathleen Turner and Linda Fiorentino played femme fatales.

Pickford, on the other hand, played an ingénue (an innocent girl) in sentimental films like *Rebecca of Sunnybrook Farm, Pollyanna,* and *Little Lord Fauntleroy* (in which she played both the boy hero and his mother). Pickford continued to play adolescents in the movies until she was thirty years old. When she tried to change her image by playing a flashy Spanish beauty in *Rosita* (1923), her fans refused to accept the personality change. She had cut off her trademark curls for the role and in later films was forced to don a curly, blond wig.

Although Pickford is generally remembered for her portrayal of children, she was actually a very shrewd businesswoman. She was one of the first

Mary Pickford in costume for the motion picture Dorothy Vernon of Haddon Hall.

film stars to have fought for the money she knew she deserved. In 1916 she signed a two-year contract that guaranteed her a total of more than $2 million in earnings, a tremendous sum of money for that time.

She was also an important force in organizing and running United Artists Corporation, which continues to be an important name in the moviemaking industry.

These first movies tended to be somewhat sentimental (with the exception of the vamp movies). Pickford and her contemporaries, sisters Lillian and Dorothy Gish, portrayed pure and noble heroines. Movies had titles like *Our Dancing Daughters* and *Orphans of the Storm.* World War I changed the direction of the movies, however, and purity and nobility became "old hat."

The 1920s

The end of World War I led into the decade known as the Roaring Twenties. The Roaring Twenties was a time when many people tried out new styles of dancing and dressing. They also rejected traditional moral standards. Hollywood reflected these feelings by introducing the "jazz baby" in movies. The jazz baby had a quality known as "it." Not innocent like Pickford, or vampy like Bara, girls with "it" were attractive, sexy, and daring. They could drink and smoke like the boys, dance the Charleston, drive fast cars, stay out all night, and be ready to start all over again the next day.

Clara Bow

Clara Bow became known around the world as the "It Girl" of the silent movie period. Bow starred in the movie *It* (1927), projecting the personality of a hyperenergetic party girl. As one of the most popular stars of the 1920s, Bow was best known for portraying a gold-digging salesgirl with designs on her rich boss (*It*) and as a boy-crazy student who thinks college is just a game (*The Wild Party*).

According to Jeanine Basinger, author of *A Woman's View,* 1920s films "were escapist, optimistic tales of love and democracy":

> [Many films] used department stores as background settings. . . . The young women stars, playing poor girls, enact the 1920s female version of the Horatio Alger story. [Horatio Alger was famous for his stories set in the nineteenth century about boys who rose from poverty to wealth.] They marry rich. The department store is seen as a setting in which it is acceptable for a woman to work, but in which her virtue will be tested. She will meet someone very, very wealthy, but if she does not maintain her own values and her own respectability, she will lose all. Perhaps she will even go to prison. . . . The department store contains all the rewards that society has to offer a woman. If she goes by the rules, she will be found ready and then removed from it into the proper world of love and marriage. All the stuff in the store will be hers, but she won't have to work for it.

Other leading actresses of the day with "it" were Polish-born Pola Negri, Swedish-born Greta Garbo, and Americans Myrna Loy, Norma and Constance Talmadge, Marion Davies, and Mary Astor.

In the late 1920s came sound movies. The first film with sound, *The Jazz Singer,* was introduced in 1927. However, many stars failed to make the move from silent movies to "talkies." The exotic Pola Negri, for example, spoke little English and was forced to return to Poland. Greta Garbo, on the other hand, made the move to sound successfully in the 1930 film *Anna Christie.* It was advertised with the slogan "Garbo talks."

Greta Garbo

Great Garbo (1905–1990) was born Greta Lovisa Gustafson in Stockholm, Sweden. She lived in poverty and was forced to seek work as a barber's assistant (she lathered faces) after her father died. She later became a salesgirl at a Stockholm department store, where she was chosen because of her beautiful face to model hats for the store's catalog. She appeared in a few low-budget films before winning a scholarship to Stockholm's Royal Dramatic Theatre Academy. While at the academy, she was spotted by an important Swedish filmmaker, who cast her in the female lead in a movie.

The filmmaker Mauritz Stiller assumed control of Garbo's life. First he changed her name, and then he insisted that she be signed to a major contract with a Hollywood studio when the studio at first wanted only Stiller. Although Stiller did not succeed in Hollywood, Garbo did, eventually making 24 films before she retired in 1941.

Garbo excelled at playing sensual, insecure women. When her last film, a comedy, failed, she refused to make another. She became a virtual recluse (an extremely private person). Her mystique grew throughout the nearly fifty years of her retirement. Garbo was rarely seen in public and seldom gave interviews. On the rare occasions when she was seen strolling near her New York City apartment, these "Garbo sightings" caused as much of a stir as "Elvis [Presley] sightings" still do among some groups of star-struck fans.

With the coming of sound, the movie screen gained many actors—and writers—from the theater. Among the new stars of distinction were names like Claudette Colbert, Bette Davis, Irene Dunn, Katharine Hepburn, Barbara Stanwyck, Ginger Rogers, and Loretta Young.

The 1930s

Gangsters and musical comedies were the focus of 1930s film. The movie industry, which had been suffering financial problems, revived during the 1930s with the arrival of new talent. Strong, independent women such as Marlene Dietrich, Joan Crawford, Mae West, and others, began to emerge as major stars. Even more popular with audiences, though, were the new female types that began to appear in films: the blond bombshell and the wisecracking dame.

Jean Harlow

Jean Harlow was one of the first blond bombshells. In the 1933 movie *Bombshell,* Harlow played a bewildered

Hollywood Gossip Columnists

Hedda Hopper and Louella Parsons are two of the most famous names in Hollywood reporting. It is said these women had so much power they could make or break movie stars. At the height of their careers as newspaper columnists in Hollywood's Golden Age during the 1920s and 1930s, Hedda Hopper and Louella Parsons had a total of about 75 million readers.

Hedda Hopper (1890–1966) was born Elda Furry to a Pennsylvania Quaker (a religious group) family. Considering her background, she took the somewhat unusual step of heading for the Broadway theater district in New York City and becoming first a chorus girl and then an actress. She married DeWolf Hopper, who suggested she change her name to Hedda and took her to Hollywood, where she played small movie roles. When she was in her forties, she changed careers and began to write a newspaper column focusing on Hollywood gossip. She sold her column to newspapers across the country and in the process became the chief rival of Louella Parsons.

Louella Parsons (1881–1966) was born in Freeport, Illinois. She lived a prosperous, small-town life, marred by the deaths of three of her four siblings. Parsons began her writing career as a reporter for the *Chicago Tribune* in 1910. Because her salary was inadequate, she also wrote scenes for a small local film company to help make ends meet. It was here that she met the movie people who would provide her with writing material for the rest of her life. Her movie column for the *Chicago Record-Herald,* which she began in 1914, was one of the earliest such columns to be written in this country.

In 1925 Parsons was hired by powerful publisher William Randolph Hearst, and a year later she moved to Hollywood. This put her close to the stars of the silver screen. Using a network of paid informers, she collected gossip and facts about the careers and private lives of Hollywood's most famous people for an audience hungry for every detail. Her column was the first of its kind and lasted nearly forty years. Depending upon how often and in what manner she portrayed an actor, Parsons helped make or break many an acting career.

Toward the end of her career, Parson's power began to fade along with Hollywood's, and she found herself out of step with the new teenage rock scene that was beginning to emerge. She wrote in her 1961 biography *Tell It to Louella,* "Hollywood is and has been my life."

but endearing personality who combined sex appeal with honesty and vulnerability. In other films Harlow combined sex appeal with a wisecracking personality to produce some of the best comedies of the 1930s.

Mae West

The wisecracking dame was best represented by Mae West, who was so much in control of her career and her image that she wrote her own scripts and more or less played the same character in all her movies. Her character was a witty woman of loose morals whom no man could resist. West, a statuesque woman with an hourglass figure, stood out among the slender, boyish women who were popular stars of the day. She especially stood apart from the biggest star to break out in the 1930s—five-year-old Shirley Temple.

Shirley Temple

Shirley Temple ushered in Hollywood's true golden age, which began in the late 1930s. The public couldn't get enough of her. Between 1933 and 1939 she danced, sang, and acted in some 21 movies, including such all-time favorites as *The Little Princess, The Little Colonel,* and *Heidi.* In 1940, she suffered her first box-office failures, and her star began to dim. At age 12, Shirley was considered too old and too ordinary to delight audiences any longer.

By the end of the 1930s, more than 400 movies were being churned out each year, bringing audiences of 80 million people (60 percent of the total population!) each week into the elaborate movie palaces that had been built between 1915 and 1920. Different movie studios turned out different styles of pictures. MGM, for example, became known for its glossy musicals. Busby Berkeley was the producer of these musical extravaganzas, which featured dazzling choreography (dance steps) and hundreds of beautiful girls in elaborate costumes.

Betty Grable and Judy Garland

Betty Grable began her career in a Busby Berkeley musical in 1930. She went on to reign as a top star for more than two decades. In Grable's musicals, the boys played football and the girls did little else but plan proms.

Judy Garland was another major star to first make her mark in 1930s musicals. Although she did several films, she is most often remembered today for her role as Dorothy in the 1939 classic *The Wizard of Oz.*

The 1940s

The early 1940s brought a string of movies featuring either strong career women or sick women. The career women, although extremely capable, nearly always came to realize by the end of the film that love was more important than their professional lives. Some examples of "career woman" movies are *His Girl Friday* (1940, starring Rosalind Russell) and *Woman of the Year* (1942, starring Katharine Hepburn).

Many movie heroines of the 1940s suffered from brain tumors or mental ill-

Latina Stars in Hollywood: Carmen Miranda and Rita Moreno

Young women have been coming to America from foreign lands to be in Hollywood movies since about 1915, when Alla Nazimova immigrated from Russia. Among those who achieved stardom are two Latina actors: Carmen Miranda from Brazil and Rita Moreno from Puerto Rico.

Carmen Miranda was born Maria do Carmo Miranda da Cunha in Lisbon, Portugal, in 1909. As a child she moved with her family to Rio de Janeiro, Brazil. She quit school at age 15 to go to work in a hat shop. By age 34, she was an established and beloved star of Brazilian radio, stage, and films, a singer and a dancer as well, despite the fact that she had been born with deformed feet.

In 1939, as World War II was being fought in Europe, Miranda came to the United States to star in a Broadway play. In 1940 she signed a movie contract and began her appearances in a series of musical comedies. Miranda's first movie, a musical called *Down Argentine Way*, provoked riots in Brazil, where it was felt she had "sold out" to Hollywood and had become too Americanized. Thereafter, her countrymen rejected her.

In 1943 Miranda appeared in her most outrageous of her musicals, *The Gang's All Here*. In it she sported the huge, fruit-trimmed hat for which she became known, while singing "The Lady in the Tutti-Frutti Hat."

The Hollywood star system turned Miranda from a vital and lively woman to a caricature (a misrepesentation of someone for comic effect). She was forced to be Carmen Miranda 24 hours a day, attending parties and other events wearing costumes that were supposed to represent a Latin look but became more and more ridiculous.

Miranda also endured life with an abusive husband and fought an addiction to pills and alcohol. At age 46, the subject of ridicule by her peers and rejection by her adopted country, she died at home, alone. Carmen Miranda was the subject of a 1995 documentary film. Titled *Bananas Is My Business,* the film is one in a series of award-winners directed by Brazilian-born filmmaker Helena Solberg.

Carmen Miranda gave Americans a stereotype of the Latin woman. Puerto Rican-

ness. In the book *Popcorn and Sexual Politics,* film historian Marjorie Rosen notes that "the list of forties female victims reads like a Who's Who hospital roster." Bette Davis may have started the trend with *Dark Victory* (1939), in which she played a wealthy woman courageously facing a fatal illness.

It became a joke in Hollywood that if an actress wished to win an Acade-

born actress Rita Moreno confronted this stereotype six years after Miranda died. Moreno refused to work in Hollywood films for seven years after she won the best supporting actress Academy Award for her 1961 performance as Anita in *West Side Story*. When she was interviewed for the documentary film about Miranda, Moreno complained that every role she was offered after *West Side Story* was another "Anita." About that experience Moreno said: "Latin actresses all had to be oversexed; we were always left by the guy. It was expected that the American man or the European would never be serious emotionally with a Latin woman. All I have to do is use myself as an example. I came here as a very young Latin girl. I quickly found out that the only way to have people pay attention to you was to be vivacious [lively]! and fiery! You had to be a very exaggerated caricaturesque person for the American movie people to pay attention to you."

Moreno was born in 1931 in Puerto Rico. Her parents divorced soon after she was born and her mother, Rosa Maria, moved to New York. Five years later, having earned enough money working as a seamstress, Rosa Maria sent for Moreno. Together they lived in poverty.

By age 13 Moreno had become an accomplished dancer and quit school to support her family. By age 19 she was appearing in movies. Her first big break came when she played a slave girl in the movie *The King and I* (1956). Good reviews for her performance led to her role in *West Side Story*. Interestingly, American-born Natalie Wood, whom many critics say could neither sing nor act, was given the lead role in the movie, playing a Hispanic girl.

Moreno has worked continuously in both movies and television and is rememberd by many children of the sixties for her stint on the educational program *Electric Company*. Recently she costarred with Bill Cosby in the 1995 television series *The Cosby Mysteries*. In 1989 she was named Woman of the Year by *Hispanic* magazine.

my Award, she had to appear without makeup or glamorous clothes in a "realistic" role. One such performance (although not an award winner) was given by Olivia de Haviland, who played a woman recovering from a mental breakdown in the harrowing 1948 movie *The Snake Pit*. Jane Wyman won an Academy Award for her portrayal of a deaf-mute girl in *Johnny Belinda* (1948). Six years later, Grace Kelly shed her glamorous image and won an Academy Award for *The Country Girl.*

World War II (1939–45) had a profound effect on the movies in a number of ways. Excessively patriotic movies (called propaganda films) were released to help the war effort. Some were very crude attempts to encourage American men to enlist in the armed forces.

Because of wartime restrictions and shortages of materials, fewer films were made during the war years, but they were all well received by a public hungry for entertainment. More than 90 million people a week went to the movies during the war years (66 percent of the total population). With millions of American men off fighting, women played a large part in the wartime movies. A number of those films had war as a theme, such as *Mrs. Miniver* (1942), which won best actress and best supporting actress awards for stars Greer Garson and Teresa Wright.

Rita Hayworth, The Ultimate Glamour "Girl"

The ultimate femme fatale of the 1940s was Rita Hayworth. Born Margarita Carmen Cansino in 1918 in Brooklyn, New York, she was the daughter of a professional Spanish dancer and a Broadway theater showgirl. Hollywood agents discovered her when she performed as her father's dance partner at a Los Angeles hotel.

During the 1930s Hayworth made a few films using her real name and her real hair color (black). Later, at the urging of her studio and her husband, she dyed her hair auburn and changed her name. Hayworth became a major leading lady throughout the 1940s. She is perhaps best remembered for her role in *Gilda* (1946), a film in which the question was raised: Is she really evil or really good? In *Cover Girl* (1944), Hayworth played a woman transformed into a star who then discovers that her celebrity status may destroy her chance for happiness as a housewife. In that movie, Hayworth combined glamour with one of Hollywood's favorite themes—career versus love.

Film Noir

Another type of motion picture appeared in the 1940s—film noir. Film noir is a name first used by the French to describe a dark, suspenseful thriller. The classic film noir picture is *Double Indemnity* (1944), in which the femme fatale role is played by Barbara Stanwyck, who talks Fred MacMurray into a murder plot. Another film noir classic is *The Postman Always Rings Twice,* first made in 1946 and starring Lana Turner as the femme fatale who seduces John Garfield into helping her kill her husband. (*Postman* was remade in 1981 and starred Jessica Lange and Jack Nicholson.)

The film noir style has been reworked from time to time, notably in 1974 with *Chinatown* (starring Faye Dunaway) and in 1981 with *Body Heat* (starring Kathleen Turner). More recent examples of film noir are 1993's *Red Rock West,* starring Lara Flynn Boyle, and 1994's *The Last Seduction,* starring Linda Fiorentino.

Marilyn Monroe's popularity during the 1950s led artist Andy Warhol to paint her image.

The 1950s

The cold war, a period of hostility between the United States and the former Soviet Union, began shortly after World War II. Seeking relief from the war's tension, audiences flocked to see movies with lighthearted themes.

The 1940s invalids and career girls were displaced by a new blond bombshell, Marilyn Monroe (see box) and

Marilyn Monroe, Screen Legend

Marilyn Monroe (1926–1962) was born Norma Jean Baker in Los Angeles, California, the daughter of Gladys Baker, an unmarried movie technician. Because her mother was mentally unstable, Norma Jean spent her childhood moving from foster home to foster home. She was both abused and neglected, and she married at age 16.

During World War II, a U.S. army photographer shot pin-up photos of her, which became very popular with soldiers and attracted the attention of other photographers. She was signed by a modeling agency and divorced her husband.

In 1946 Norma Jean was signed by a major movie studio, and her name was changed to Marilyn Monroe. She appeared in a few very bad movies, and her career seemed to be going nowhere. Then, with the help of some older men, she began to appear in small roles in more respected movies, including *All About Eve* in 1950. The movie studio that held her contract began to promote her through publicity campaigns, and she was soon given a series of starring roles. Monroe became a hit with moviegoers.

But Monroe was not happy with the way she was being promoted—as a dumb blond sex symbol. She remarked, "A sex symbol becomes a thing. I just hate to be a thing." Monroe announced that she wanted to play serious roles, and began studying with acting teacher Lee Strasberg. She then appeared in several critically acclaimed dramas. Her last film, *The Misfits* (1961), written by her playwright husband Arthur Miller, was greeted by critics and audiences with indifference, however. During filming, she was fired for lateness, and just days before it opened, she divorced her husband. Monroe became increasingly unstable and attempted suicide several times. On August 4, 1962, she died of an apparent drug overdose. It is not known whether she really intended to kill herself.

Monroe was a "sex goddess" who wanted to be taken seriously as an actress. Although she was not considered an especially great actress, the personality she displayed on screen was extremely popular with audiences. As a result, Monroe has become a screen legend.

good girls Debbie Reynolds and Doris Day. Reynolds danced and sang her way through musicals and looked for romance in the *Tammy* series. Day starred in a series of "sex war" or "battle of the sexes" comedies like *Pillow Talk,* in which she plays a very prim and proper but capable career woman. Meanwhile, Betty Grable continued to be a big box office draw, appearing in playful roles such as those in *How to Marry a Millionaire* (1953) and *How to Be Very, Very Popular* (1955).

Movie critic Marjorie Rosen defined the decade this way: "Women's films became 'how-to's' on catching and keeping a man." However, by the late 1950s, television was challenging the popularity of motion pictures.

The 1960s

The wide availability of television sets in American homes during the 1960s had a profound effect on the movie industry. Fewer films were made because there was no longer a guaranteed audience for them—everyone was watching television. By 1968 fewer than 175 motion pictures were being released each year to audiences of fewer than 20 million people a week, a great deal less than the 90 million a week of the World War II years.

Increasing costs in the United States led to the production of films overseas. When lawsuits forced the breakup of the major studios, the star system—in which studios spent millions of dollars promoting the people under contract to them—came to an end, and Hollywood's place as a major production center diminished.

During the 1960s the strict Production Code adopted by American producers in 1934 was relaxed. What resulted were more and more movies featuring nudity, sex, and gore. Studios began targeting younger audiences, turning out a flood of "slasher" movies and big-budget fantasy films for young people. Consequently, there were fewer starring roles for women.

The 1970s through 1990s

The 1970s saw a revitalized American women's movement and Hollywood movies flirted briefly with the theme of independent women. In movies like *Alice Doesn't Live Here Anymore* (1974), *Kramer vs. Kramer* (1979), and *Private Benjamin* (1980), women left home to find their own voice. Activist movies were also something of a trend, notably *Norma Rae* (1979), in which Sally Field played a poor southern textile worker won over to the labor union movement. This film was soon followed by *Silkwood* (1983), starring Meryl Streep and Cher. In the film, Streep plays Karen Silkwood, a worker in a nuclear-parts factory who discovers the employees are being contaminated by nuclear radiation.

The top female draw at the box office for most of the 1970s was Barbra Streisand, whose hits included *Hello Dolly!* and *The Way We Were,* both showcases for her singing and acting talents.

But the 1970s were more given over to the "blockbusters," which have wide popular appeal and achieve enormous sales. In this category fall popular fantasies and male-driven fare such as *Close Encounters of the Third Kind* (1977), *Star Wars* (1977), *Superman* (1978), and the *Star Trek* series.

The top moneymakers at the box office in the early 1980s were escapist

Barbra Streisand in a scene from the film version of Hello Dolly.

and fantasy films like *The Empire Strikes Back* (1980), *Raiders of the Lost Ark* (1981), and *ET: The Extraterrestrial* (1982). Later in the decade, audiences turned out for action movies, including *Top Gun* (1986) and *Beverly Hills Cop II* (1987). In these kinds of films, women usually played the love interest.

After Hollywood's brief flirtation in the 1970s with the theme of the liberated woman, some late 1980s movies saw women pitted against women. In 1988's *Working Girl* we have career "girl" Melanie Griffith pitted against career "girl" Sigourney Weaver, who plays Griffith's boss and the villainess. In movies like *The Good Mother* and *Three Men and a Baby,* either the "good mother" wins or the independent career women is punished. Two of the most talked-about "women's movies" of the late 1980s and early 1990s were *Fatal Attraction* and *Thelma and Louise*.

Fatal Attraction

Fatal Attraction (1987) tells the story of the terrible (and terribly unbelievable) things that can happen when a man cheats on his wife. Glenn Close plays the "other woman," who is a raving lunatic. Movie critic Pauline Kael wrote in her review, "This film is about men seeing feminists as witches, and the way the facts are presented here, the woman *is* a witch . . . . Basically, this is a gross-out slasher movie in a glossy format."

Thelma and Louise

Thelma and Louise was released in 1991. It starred Susan Sarandon and Geena Davis as two friends who leave their responsibilities (including men) behind to take a short trip. They encounter and react to violence from other men along the way, which turns them into fugitives from the law.

New York *Daily News* columnist Richard Johnson called the movie "degrading to men." Many other men and some women felt the same way. Callie Khouri, who wrote the screenplay (and won an Oscar for it), says she intended the movie to be a story of two women who "go on a crime spree." Other movies of this type—called "road movies" or "buddy movies"—had nearly always starred men. Seldom, if ever, had they generated as much controversy as this female road movie.

By the end of the 1980s, it appeared that Hollywood was warning women: "You can't have it all." Buddy movies, where the buddy could be another man or even a dog, were packing audiences in. There were few strong roles for women in movies, and in fact women had almost disappeared from film. Male roles outnumbered female roles by two to one.

As a matter of fact, during the late 1980s and early 1990s, Academy Award officials found themselves in the embar-

Window on the World: A Film is Banned in India

In 1995 famed Indian film director Shekhar Kapur submitted his movie *Bandit Queen* to India's board of censors, which reviews all Indian films before release. The movie was based on the life of Phoolan Devi, an peasant from India's lower class. She is a folk hero who became an outlaw and spent 11 years in prison for her crimes. Because she directed her banditry against the country's higher castes, she earned a reputation as a female Robin Hood.

The movie, which stars Seema Biswas, is a stunning and graphic condemnation of India's caste system. Devi herself, who was released from prison in 1994, ran for parliament in 1996 for a political party that claimed to represent India's underprivileged. She describes the movie as an accurate portrayal of her life.

Although *Bandit Queen* has been shown at film festivals around the world, it has been banned in India because of the director's refusal to make what he considers drastic changes that the censors ordered that would portray the Indian social system in a more favorable light.

Actresses Susan Saradon and Geena Davis in a scene from the film Thelma and Louise.

rassing position of scrambling to find five nominees to name in the best actress category. All but one woman nominated for the best actress award in 1988 played a victim. The winner that year, Jodie Foster, played the victim of a gang rape in *The Accused.*

The lack of female nominees was no longer a problem by 1995. But the grim joke was that many of the best actress nominees played prostitutes, while one played a nun (Susan Sarandon, *Dead Man Walking*).

By the mid-1990s, it appeared that the trend of few women in strong female roles was reversing itself. Several films about women and girls were released in 1995, movies including *How to Make an American Quilt, Little Women, Waiting to Exhale,* and *Now and Then.* Unfortunately, the public's perception was that those movies were strictly for women ("chick flicks"). Few men (and boys) went to see them. In the case of *The Little Princess,* for example, critics praised the movie, and test audiences of both boys and girls loved it. Boys would not go into movie theaters to see it, however. The reception these movies get from audiences may well determine whether more such movies are made.

"Boy" Movies and "Girl" Movies

In a November 24, 1995, *Oakland Press* article, director Martha Coolidge (*Rambling Rose, Angie, Valley Girl*) commented on Hollywood's recent efforts to make movies that appeal to women: "I think it's gotten really extreme, now. You walk into the theater and there are the boy movies over here and the girl movies over there. It's like pink and blue toys." Coolidge hopes audiences will come to realize that the best movies combine the qualities of women's movies (character-driven) with the qualities of men's movies (action/adventure). She cites *The Fugitive* as an example of a "character-driven action movie."

Current Trends

By 1996 Hollywood was making about 185 movies a year, up from the 1968 figure of 175. However, the average cost to produce and promote a single major movie was $50 million. This figure is double the cost from a mere six years earlier. (In 1913, the average budget for a feature film was $13,000; in 1987 it was $12.5 million.) A large part of today's cost goes for the outrageous salaries demanded by movie stars. How have things come to such a pass?

Stars' Salaries Reach Astronomical Proportions

The movie legends of the 1940s and 1950s, such as Marilyn Monroe, Bette Davis, and Joan Crawford, made one popular movie after another. Their name on the marquee (the sign outside the movie theater) was enough to guarantee a picture's success. This is no longer true of modern movie stars. One of today's highest paid female stars, Demi Moore, has followed hugely successful movies, like *Ghost* (1990), with spectacular failures, such as *The Scarlet Letter* (1995), for example. Still, women such as Moore demand—and get—big salaries.

Experts say one reason for this is that a guaranteed star has to agree to be in a picture before the moviemaker can get money to make it. The number of these "sure stars" is fairly small, so the competition to snare them is great. This drives up the stars' salary demands for each picture. Thus, even though Moore had some hits and some misses in the 1990s, she was able to demand $12.5 million for her 1996 film *Striptease*, the largest salary ever received by a woman up to that time.

Alicia Silverstone, who made the hugely successful *Clueless* for $250,000, demanded and got $5 million for her next film. Sandra Bullock's salary went from $600,000 for *Speed* (1994) to $6 million for *A Time to Kill* (1996). It is important to keep in mind, though, that while female stars were getting these high salaries, Jim Carrey was paid $20 million for the dud *Cable Guy* (1996).

This tremendous increase in the cost of making movies inhibits creativity. As a result, moviemakers now tend to play it safe, making movies they know will appeal

Asian American Actors in Hollywood

Asian American actor and filmmaker Thi Thanh Nga (*From Hollywood to Hanoi*), who goes by the stage name of Tiana, recently discussed the image of Asians that is projected by Hollywood. Writing in *Cineaste,* a magazine "on the art and politics of the cinema" (Vol. XXI, No. 4, 1995), she said that between 1919, when Anna May Wong appeared as an extra in the silent film *The Red Lantern,* and 1994, when leading Hong Kong director John Woo made his first Hollywood film:

"Hollywood's perception of the Asian seemed to have been derived directly from the nineteenth-century frontier view of Chinese as a subhuman species suitable for building levees, laying railroad track, doing laundry, or being dangled from trees by those ridiculous pigtails. Moviegoers were fed . . . images of the China Doll. . . supple in [native] attire, secret danger cocked in her eyes, graceful as a snow leopard. But look out! There's a dagger up her silk sleeve."

Tiana believes the stereotypes and the scarcity of roles for Asian Americans in Hollywood films is slowly changing. "The long march isn't complete, but maybe we do see the hint of light at the end of the Hollywood tunnel," she writes.

to audiences. Usually this means repeating the same type of movie that succeeded the last time or remaking an old hit. This is why we see stars such as Sylvester Stallone or Arnold Schwarzenegger playing essentially the same role in movie after movie.

More Movies Being Made

As the twentieth century draws to a close, more and more movies are being made. Film companies like Paramount are producing and distributing far more films than in the past. The reason is that they are owned by much bigger and wealthier companies like Walt Disney and Turner and have more money to make films. The foreign market (American movies being shown around the world) has grown enormously and now accounts for at least one-half if not more of what a film earns. Videos, cable, and network television also create a continuous hunger for movies. This being the case, movies continue to play an important part in American culture.

Minorities Underrepresented in Films

African Americans complain that blacks, especially black actresses, continue to play only a small role in the film industry. When Whoopi Goldberg won an Academy Award for her supporting "buddy" role in *Ghost* (1990), she was only the second black woman ever so honored by Hollywood. In fact, major black organizations considered boycotting the Academy Awards presentation in 1996 to protest the scarcity of blacks in the movies.

Ellen Holly, author of *One Life: The Autobiography of an African American Actress,* says:

> Back in November 1981, the NAACP [National Association for the Advancement of Colored People] had to eliminate the category of best actress when giving out its annual Image Awards because there was only one performance by a black actress in a major role that year (Cicely Tyson in *Bustin' Loose*). [There is a] paucity [lack] of roles for black actresses . . . [who] face additional problems. The film industry creates white female stars by casting gifted but unknown actresses in career-building roles. . . . The industry has preferred to . . . borrow them [black female stars] ready-made from the field of entertainment. The history of black women in film has not been one of actresses but of international singers who are already celebrities: Lena Horne, Dorothy Dandridge, Leslie Uggams, Diana Ross, Whitney Houston, Janet Jackson.

Blaxploitation Movies

The real heyday for blacks in the movies was the 1970s, when a group of movies with mostly black casts was released. Often referred to as "blaxploitation" films, these movies revolved around black revenge against whites. (The movies came out not long after riots and unrest in urban areas during the 1960s.) The movies were mostly male-centered and relied heavily on sex and violence. A notable exception was *Foxy Brown,* starring Pam Grier. Audiences cheered as Grier got revenge against a

Whoopi Goldberg became only the second African American woman in history to win an Academy Award.

ranch full of drug-dealing white men who had killed her lover.

A series of nonblaxploitation films was also released between 1972 and 1978, but unfortunately the movies were ignored by critics and audiences alike. Among them were:

- *The Wiz* (1978), starring Diana Ross
- *Georgia, Georgia* (1972), starring Diana Sands
- *The River Niger* (1976), starring Cicely Tyson
- *Black Girl* (1972), starring Leslie Uggams and Ruby Dee, with a script by Maya Angelou

Oprah Winfrey: Talk Show Host Extraordinaire

Oprah Winfrey, television and film star, was born in 1954 in the small town of Kosciusko, Mississippi, to a single mother. She spent her early years on her grandparents' poor pig farm while her mother sought work in the North. Her life on the farm was lonely and isolated, and much of her free time was spent acting in church pageants and reading. She became so skilled at public speaking that she became known as "Preacher."

Between the ages of seven and fourteen, Winfrey moved back and forth from her mother's home in Wisconsin to her father's home in Nashville, Tennessee. At age fourteen, Winfrey permanently went to live with her father in Tennessee. With him and his wife, she found the discipline and structure that gave direction to her life.

In 1973, after studying theater arts at Tennessee State, Winfrey accepted a job as Nashville's first black newscaster. She was only nineteen. At age twenty-two she moved to Baltimore, Maryland, and delivered the news on television there. Over the next six years she became cohost of a celebrity interview program, to rave reviews from the critics. In 1979, she moved to Chicago, Illinois, which was considered by some to be a racist city, to host her own morning talk show. Audiences responded with enthusiasm to her warm, friendly style and her sense of humor. In 1986, Winfrey's talk show went national and has remained an audi-

---

Two of the best black films to come out of the decade and to achieve some commercial success were:

- *Sounder* (1972), starring Cicely Tyson
- *Claudine* (1974), starring Diahann Carroll, with a script by Tina and Lester Pine

During the 1980s, the film that stands alone in featuring strong black women characters is *The Color Purple* (1985), based on Alice Walker's book. The movie starred Whoopi Goldberg, Margaret Avery, and Oprah Winfrey. Although nominated for 11 Academy Awards, the movie received none.

The continuing popularity in the 1990s of black women's novels prompted a call for more films by black women directors. Julie Dash has emerged as the director to watch with films like *Daughters of the Dust*.

Early Women Movie Directors

Lois Weber

Lois Weber began her movie career in about 1912, writing, directing, and starring in her first film. By the follow-

ence favorite ever since. Winfrey attributes her success to her "ability to be myself in front of the camera, which is a gift."

Winfrey has appeared in movies, such as *The Color Purple,* and today owns her own production company, HARPO Productions, Inc. (HARPO is Oprah spelled backwards). She was the third woman and the first black woman in American history to own such a company (Mary Pickford and Lucille Ball were the other two). At the HARPO studios, Winfrey's television show and other films are taped. In 1992, *Forbes* magazine reported that she and Bill Cosby, also African American, were the world's top two moneymaking celebrities.

ing year she was a leading American director. Weber's films were popular because they were about unusual topics that no one else would touch. For example, her movie *Where Are My Children?* (1916) was about abortion. She tackled other topics such as capital punishment (receiving a death sentence for committing a crime), birth control (at a time when sharing birth control information with another person was illegal), and racial prejudice. Weber directed Russian ballerina Anna Pavlova in the only film Pavlova ever made, *The Dumb Girl of Portici.*

Dorothy Arzner

At about the same time Weber was making her mark, Dorothy Arzner began directing films. She had quit medical school to enter the film industry. Arzner worked her way up from being a typist to directing her first film in 1927. Called *Fashions for Women,* it was a great success with women, who were then the majority of moviegoers. Arzner became known as a maker of "women's films" (see box), a title that may have been meant to belittle her but in fact delighted her. She reasoned that if her movies were popular with women, her services ought to be in demand. And she was right. Arzner worked with some of the greatest acting talents of her time, including Katharine Hepburn in her second film, *Christopher Strong* (1933). In that film, Hepburn portrayed a flier with a mind of her own (she had an affair with a married man). The movie's message was considered a strong statement for the time.

Ida Lupino

A third notable early woman director was Ida Lupino, a British movie actor who went to Hollywood in 1933. Although she was very popular with the public, Lupino was not satisfied with merely acting. In 1949 she began her own production company—acting, writing, producing, and directing a number of films. Her movies often explore the tensions involved when women experienced a conflict between home and career. She confronted intimate issues such as rape, polio, and illegitimate children at a time when the big studios were turning out war films. Lupino was one of the first major directors to make the move from movies to television in 1959. She directed episodes of several popular shows and also starred with her husband, Howard Duff, in a comedy about a husband-wife detective team.

Weber, Arzner, and Lupino all touched a nerve in the moviegoing public. They directed films that dealt with the real problems women faced—and still do.

The Modern Directors

Barbra Streisand

Women still have difficulty being accepted as film directors, a position long reserved for men. Even when women do direct successful films, they are often judged using standards different from those applied to men. For example, Barbra Streisand has directed the successful films *Yentl, The Prince of Tides* and *The Mirror has Two Faces.* Yet she is still considered by her Hollywood peers to be an intruder in the directing field. This attitude makes it harder for women directors to secure financing for new films.

Jodie Foster

In the 1990s, Jodie Foster, after appearing in some thirty films, emerged as one of the most powerful women behind the scenes in the movie business. Her first directing effort was *Little Man Tate,* which was well received by movie critics. She followed this with *Home for the Holidays* in 1995, which was also well received and found an even larger audience.

Diane Keaton

Diane Keaton is another actress turned director, first of music videos, then after-school television specials, and recently the feature film *Unstrung Heroes.* Both Foster and Keaton turn out studies of people coping with real-life, emotional issues in an era of R-rated shoot-em-ups.

Penny Marshall

When Penny Marshall's movie acting career failed to take off, she turned to directing—with great success. Among her directing efforts is *Big,* the story of a child who magically turns into an adult overnight, and *A League of Their Own,* which brings to life the long-neglected story of the women's baseball league that was formed when American men marched off to fight in World War II.

Television

Few inventions of the twentieth century have had a more profound impact on our lives than radio and television. Long before there was television, families gathered around the hearth in the evening to share its warmth and to converse with one another. When radio replaced the hearth, family members still sat facing one another and shared their reactions to what they heard. The mass distribution of television sets in the 1950s changed everything, though. Now people faced a screen instead of one another. This section gives an overview of how women have been depicted on television shows through the decades.

The 1950s: Two Interpretations of the Housewife

One of the most popular television programs ever produced came out of the 1950s—*I Love Lucy*—starring Lucille Ball. Ball played the well-meaning but scatterbrained wife of Ricky Ricardo, a

Jodie Foster has become the latest female film director to make hit movies.

Cuban bandleader. Although he considered her a housewife, she longed for a career in show business. As a result, Lucy spent most of her time cooking up ridiculous schemes to become a star.

The 1950s also brought audiences the character of June Cleaver, the perfect homemaker and mother, on the television show *Leave It to Beaver.* Barbara Billingsley played June on the show, which ran from 1957 to 1963. June was calm and unflappable in the face of the rather mild mischief her sons got into. She presented American women with an

Lucille Ball

Bewitched

Bewitched appeared just as the 1960s women's movement was gathering momentum. It starred Elizabeth Montgomery as Samantha, a beautiful witch who tries to adopt the role of a housewife, while her husband, Darrin, frets about curbing and trying to conceal her extraordinary powers. Darrin feels strongly that his job is to be the family's only breadwinner, while Samantha's job is to be a perfect homemaker. Unfortunately for Darrin, in episode after episode it proves impossible for him to succeed without Samantha's magical assistance.

I Dream of Jeannie

I Dream of Jeannie starred Barbara Eden as a genie with magical powers who is "owned" by Captain Tony Nelson, an astronaut. She even calls him "Master." For his sake she must, like Samantha on *Bewitched,* conceal her powers. Jeannie, who does not have to pretend to be a housewife, spends considerable time getting into and out of mischief. When her "Master" wishes her to, she can conveniently disappear.

That Girl

On a more realistic note, *That Girl,* another popular series of the 1960s, starred Marlo Thomas as a young woman struggling to become an actress as she supports herself with a variety of part-time jobs.

Hillbillies and Angels

The late 1960s and early 1970s are notable for a series of country-bumpkin

impossible ideal—she did all of her housework and cooking without any help—and while wearing a dress, high-heeled shoes, and pearls.

The 1960s and 1970s

The top-rated shows throughout the 1960s were male-dominated westerns with titles like *Gunsmoke, Have Gun Will Travel,* and *The Rifleman.* Some television shows did, however, grapple with the notion of powerful women. This was reflected in two hit television series with somewhat similar themes, *Bewitched* and *I Dream of Jeannie.*

shows featuring a bevy of scantily-clad young women. Among them are *The Beverly Hillbillies, Petticoat Junction, Hee Haw,* and *Green Acres.*

Featuring not one but three women in leading roles, *Charlie's Angels* was the story of three young detectives who took orders from a male boss whose voice was heard but he was never seen. The show first aired in 1976 and became an instant hit. All the "Angels" were glamorous, of course. Within months of the show's premiere, one of the show's stars, Farrah Fawcett, was on dozens of magazine covers, and women all over the country were imitating her hairstyle.

Social Relevance on the TV

Just as Hollywood paid tribute to the women's movement in the 1970s by producing movies on that theme, so did television shows of the 1970s acknowledge the women's movement. In the 1970s, shows like *All in the Family, Maude,* and *The Mary Tyler Moore Show* discussed and argued women's issues in many episodes.

The 1980s

Soap operas have been around since the radio days of the 1930s. They were originally aimed at housewives and got their name because they were dramatic stories sponsored by soap companies. Soap operas were transplanted to television in its very earliest days.

Soap operas, however, reached their greatest popularity in the early 1980s.

By this time their themes had become a mixture of sex and an earnest handling of popular issues of the day (AIDS, homosexuality, and homelessness are some of the issues that have been tackled). Soap operas involve many plot twists, trauma and heartache, and a cliffhanger ending that keeps audiences tuning in day after day (the phrase "Tune in tomorrow" is said to have originated with soap operas). Lynn Leahey, editor-in-chief of *Soap Opera Digest,* calls soap operas "great dramas that draw you in for years." These shows allow their audiences to watch how characters are handling familiar problems.

Dallas

The top-rated television program during the 1980s, and a smash hit around the world, was the nighttime soap opera *Dallas.* The popularity of *Dallas* coincided with the presidency of Ronald Reagan, a time of self-indulgence throughout the country. (Self-indulgence means that people do not deny themselves material goods.) The show centered on an extremely wealthy and self-indulgent family, and it featured several glamorous leading ladies.

Although many people dismiss soap operas as "women's programming" not worthy of serious consideration, others praise them. Feminist writer and critic Camille Paglia loves soap operas, claiming they present many examples of strong female characters. In fact, soap operas are notable for their aggressive female characters.

Today it is believed that about 40 percent of all Americans watch at least one soap opera a week, and this figure does not include those who tape soap operas for viewing at a more convenient time. Most soap operas are still on in the daytime, but some have appeared weekly during prime time, including *Dallas, Dynasty,* and *Melrose Place.*

American soap operas are wildly popular in India, and Latin America produces its own. Even the World Wide Web has soap operas. The first one was "The Spot," which is visited by up to forty thousand people a day.

Moonlighting

One of the most popular 1980s shows featuring a strong woman character was *Moonlighting.* It starred Cybill Shepherd as Maddie Hayes, head of her own detective agency, and Bruce Willis as her immature, wise-cracking employee David Addison. When the show first appeared on the air, Maddie Hayes was an elegant and confident character. By the time it ended, though, Maddie had succumbed to the charms of David and had been subjected to a variety of humiliations.

Susan Faludi, author of *Backlash,* relates that during the filming of the series, costar Bruce Willis and the show's executive producer were unhappy with the way Shepherd was always voicing her opinion about how the show should be going. Behind the scenes there was a "long-running campaign to cow this independent female figure." Finally Shepherd was sent a disciplinary letter telling her that she would be sued or the show canceled if she did not follow the director's orders. "I felt ill when I received it," Shepherd said. "It was like reform school." *Moonlighting* was canceled in 1989 in part because of the personality conflicts among the stars and the show's producer.

Cagney & Lacey

Another show popular with audiences and featuring two strong, mature female characters was the critically acclaimed *Cagney & Lacey.* The show revolved around two partners on the police force. *Backlash* author Faludi, relates that during the six years Barney Rosenzweig spent trying to get the show produced, he was told, "These women aren't soft enough. These women aren't feminine enough."

The show finally did air as a made-for-TV movie in 1981, and it was a smash hit. However, after two episodes, *Cagney & Lacey* was abruptly canceled. Rosenzweig convinced the network to give it another chance, but to do so he had to hire a different star, someone more "vulnerable" than original cast member Meg Foster. Even though Foster's character was a police woman, vulnerable is "the way the vast majority of Americans feel women should be." Foster was replaced by Sharon Gless.

The network refused to allow the show to deal with "feminist issues," and Rosenzweig continued to do battle with the network executives to keep the show on the air. One network executive told

Two Mid-1980s Shows Are Hits With Women

In the mid-1980s two television show appeared that portrayed women in a positive light: *The Golden Girls* and *Designing Women.* Each of these shows revolved around a group of strong, independent women.

The Golden Girls premiered in 1985, and it became the first successful modern sitcom in which all the central characters were women. Even more unusual, all of these female characters were over the age of fifty. The show centered on the lives of four women who shared a house in Miami, Florida. Humor was often the result of each story as the women tried to overcome the stereotype of the "middle-aged woman." The stars of *The Golden Girls* were Bea Arthur, Betty White, Rue McClanahan, and Estelle Getty.

Like *The Golden Girls, Designing Women* also revolved around a group of four women. Originally starring Dixie Carter, Annie Potts, Jean Smart, and Delta Burke as the four very different women who run a decorating business in Atlanta, the show was successful in portraying businesswomen fairly and positively. First airing in 1986, *Designing Women* was paired with *Murphy Brown* and established a block with strong female appeal.

TV Guide magazine that "the heroines seemed more intent on fighting the system than doing police work." Although it was enormously popular with its audience, the show was finally canceled in 1983. One of its stars, Tyne Daly, went on to win an Emmy for the program, which was shown in summer reruns and scored number one in the ratings. The following year, the network put the show back on the air. It went on to win five more Emmys, until it was finally canceled again in 1988.

Wooing Back Women Viewers

By the late 1980s, male-oriented shows dominated the airwaves, and women had just about disappeared from television (as they had from the movies). During the 1987–88 television season, only three of twenty-two new prime-time dramas featured female leads, and only two of the female leads were adults. Women responded to this turn of events by turning off their television sets. The 1987–88 season is said to have been one of the lowest-rated in television history.

The networks responded to this mass turn-off by giving women some new shows. Among them were *Roseanne, Murphy Brown,* and two shows featuring black women in leading roles, *The Bill Cosby Show* and *I'll Fly Away.*

Roseanne: Hollywood Powerhouse

Roseanne is a comedian and star of her own television program. According to her autobiography, her childhood years were filled with chaos. A serious auto accident at age 16 affected her so strongly that she was admitted to a mental institution. Upon her release, she became pregnant, bore a daughter, and gave her up for adoption.

Roseanne began her career as a comedian while working at a feminist bookstore in Denver, Colorado. She would tell jokes in the parking lot of the bookstore, and her reputation spread by word of mouth. She began appearing in comedy clubs, and eventually Las Vegas nightclubs, earning about $2,000 a month. Roseanne was finally offered her own show after appearing as a guest on *The Tonight Show.*

Of her experience as the star of her own show Roseanne has written:

"When I took that stage, I had earned it, it was mine . . . and I was gonna get rich. Rich as Eddie Murphy, Bill Cosby, Richard Pryor, Bette Midler, all of them. . . . All of my little life I wanted to be a 'star,' to get out, rise above, transcend, shine, burn. I was twenty-eight now and had found that stage."

Roseanne's show consistently ranks among the twenty most popular shows on television. Her style of comedy has been called crude. Her talent, however, is undeniable, and she has made herself one of the highest-earning women in television through determination and hard work. She says: "I wanted to bring to the stage, to the media, to the arts, and *to my own life,* the idea of a woman who was strong and brave, sly and mouthy. . . . In *my* show, the Woman is no longer a victim, but in control of her own mind."

Roseanne and *Murphy Brown*

Roseanne (see box) and *Murphy Brown* were two of the highest-rated television shows of the late 1980s and were still on the air in the mid-1990s. Both series were written by women and became instant and huge hits. Members of the media immediately began to mock and ridicule the real-life Roseanne, at one point declaring her "the most hated woman in America." Despite its huge popularity with audiences, her show has never won an Emmy. Defenders of the program praise Roseanne because unlike other television women, she has qualities that women can relate to. She has an imperfect figure and wears comfortable (not glamorous) clothes. She also has a sense of humor, a job, and a mind of her own.

Phylicia Rashad and the cast from the long-running Cosby Show.

Murphy Brown is played by Candice Bergen. Brown is a recovering alcoholic and star news reporter who is outspoken about politicians. Vice-President Dan Quayle made Murphy Brown famous by singling her out as a bad role model because she had a child without benefit of marriage and seemed to be glamorizing the situation. The controversy only boosted the show's already high ratings.

Jane Seymour in her role as Dr. Quinn.

ics of the program complained that it did not represent reality for most black people, the show was something of a breakthrough. It presented affluent blacks in intact families who were excellent role models. *The Cosby Show,* along with its spinoff *A Different World,* controlled the NBC Thursday night lineup through the late 1980s and continue to be seen in reruns.

Regina Taylor played the role of Lilly, maid to the Bedford family, in the critically acclaimed dramatic series *I'll Fly Away,* which aired from 1991 to 1993. The show was set in the South during the early years of the Civil Rights movement. Unusual for its lack of sex and drugs, the show never found an audience large enough to satisfy NBC and was finally canceled. Black actor Mary Alice received an Emmy in 1993 for her performance on the show.

Heroines From Another Era

Two popular mid-1990s television programs offer us heroines from another age: *Dr. Quinn: Medicine Woman* and *Star Trek: Voyager.* These shows seem to be telling us that audiences can handle strong female characters as long as they are from another time period.

Dr. Quinn: Medicine Woman

The success of *Dr. Quinn,* called "a feminist Western," took many television people by surprise. The title role is played by Jane Seymour. Dr. Quinn is unusual in that she is juggling her roles as wife, mother, and career women on

The Cosby Show and I'll Fly Away

A major showcase for black actors in the 1980s was *The Cosby Show.* It starred Bill Cosby as Dr. Heathcliff Huxtable, and Phylicia Rashad as his wife, Clair, an attorney. Although crit-

the American frontier, when this wasn't the norm. The show appeals to an audience hungry for wholesome programming and good role models.

Star Trek: Voyager

Kate Mulgrew plays Kathryn Janeway, captain of the USS *Enterprise* in a spinoff of the 1960s *Star Trek* series. The show has inspired tremendous loyalty among its fans (called "trekkies").

Although some women have become film and television stars, most actresses continue to struggle for the few select roles. It is even more difficult for Hispanic and Asian American women to find quality roles that aren't stereotypical. It is important to keep in mind that film and television have a profound influence on people, especially children. In order to break society's stereotypical view of both women and men, the film and television industries need to produce motion pictures and programming that portray both genders in a positive way.

Hispanics Missing From Prime-Time Television

The Center for Media and Public Affairs is a Washington, D.C., group that studies the news and entertainment media. In 1996 the center released its study of the 1994–95 television season, which was conducted for the National Council of La Raza, a Hispanic organization.

According to the study, Hispanics made up only 2 percent of the TV world in the 1994–95 season, although they make up 10 percent of the United States population. Of 139 television programs examined for the study, only 18 featured a continuing Hispanic character. And at least two of the television series that did not feature regular Hispanic characters took place in states with large Hispanic populations—Texas and California. These programs were *Walker, Texas Ranger* and *Baywatch.* A spokeswoman for La Raza said, "We're still very much invisible on television. We're not there as writers, we're not there as producers."

22

Journalism

"Journalism" is the collecting, writing, editing, and presentation of news or news articles in the media. The word "media" refers to the means of communicating on a large scale (such as newspapers and magazines, radio and television). It also refers to skilled people—the group of journalists, photographers, and others who make up the communications industry and profession.

This chapter discusses the evolution of print media, such as newspapers and magazines, and broadcast media, including radio and television. Some women who have made names for themselves in those media are profiled. The latest development in human communications, the Internet, is also discussed.

Television Today

In 1953 the Amana television company was proclaiming that the number of televisions surpassed the number of bathtubs in many American cities. In 1950 an average of four hours and thirty-five minutes was spent watching television in each home with a

Timeline: Women in the Media

1825 Anne Newport Royall, possibly the first woman newspaper reporter, is the first woman to have an exclusive (her alone) interview with a president (John Quincy Adams).

1830 *Godey's Lady's Book,* the first American magazine for women, is founded by a man, but it is edited by poet Sarah J. Hale, who intends "to make females better acquainted with their duties and privileges."

1833 Abigail Goodrich Whittelsey is editor of the first American magazine for mothers, *Mother's Magazine.*

1849 Amelia Jenks Bloomer publishes and edits the first prominent women's rights newspaper, called the *Lily.*

1855 The weekly *Women's Advocate,* the first newspaper entirely operated by women, is published by Anne E. McDowell.

1861 Emily Edson Briggs becomes the first female reporter to make regular visits to the White House for news. In 1882 she becomes the first president of the Women's National Press Association, dedicated to supporting professional female reporters.

1889–90 Journalist Nellie Bly is the first woman to circle the globe alone.

1904 Ida Tarbell publishes the *History of the Standard Oil Company,* which causes the company's breakup.

1915 Mary Roberts Rinehart is the first woman to report from the front lines (France and Belgium) in World War I (1914–18).

1918 Peggy Hull is the first woman correspondent given credentials by the U.S. War Department to cover a war zone. The war, however, is over by the time she arrives in Siberia (Russia).

set. By 1994 however, the time had increased to an astounding seven hours and sixteen minutes.

Television has reshaped the United States's culture. Today, nearly every household in the country has at least one television set. Average American children have watched thousands of hours of television by the time they enter first grade. And by the time today's children reach age seventy, they will have watched seven to ten years of television.

"Everything we learn about the world comes from media, particularly television," according to Jeff Cole of the Center for Communications Policy in Los Angeles, California. "Television opens the whole world to us and broadens our horizons. It can be terrible, but it can also be wonderful." Where previous genera-

1939 Pauline Frederick is American radio's first network news analyst and diplomatic correspondent. In 1960 she is the first woman to anchor network radio's coverage of the presidential conventions, and in 1976 she is the first woman to moderate a presidential debate.

1942 Irene Corbally Kuhn makes the first radio broadcast from China.

1948 Frieda B. Hennock is the first woman appointed to the Federal Communications Commission (FCC), the U.S. agency responsible for the regulation of radio and television communication.

1951 Maggie (Marguerite) Higgins wins the Pulitzer Prize for her reports on the war in Korea. She is the first woman to win the prize for international reporting.

1964 Hazel Brannon Smith is the first woman to win a Pulitzer Prize for editorial writing. (She wrote about corrupt politicians.)

1971 Esther Van Wagoner Tufty is the first woman elected to the National Press Club, two days after the Women's National Press Club had voted unanimously (all in favor) to admit men.

1974 Helen A. Thomas is the first woman to head the White House Bureau of a major news service (United Press International; UPI).

1976 Barbara Walters becomes the first woman to anchor a television network newscast.

1991 Pauline Kael retires. For thirty years she reigned at the *New Yorker* as America's top movie critic.

1996 Statistics show that women are still underrepresented as journalists and as subjects of news stories.

---

tions read books and newspapers and listened to the radio, today's generation gets most of its information from television.

Women in Television

As discussed in Chapter 21: Film and Television, women as characters on television shows were generally portrayed as stay-at-home mothers until the late 1960s. At the same time, only a handful of women were reporting the news. Liz Trotta, an Emmy Award-winning journalist who covered wars in Vietnam, Israel, Ireland, and Iran, describes the situation at NBC during the 1960s in *Fighting for Air: In the Trenches With Television News:*

> Women remained virtually invisible in network news. At NBC, the most progressive at the time, Pauline Frederick covered the United Nations and Nancy Dickerson covered the White House. Bar-

On Women Having Opinions

In 1993 *New Republic* magazine published an article entitled "Are Opinions Male? The Barriers That Shut Women Up." The article, written by Naomi Wolf, asserts that sexism in publishing and broadcasting still exists. She noted that women have a problem getting ahead in the media because they are brought up to believe that they should not be too opinionated—that is, they should not be too free and aggressive in expressing their opinions because it is unattractive to men. The best media jobs, according to Wolf, go to those who express strong opinions.

Wolf also quotes statistics. Before reading them, remember that women make up approximately 52 percent of the U.S. population. She writes:

> In 1992, the [so-called] Year of the Woman, the television program *Crossfire* presented 55 female guests, compared with 440 male guests. Of the print media . . . according to a survey conducted by Women, Men and Media, during a one-month period in 1992, 13 percent of the op-ed [opinion-editorial] pieces published in the *Washington Post* were written by women; 16 percent of the articles on the *New York Times* op-ed pages were by women. Over the course of the year, the *New Republic* averaged 14 percent female contributors; *Harper's,* less than 20 percent; the *Nation,* 23 percent; the *Atlantic Monthly,* 33 percent. The *National Interest* ran the remarkable ratio of eighty male bylines [the line at the head of the story with the author's name] to one female. The *Washington Monthly* ran 33 women to 108 men; *National Review,* 51 female bylines to 505 male (and 12 of those female bylines belonged to one columnist, Florence King). Talk radio, an influential forum for airing . . . grievances, counts 50 female hosts in its national association's roster that totals 900.

bara Walters had not yet arrived to cohost the 'Today' show, which in any event was not considered 'news.' There was no female general assignment reporter—a reporter on call to cover whatever the [editor's] desk ordered anywhere in the world. Most perceived this as men's work; women weren't tough enough, and besides, after you train them, they go off and have babies. Behind the cameras, too, editorial and technical staffers were with one or two exceptions—or flukes—solidly male and white.

Since the 1960s women have made gradual inroads into television. Susan Zirinsky, executive producer of CBS, says women television and radio correspondents are more sincere and enthusiastic and less scornful about the subjects they cover than men are. She thinks this is because women "had to fight to get there. . . . [And] the deliciousness of it all has never worn off."

Some of the women who achieved highly visible positions on TV say that women are held to different standards from men. "Men are allowed to be bald and fat and ugly and still deliver the news. There are no bald, fat, ugly women delivering the news," says Connie Chung, former CBS anchor. Former Kansas City television news anchor Christine Craft echoes Chung's sentiments. "The men could be balding, jowly, bespectacled, even fat and encased in double knit, yet the women had to be flawless." Although women have had a difficult time breaking into television news, more women are entering the field thanks to a few pioneers. Some of these groundbreaking women are discussed below.

Barbara Walters

Barbara Walters (1931–) is one of the most visible early female success stories in television journalism. She attributes her success to "hard work and perseverance." She joined the *Today* show as a writer in 1961 and eventually became the program's cohost. (It is interesting to note that the *Today* show more than any other television show influenced the style of modern talk shows.)

In 1974 *Time* magazine named Walters one of the 200 Leaders of the Future. In 1975 she became the highest-paid TV news personality in history when she was made coanchor of ABC's nightly news with Harry Reasoner. Reasoner's resentment of Walters was obvious to viewers from their first night on the air together. Walters recalled in a 1996 interview with the *New York Times* that her coworkers resented her too. "No one would talk to me," she says. Today Walters is famous for her interviews with

Barbara Walters was one of the first women to break into the field of television journalism.

celebrities and is given prime assignments. She has also won many journalism awards throughout her career.

The Story of Christine Craft

Christine Craft was unknown outside of Kansas City, Missouri, until she made news headlines around the country in 1983. That year she was removed from her news anchor chair because, she says, she would not "hide [her] intelligence to make the guys look smarter." When she had been hired, Craft was told that the station loved her "look." When she was fired nine months later, she was told,

"You are too old [she was 38], too unattractive, and you are not sufficiently deferential to men."

Craft sued her former television station for sex discrimination and fraud. She successfully argued her case before two juries. Then she lost her suit when it was heard—on appeal by the television station—by a panel of three male judges.

Craft says her experience has prompted newsmen and newswomen to tell her that her "battle made a positive difference for them. The [usual] story [involves] an anchorwoman or reporter approaching middle age whose contract has run out. She or he is sure that there will be no renewal [because she or he is 'too old']. Surprise of surprises, the contract is renewed. . . . A nervous joke or two is made about the Christine Craft case. The new contract is signed."

Charlayne Hunter-Gault

The most visible African American journalist on public television has been correspondent Charlayne Hunter-Gault, a former *New York Times* reporter noted for her in-depth reporting. Hunter-Gault has become a role model for women of all colors. Her autobiography *In My Place* tells the story of her life from birth to her integration (opening to people of all racial or ethnic groups) of the all-white University of Georgia in 1961. There she faced racial slurs, burning effigies (a dummy representing a black person), and even a riot outside her dormitory window. Referring to that time she wrote:

"With a passion bordering on obsession, I wanted to be a journalist. . . . No one ever told me not to dream, and when the time came to act on that dream, I would not let anything stand in the way of fulfilling it." She went on to become an award-winning journalist and anchor for public television's *News Hour With Jim Lehrer.* (Formerly *The MacNeil-Lehrer News-Hour*).

Women Television and Radio Sportscasters

It was former Miss America Phyllis George who broke the barrier against women in sportscasting. Women were often barred from sportscasting because of the longstanding concern that women in the locker room would destroy male comradeship there. George appeared to report on the National Football League on *The NFL Today* on CBS from 1975 to 1984. Since then televised sports have been slowly warming up to women sportscasters, but they remain rare.

In 1992 an estimated 50 female sportscasters worked at 630 major television network local branches. Among the women covering sports for the national networks are Lesley Visser and Andrea Joyce (CBS); Gayle Gardner and Paula Zahn (NBC); and Donna DeVarona and Beth Ruyak (ABC).

Cable network ESPN is credited with being especially enlightened when it comes to hiring women to cover sports and other topics on the air. Many of ESPN's female sportscasters have gone on to cover sports for other networks. For example, ESPN's Mary Carillo went on to cover tennis for CBS. ESPN's Hannah Storm has covered sports for CNN. The presence of women in visible spots in TV sports sends a powerful message—one that says women belong everywhere. Some women who have made it big continue to complain, however, of grudging acceptance by sports fans.

Michele Tafoya, host of a radio sports show and a sportscaster for CBS television, remembers a job she held in 1993: "There were a lot of people who didn't want me to be there. Because I was female. Guys were calling in and saying sports is the last safe haven for men—why bring a woman into it?"

Kathy Jordan made history in 1993 when she became the first woman to host the TV football review program of Alabama A & M University. According to Jordan: "In the old days they [men] didn't mind us [women] serving them sandwiches while they watched the game, but we hope to break down those kinds of stereotypes."

Women on Cable Television

Writer Elayne Rapping asserts that the explosion of cable TV channels is opening a new forum for programs of interest to women, the type of programming that is ignored by regular TV. Writing in *The Progressive* magazine (September 1994), Rapping declared:

> I am often amazed at the number of places (mostly hidden away at odd hours and addresses) where all-woman panels of

commentators can be found discussing world events. These women are generally more interesting than their male counterparts, if only for their novelty, and sometimes they are great.

Geraldine Laybourne, Network President

Geraldine Laybourne became program manager of Nickelodeon, a basic-cable television network aimed at kids, in 1980, when the network was only a year old. Four years later, she became president. When she left the network in 1996 to become president of Disney/ABC Cable Networks, Nickelodeon was the top-rated basic-cable network, and Laybourne was considered one of the most powerful women in television.

Laybourne worked her way to the top by defying what she called "standard broadcast mythology." That mythology included the myth that one should "program only to boys; girls will watch anything." Laybourne said, "Hooey," and started the popular program *Clarissa Explains It All.* Another myth was, "Kids never watch news." Laybourne said, "Not true. Kids want to be connected to the world. They just don't like all the bad news hyped by adults."

A third myth that Laybourne dealt with was, "Kids only watch shows with toy-related characters they already know." According to Laybourne, "We went with fresh, new characters, and a fresh approach to talk. Kids knew Nick was theirs and on their side, that we like them and we think they're really smart." Laybourne says now that she has turned Nick into "an incredible force" for kids, she hopes to do the same for other audiences, such as women.

Radio Days

Many people thought radio would lose its audience to television. This has not been the case, though. Americans today own about 550 million radios, which they listen to in their cars, while jogging and rollerblading, while sitting in the dentist's waiting room, and while shopping. In the 1950s radio was the place for teens to hear the then-developing musical form of rock and roll.

Women Speak on the Radio

A list of radio's star reporters from its early days to the 1960s includes no women. Alison Steele became one of radio's first female disc jockeys (deejays) when she was hired by WNEW-FM in Chicago in 1966. That year the station took the highly unusual step of hiring only female deejays. Although that idea was given up, Steele stayed on in radio until her death in 1995.

African American Yvonne Daniels was another Chicago disc jockey and radio pioneer famous for her jazz programming. Daniels was inducted into the Chicago Radio Hall of Fame in 1995.

Talk shows are among the most popular radio formats of the 1990s. Robin Quivers, a black woman, reads the news and functions as Howard Stern's sidekick on his popular national talk show. Dr. Laura Schlessinger dispenses advice on "character, courage and conscience" to more than ten million people a week (an audience second in size only to conservative radio personality and controversy-raiser Rush Limbaugh's).

National Public Radio

National Public Radio (NPR) has a reputation for being more open to hiring women than other radio networks. According to NPR journalist Nina Totenberg: "NPR's wages were at least a third lower than elsewhere in the industry, and for what they paid they couldn't find men. . . . It was and still is, a shop where a woman could get considerable visibility and responsibility." Totenberg is famous for helping to break the Anita Hill story (see Chapter 9: Politics). Totenberg, Cokie Roberts, and Linda Wertheimer, veteran NPR reporters known as "The Three Musketeers," have all branched out into television, as have other journalists who got their start at NPR. According to writer Lisa Schwarzbaum, "NPR provides the opportunities for journalists to hone the skills that attract network attention." It is interesting to note that with the help of women broadcasters, NPR went from being a little-known network to its current highly respected position in the radio world.

Cokie Roberts

Cokie Roberts (1943–) is the daughter of former U.S. Representative Lindy Boggs (1973–90) and U.S. House of Representatives Majority Leader Hale Boggs, who disappeared in an Alaskan plane crash in 1973. Born in 1943, Roberts has spent much of her life in the nation's capital. Because of her intimate knowledge of how government works, she is referred to as a "Washington insider."

Despite her knowledge of Washington and her degree from Wellesley College, Roberts did not find it easy to break into journalism. "For eight months I job-hunted at various New York magazines and television stations," she says, "and wherever I went I was asked how many words I could type." She eventually found work and moved up the ladder. Roberts has worked as a reporter for National Public Radio, at first covering Congress with partner Linda Wertheimer. She later became a regular on ABC's *World News Tonight* and *This Week With David Brinkley* while continuing to work as a political correspondent for NPR.

Linda Wertheimer

Linda Wertheimer, born in Carlsbad, New Mexico, in 1943, is one of a small group of women who broke the gender barrier in radio broadcasting. She is a role model to many young women journalists. In an interview with Wertheimer for the *New York Times Magazine* (January 2, 1994), reporter Claudia Dreifus asked her: "How do you feel when you meet younger women in journalism who haven't any idea how rough things used to be in the 'bad old days?'" Wertheimer responded:

I think what happens now is that the young women get the first job, and the next job, and achieve some level of suc-

Robin Quivers, cohost of Howard Stern's radio program.

cess. But at some point they hit a wall and they find out that until and unless a substantial number of mostly white men die, they may not be able to move up. It's a shock to their systems.

Publishing: Newspapers and Magazines

In the early days of the United States, weekly newspapers were the most widely available form of mass communication. People wanted to read about politics. They also wanted to read about the wonderful and the horrible. The first woman newspaper editor in America is said to

Trend Stories

In the late nineteenth century, newspapers and magazines jumped on the bandwagon to attack women's rights. Women were told over and over again that education would make them spinsters (old maids, unmarried women), that equal employment would make them sterile, and that equal rights would make them bad mothers. These kinds of stories are sometimes referred to as "trend stories." Journalist Kathleen Parker says that "in journalism, any observation that occurs more than once constitutes a trend."

In her book *Backlash,* writer Susan Faludi discusses modern trend stories. According to Faludi, beginning in the 1980s trend stories began to appear in newspapers and magazines stating that women were not happy with the gains they had made as a result of the women's movement of the 1960s and 1970s. These stories went on to "prove" that if women were not happy with their gains, their unhappiness must be because of feminism.

Modern trend stories speak of the ticking of the "biological clock," telling women that they'd better give up their careers and start having children before they are too old or find themselves infertile (unable to have children). "Hurry up, ladies," the trend stories say, "or you will never get a husband. There's a man shortage out there." Headlines have featured stories titled: "Loveless, Manless: The High Cost of Independence," and "Too Late for Prince Charming?"

Another modern trend story reports that women are fleeing corporate life and returning to home and hearth. However, U.S. Department of Labor statistics show there is no such mass flight.

Faludi suggests that readers use caution when reading trend stories with themes like these. She says the flimsy trend stories often have these characteristics:

- an absence of factual evidence or hard numbers

- a tendency to use phrases like: "No one knows how many career women each year leave jobs to be with their children"

- a tendency to cite only three or four women, often anonymously (without giving real names), to support the story, or the story includes no real women at all

- a tendency to use vague phrases like: "There is a sense that . . ."

- a tendency to quote "authorities" who cite other trend stories to support their argument

The next time you read a story that claims to be telling you that a certain phenomenon is affecting large numbers of women, ask yourself: "Is this story reporting real events or is it a trend story?"

have been Ann Franklin, Benjamin Franklin's sister-in-law. She took over the editorship of the Newport, Rhode Island, *Mercury,* on the death of her son in 1762. She continued to edit the paper until her own death a year later. She was soon followed by Sarah Updike Goddard, who, together with her son William and daughter Mary Katherine, established three major newspapers in the 1760s and 1770s.

Magazines for Ladies

Magazines stepped in to reach the people whose interests did not lie in newspapers. Two of the most famous early magazines were *Godey's Lady's Book* and *Peterson's Ladies' National Magazine. Godey's Lady's Book,* founded in 1830 by Louis A. Godey, was the first American magazine for women. It was edited by poet Sarah J. Hale (author of "Mary Had a Little Lamb"). *Godey's* offered women advice ("Earrings are out. Archery is in. Fresh air is in."). According to Hale, who shaped the magazine's philosophy, "The most important vocation on earth is that of the Christian mother in the nursery." Attitudes like this helped shape how American women were expected to behave and dictated to some extent the jobs open to them. By the 1860s, *Godey's* and *Peterson's* each had circulations (number of copies sold) of 150,000 readers.

Social reformers and religious groups soon began publishing their own periodicals. One of the most influential magazines of this type was *The Dial,*

Diana Vreeland: The "High Priestess of Style"

Diana Vreeland is the most famous name in twentieth-century fashion journalism. She was born to English parents in Paris, France, in 1901 and emigrated with them to the United States at the start of World War II (1914–18). In 1935 she began her journalistic career as fashion editor of *Harper's Bazaar.* She acquired fame with her "Why don't you?" column, featuring suggestions like "Why don't you wash your child's hair in champagne?" Vreeland moved to *Vogue* magazine in 1962, where she remained a consultant even after her retirement in 1971. She also served as a special consultant to the Metropolitan Museum's Costume Institute, where she organized exhibits showcasing the history of fashion and design.

which was published by New England transcendentalists. Transcendentalists believe knowledge comes from within and not from what can be observed. *The Dial* was edited by Margaret Fuller, an early critic of discrimination against women. She is discussed in detail later in the chapter.

The *Ladies' Home Journal,* founded in 1883, began to work for social causes in 1889. Where magazines had mainly been published for wealthy people in the

Ida Tarbell is one of the most famous muckrakers.

from about 1880 to World War I (1914). Men became millionaires through industry and business (J.D. Rockefeller started Standard Oil, Andrew Carnegie ran the steel industry, Andrew Melon was the big name in banking, and Cornelius Vanderbilt became the richest man in America through railroads). The gap between the very rich and the very poor was wider than ever.

One of the most famous of the muckrakers was Ida Tarbell, who took on J.D. Rockefeller. The founder of Standard Oil, Rockefeller was a powerful man who eventually became the richest man in the world. Tarbell's exposure of him as a cutthroat monopolist (one who used unfair business practices to stifle competition) led to the breakup of his Standard Trust company.

1800s, by the 1920s the *Journal* and other magazines like it were fixtures in many middle-class homes.

Muckraking

A new kind of print journalism had emerged around the turn of the century (1900). It was called "muckraking," a term said to have been coined by Theodore Roosevelt. Muckrakers were investigative reporters, both men and women, who exposed corruption in our political system and greed in business.

The muckrakers were active during a time in American history known as the Age of Extremes, which lasted

Women Work for Newspapers

Newspapers lagged behind magazines in hiring women. When newspapers began to get larger in the late 1800s, though, newspaper publishers divided into departments. Women were hired to report on home and society news in the newly created "women's sections." Women were also considered especially suited to "sensation" writing. Soon women were being sought as stunt girls, after the example of Nellie Bly. Bly was stunt girl, sensation writer, and "sob sister" (a journalist , especially a woman, employed as a writer or and editor of sentimental stories) all rolled into one. She is discussed further in this chapter and in Chapter 14: Science and Exploration.

During the years of the Great Depression (1930s), many people, including journalists, lost their jobs. At newspapers all over the United States there might be a woman here, or a woman there—covering trials in courts of law, investigating mental hospitals, advising those unhappy in love. They had experience but were given little opportunity. It wasn't until the 1970s that newspapers began gradually adding women staffers to the "serious" pages. Often this meant there was now one woman where before there had been none.

Television Supplants Magazines

The growth of television in the 1950s had a major impact on magazine publishing. Advertisers, who are the source of much of the money earned by publishers, saw that they could reach a far larger audience by advertising on television. They began to abandon magazines. That abandonment, plus rising costs of production, caused many general magazines (such as *Life, Look,* and the *Saturday Evening Post*) to either stop publishing or to publish less frequently.

Niche publications stepped in to fill the gap left by the general magazines. Niche publications are those targeted to a particular audience, such as gardeners or music lovers. Advertisers like niche publications because they are able to reach the audience that will most likely use the product being advertised. Two completely new kinds of niche publications were introduced in the 1970s.

Helen Gurley Brown, the founder of Cosmopolitan magazine.

Cosmopolitan and *Ms.*

Sometimes editors have a great impact in shaping the content and style of magazines. Such was the case with *Cosmopolitan* and *Ms.,* women's magazines created by Helen Gurley Brown and Gloria Steinem, respectively.

Helen Gurley Brown first earned international fame with the publication in 1962 of *Sex and the Single Girl.* That book seemed to capture the spirit of a new freedom being enjoyed by women, who were finally earning a living wage and becoming independent. In 1965 she

Gloria Steinem holds a mock-up of her Ms. magazine cover during the 1970s.

became editor-in-chief of *Cosmopolitan,* which was soon among the five top-selling magazines in the country. The magazine promoted the image of a "Cosmo Girl," a woman whose major concerns were attracting and pleasing a man.

With a somewhat different focus, *Ms.,* a magazine published and edited by women, was founded by feminist leader Gloria Steinem in 1972. Steinem says she started the magazine because other publications were either ignoring feminist activities or ridiculing them. *Ms.* told women about career opportunities and ways to lead a meaningful life.

General magazines (featuring articles of general interest rather than niche articles) experienced something of a comeback in the late 1980s, when British-born editor Tina Brown revived *Vanity Fair.* In 1992 she became the first female editor of the *New Yorker.*

Women's Magazines Today

Today's high costs of producing and mailing magazines limit the number that can be published. Many magazines stop publishing each year. At the same time, up to 750 new magazines begin to be published, but many of them fail in the first year or two.

The publishing industry's top women's magazines are known as the "seven sisters." They are: *McCall's, Better Homes & Gardens, Family Circle, Good Housekeeping, Ladies' Home Journal, Woman's Day,* and *Redbook,* all magazines devoted to the glories of home and hearth. The circulation (number of copies sold) of these magazines began to decline in the early 1990s, however, and most of them were redesigned. Today they feature articles more sensitive to the needs of modern working women: quick-cooking recipes, simpler crafts and redecorating projects, stress relief, and exercise tips.

Cosmopolitan magazine remains popular under the continuing direction of Helen Gurley Brown. *Ms.* magazine saw its circulation fall from a high of 550,000 to 164,000 in 1996. This pioneering feminist magazine has since been taken over by a male publisher, and many people blame its declining popularity on feminism's falling out of favor with the public.

Window on the World: Egypt's Woman Journalist

Prominent Egyptian journalist 'Aminah Al-Sa'id was born in Cairo in 1914. Her upbringing was remarkable in that her father believed in the education of women. Al-Sa'id was one of the small group of women who were the first to graduate from Cairo University in 1935.

A long time supporter of women's rights, Al-Sa'id was an editor for the weekly magazine *Hawā* (Eve), which was said to circulate in more foreign countries than any other Arabic paper (and it still exists). She was president of the oldest publishing firm in the Arab world and was the first woman to be elected to the Egyptian Press Syndicate Executive Board.

Al-Sa'id was a frequent speaker at international conferences. One of her primary topics was Arab women and how they are alike and how they differ from Western women (women of European and Northern American heritage) in their struggle for equal rights.

Egypt is one of a large number of countries in which the press is subjected to strict censorship from government and religious bodies. Although an Egyptian publisher can run into problems with censors for printing "lies" from foreign publications Al-Sa'id's political connections rendered her immune from these censors.

Freedom House, a New York-based human rights organization, reported in 1994 that 113 of 186 countries placed restrictions on freedom of the press. Freedom of the press is the right to circulate opinions in print without censorship. The report also noted that in 1993, 76 journalists from 27 nations had been killed while engaged in their profession.

The largest U.S. magazine aimed at working women at the management level is *Working Woman,* with an annual circulation of 700,000. It is one of only a few magazines that concentrates on the business needs of career women.

Women's Voices in the Newspaper Today

According to Kay Mills, author of *A Place in the News: From the Women's Pages to the Front Pages* (which was published by Columbia University Press in 1991), until about the mid-1970s women journalists "were expected to write the same thing as the guys did." Today more and more women are writing newspaper columns in which they comment on the issues of the day, and some of them are bringing up issues that have long been ignored. Issues such as the lack of affordable child care, sex discrimination in the workplace, abortion, and parenting are being discussed.

Window on the World: Argentina's "Queen of Letters"

Victoria Ocampo (1890–1978) was born of wealthy parents in Argentina. She received a good education and learned to speak several languages. She was married to a man her family chose but took the highly unusual step of leaving him to live independently. Ocampo was a woman of many interests, one of which was the introduction of the works of foreign writers (especially female writers) into Latin America. To further that end she published a literary magazine called *Sur.* (A literary magazine contains writings that are considered literature rather than news stories.) As a result of her efforts, Ocampo became known as the "Queen of Letters" in Argentina. She was also a fighter for women's rights.

For instance, *Washington Post* columnist Donna Britt has discussed issues like her fear, as she celebrated her son's twelfth birthday, that he would soon be perceived as the stereotypical frightening young black man instead of the honor-roll student he actually was. While some people applaud this type of writing, others criticize it as not being "serious" news.

Some critics also blame women reporters for the emerging trend of dragging the private lives of public people out for discussion. These critics say that issues like whether or not a candidate is cheating on his wife is not relevant to his being able to perform well in public office. This is sometimes referred to as the "character issue." Defenders of the new trend of probing into a person's private life say that knowing a person's character is important when deciding whom to vote for.

Women on the Front Pages

In the mid-1970s, more women read newspapers than men. Two decades later, readership surveys show that women lag behind, and the younger the reader the greater the gap. Critics say the reason women are showing less interest in newspapers is that the newspapers show no interest in women.

A survey conducted for Women, Men, and Media, an organization that monitors how women are covered, hired, and promoted by the press, reported on women as the subjects of newspaper stories. The survey, released in 1996, shows that although women make up 52 percent of the United States's population, they are the subject of only 15 percent of front-page newspaper articles.

The survey looked at twenty newspapers around the country. Ten of the twenty newspapers are considered "major" papers. They are: the *Atlanta Journal-Constitution,* the *Chicago Tribune,* the *Houston Chronicle,* the *Los Angeles Times,* the *Miami Herald,* the *New York Times,* the *Seattle Times,* the *St. Louis Post-Dispatch, USA Today,* and the *Washington Post.* According to the survey, in the twen-

Katharine Graham, Publisher

Katharine Graham was called "the most powerful woman in America" at a 1974 breakfast held in her honor. She achieved that power, she says, "by birth and by death." By birth, because her father owned a newspaper called the *Washington Post,* which she and her husband bought from him in 1948 for $1. By death, because when her husband died in 1963, Graham took over the job of running the paper, today considered one of the most influential and powerful news sources in the country. She was publisher of the *Post* from 1969 to 1979. Thereafter she became chairperson of the board of the Washington Post Company.

Graham was a "hands-off" publisher, which meant that she gave her reporters considerable freedom when they were pursuing stories. In 1972 that policy allowed two of her employees to continue their investigation into what became known as Watergate and eventually led to Republican President Richard Nixon's resignation. Graham let reporters Carl Bernstein and Bob Woodward pursue their investigation of the infamous break-in at Democratic Party headquarters, even though she was being attacked by members of President Nixon's staff and the president himself.

ty newspapers studied, coverage of men not only dominated the front pages but also the local news and business pages.

Nancy Woodhull, a spokesperson for Women, Men, and Media, commented: "A free press in a democracy should reflect all its voices. None should be invisible. The press needs to focus on this trend toward the invisibility of women and their concerns."

Another survey asked women what they would like to see covered in the news. Women responded that they are interested in topics such as their children's education and how they learn; how to save time and money; safety and health issues; women in the workplace; social issues like homelessness; and family and personal relationships. The female respondents also complained about reporters who invade privacy or are insensitive to disaster and crime victims.

Trendsetting Print Journalists

"Sob Sisters" and "Sensation Writers"

A sob sister writes sob stories, tales of personal hardship or misfortune intended to arouse the reader's pity. The women

The Media Describe Women Running for Office

Women running for political office (and those who read about them in newspapers and magazines) complain that women candidates are often described differently from men. When Carol Moseley-Braun and Richard Williamson ran against each other in 1992 for the office of U.S. Senator from Illinois, the *New York Times* described them this way: "She is commanding and ebullient [enthusiastic], a den mother with a cheerleader's smile; he, by comparison, is all business, like the corporate lawyer he is." In the twenty-second paragraph of the article, it was finally noted that Moseley-Braun is also a lawyer and a former federal prosecutor. Many articles still focus on how a woman looks or sounds, rather than on the content of her message.

(and occasionally men) who wrote this type of story were performing a valuable function in exposing the misery and poverty they discovered. The dismissal of their efforts as "sob stories" is an example of sexism.

Sensation writing is designed to make the reader excited and ready to take action. Among those who went in for sensation writing were Ida B. Wells-Barnett and Mary Ann Shadd Cary, both African American women.

Ida B. Wells-Barnett, a former slave and at one time a reporter for a Tennessee newspaper, was known for her campaigns against the racially motivated lynching of blacks. Lynching is the killing, usually by hanging, of a person suspected of a crime who has not had a trial. She is credited with bringing this outrageous practice to national attention and for organizing efforts that led to its outlaw.

Mary Ann Shadd Cary, a journalist and teacher, moved to Canada in 1851 to help slaves fleeing the United States. In 1853 she helped found *Provincial Freeman,* a weekly newspaper for blacks. Thus she became the first black woman in North America to edit and found a weekly paper. She was working before the Civil War (1861–65) and helped publicize the horrible conditions of American slaves.

Nellie Bly, "The Best Reporter in America"

Nellie Bly was the best known of the sensation writers, a truly remarkable woman and a trendsetter for the women journalists who followed her. She was born Elizabeth Jane Cochran in Cochran's Mills, Pennsylvania, in 1865. In 1885 she landed her first newspaper job on the *Pittsburgh Dispatch* after writing an angry letter opposing the paper's stand against women's right to vote. She took the pen name Nellie Bly from a song by that name written by Stephen Foster.

Bly soon left for New York City, the publishing capital of the world, determined to be hired as a reporter. She settled for a job writing descriptions for the New York *World* of what fashionable New York women were wearing. Annoyed by the boredom of her job, Bly soon staged her first stunt. She proceeded to interview three of the country's most powerful men in journalism, asking them if they thought New York was a good place for a woman to get started in journalism. None of them did. One of them told her that women were "not regarded with editorial favor in New York." Bly's story resulting from these interviews caused a furor across the United States, where women had been making some inroads into publishing.

Bly also exposed the terrible working conditions in big-city factories and wrote dramatic stories about them. During the last part of her career, she wrote an advice column. Among her words of wisdom were these: "The world would be a happier and better one if everybody cultivated happiness. Don't be a grouch and waste life; don't be disgruntled and dissatisfied, don't be a growler; don't be a crank." (Other adventures of Nellie Bly are discussed in Chapter 14: Science and Exploration.)

Alma Reed

In a 1925 *New York Times* profile, Alma Reed was hailed as "the only archaeological reporter in the world." (An archaeologist studies the life and culture of our past.) She led an extremely colorful life.

Nellie Bly

Alma Reed was born in 1889 in San Francisco, California, a city still prosperous from the gold rush of the 1840s. Her family was shocked when she expressed her determination to become a writer rather than to marry and settle down, as was expected of a young lady. She managed to secure a job on the *San Francisco Call* writing stories about the poor, the proper topic for a woman reporter at that time. Reed used this opportunity to ignite the public's conscience, documenting cases like that of a poor Mexican boy sentenced to death although he did not speak English and did not understand the case against him.

On a tour of Mexico, Reed met and fell in love with the governor of the Yucátan (a region in Latin America), Felipe Carrillo Puerto. Puerto was founder of the "Feminista Leagues," groups of women dedicated to overcoming illiteracy and improving the lot of Mexico's poor.

It was in Mexico that Reed discovered a passion for archaeology. She was the major reporter covering exciting archaeological finds in exotic locations all over the world. She even became a deep-sea diver and searched for the lost continent of Atlantis in 1925. Around the world newspaper headlines read: GIRL TO PROBE DEPTH OF SEA. The story continued: "The first to explore the depth of the ocean 500 feet below the surface will be a woman . . . [on a] deep sea expedition to the Gulf of Naples, who will probe for a buried city in a specially constructed diving bell."

Reed died of cancer in 1967 and was buried in the Yucátan next to Puerto, her longtime love. At her funeral the U.S. consul to Mexico spoke of her contributions to reach a more harmonious relationship between the United States and Mexico.

Women Journalists in the White House

White House correspondents attend press conferences at the White House, where either the president or his spokesperson will meet with the correspondents and answer questions they pose. The correspondents then report to their employers (radio or television broadcasters or newspapers or magazines) on what they have learned, and the information is broadcast or published.

In 1879 the mostly male members of the press assigned to the White House noticed there were quite a few women in attendance. As a matter of fact, the Congressional Directory showed that a grand total of 20 women correspondents had been granted press gallery privileges, about 12 percent of the total of 166 correspondents. Most of the male press members felt that this was 20 women too many. The male press banded together to prohibit women from the White House press room. Within two years after the ban, an increasing number of women correspondents could be found writing society gossip instead of covering politics. With few exceptions, women continued to be banned from political reporting, or what was known as "hard news," for most of the next 100 years. The ban put women in their place, in the "soft news" sections and "society" pages.

Eleanor Roosevelt, herself a journalist (for twenty years she wrote a daily newspaper column called "My Day") helped bring a few women back into the White House. During the 1940s, she refused to be interviewed by anyone but female journalists. Since she was a newsmaker herself, newspapers were forced to hire at least one woman to cover Roosevelt's activities.

Sarah McClendon has been a White House correspondent since 1944, when

Franklin Delano Roosevelt was president. In the mid-1990s she owned and operated McClendon News Service, which is responsible for a weekly syndicated newspaper column, a biweekly newsletter, and a weekly radio show heard across the nation.

In an interview with *Mother Jones* magazine (May/June 1996), the 85-year-old McClendon commented on the state of journalism today. She said:

> The sad thing about the United States today is the American people are informed only on a few issues. They don't know anything about welfare. They don't know that we're selling arms [weapons] to every country in the world. The public has no idea about what's going on.

> [The reason for this is] the press. They stick together and circle around one subject. You go to a press conference at the White House and there'll be 55 questions. All but one or two will be on the same subject. They ask the same question over and over in different ways.

Women in the Locker Room

It was not until 1977 that a federal judge ordered that female reporters have the right to enter male players' locker rooms to conduct interviews. Today women covering sporting events are no longer a novelty—most major daily newspapers have one. But women still have problems being accepted.

For example, *Boston Herald* sports reporter Lisa Olson made headlines in 1990 over an incident that occurred when she entered the locker room of the National Football League's (NFL) New England Patriots for an interview. The football players behaved in such an obnoxious manner that they were forced by the NFL to pay a $72,500 fine. This type of incident can have a chilling effect on women journalism students considering entering the field of sports reporting.

America's Foreign Correspondents

Foreign correspondent is the term used to describe people who travel to other countries to gather news and report back to their employers—a newspaper, for example—back home.

American women have been foreign correspondents since at least the time of Margaret Fuller, who covered the French attack on Rome, Italy for the *New York Tribune* in 1849. Her exploits and those of other female foreign correspondents are even more remarkable because these women often had to overcome obstacles designed to keep them out of the action. Reporting on military activities had long been considered too dangerous and most unsuitable for women.

Margaret Fuller

Margaret Fuller, self-described as "bright but ugly," had an unusual upbringing. She was educated at home by her congressman father. She was so well educated, in fact, that she became the first woman permitted to use the Harvard College library, although she was not permitted to attend college (no woman could back then).

Margaret Fuller opened the door for female foreign correspondents.

women to cover stories in Europe for newspapers that would not hire them at home. Like Nellie Bly, these women often used pen names to avoid the disapproval reserved for nontraditional women. One example is Sara Jane Clarke, who sent stories home from Paris using the pen name Grace Greenwood.

Mary Roberts Rinehart

Novelist Mary Roberts Rinehart was already one of America's favorite writers when she became one of America's first correspondents to reach the scene of the fighting in Europe during World War I (1914–18). Of the experience she wrote, "I have done what no woman has done before, and I am alive." It may have been her fame that convinced her employer, the *Saturday Evening Post,* to permit her to cover the war for them when other women were not permitted to go. She told the *Post,* "I do not intend to let the biggest thing in my life go by without having been a part of it."

Rinehart's stories from Europe described the terrible conditions being endured by the wounded and dying. Rinehart—in part because of her fame—was able to obtain exclusive interviews with famous people. A woman of many talents, she had also trained as a nurse. This training allowed her to make recommendations to the U.S. War Department on medical matters.

Despite her work, Rinehart received little recognition for her efforts from the male-dominated press, the reason for this

Fuller became one of America's first foreign correspondents in spite of the fact that it was not considered proper for women to travel alone. Fuller sent home riveting accounts of the fighting and bloodshed in Rome. She opened doors for American women who wanted to become foreign correspondents. She once remarked: "'Tis an evil lot, to have a man's ambition and a woman's heart." On her way home from Italy, Fuller and her infant son died in a shipwreck.

Male journalists of the time were for the most part uninterested in jobs overseas. Fuller's example led other

being that she was a woman, and she had been a fiction writer—positions not held in high regard.

Anne O'Hare McCormick

In her book titled *Women of the World: The Great Foreign Correspondents,* Julia Edwards writes:

> In World War II, women won overseas assignments by agreeing that they were different from men. They argued that as they were more sensitive and more opposed to war than men, they should be sent to write 'the woman's point of view.' Once overseas, they took off their kid gloves, put on their helmets, and raced the men to the front and back to the cable desk.

One of the most famous of the many women who covered World War II (1939–45) was Anne O'Hare McCormick of the *New York Times.* McCormick interviewed the most prominent world leaders of the time—Franklin Delano Roosevelt, Adolf Hitler, Joseph Stalin, and Benito Mussolini. In 1937 she became the first female journalist to win a Pulitzer Prize, one of many awards and honors she received during her lifetime in the profession.

McCormick was born in England to American parents and grew up in Ohio. Her mother was a poet and the women's page editor of an Ohio newspaper. In 1921, at age 39, McCormick wrote the managing editor of the *New York Times* informing him that she was taking a trip to Italy and humbly asking if he would permit her to submit articles from there. McCormick's vacation brought her to

Window on the World: Italy's Woman Journalist

Italian-born Oriana Fallaci is one of the most famous women journalists in the world. Born in Florence, Italy, in 1930, she began her career in journalism while still in her teens and became a special correspondent for an Italian newspaper by age twenty.

During her long career (she was still writing in 1996), she has filed news reports from the wars in Vietnam, Pakistan, the Middle East, and South Africa. Fallaci is famous for her confrontational style (she virtually refuses to allow her subjects to avoid answering). She is also famous for the clever way she encourages famous people to open up to her. Fallaci has twice won Italy's prestigious St. Vincent Prize for journalism.

Italy at a very exciting time in history, and she happened to be one of the few journalists reporting from the scene.

Because of her training in Latin, the parent language of Italian, McCormick was able to understand some major political speeches being made. She became an important regular contributor to the *Times* and was later appointed to the board that makes decisions about what kinds of stories would be published. She was also made the paper's "freedom editor," whose job it was "to stand up and shout whenever freedom is interfered with in any part of the world," a job she performed for nearly twenty years.

Margaret Bourke-White

Margaret Bourke-White also covered World War II—on the North African front. Although she considered herself primarily a photographer, Bourke-White wrote moving stories of her wartime experiences, thus becoming one of the first in a now distinguished profession called photojournalism. In 1943 she became the first American woman permitted to go on a bombing mission. Bourke-White is discussed in greater detail in Chapter 24: Fine and Applied Arts.

Dickey Chapelle in Vietnam

American involvement in Vietnam was covered by the daring and colorful Dickey Chapelle, who had learned to fly a plane and to use a parachute while still a teenager.

Born Georgette Meyer in Milwaukee, Wisconsin, Chapelle married her photography teacher when she was 19 years old. He started her on a career selling stories for magazines, and she eventually became a correspondent for *Look*. She photographed scenes during World War II for Fawcett Publications. By the time the war was over, Chapelle was divorced and out of a job. She finally found work as an assistant to Leo Cherne, who was in charge of an organization that aided refugees around the world. (Refugees are people who flee their native country because of problems there.) After World War II, Europe was full of refugees fleeing Russia.

Chapelle earned fame by trying to help the refugees. As a result, she was captured and imprisoned by the Russians. Risk-taking became a way of life for her after this experience. She traveled the globe taking photos of fighting in Algeria, Lebanon, Cuba, and Korea. When she could find no publisher willing to sponsor her trip to Vietnam in 1961, she set off on her own. While there, Chapelle used her parachute training to get the kind of photographs no one had ever gotten before. Where other photographers sought action shots, Chapelle chose to focus on individual acts of heroism. She photographed men who had been shot in the back and men who had stepped on land mines.

For her coverage of fighting in Vietnam and neighboring Laos, Chapelle won a prestigious award "for the best reporting . . . requiring exceptional courage and enterprise abroad." In 1965, in Vietnam again, Chapelle stepped on a land mine, becoming the first American woman war correspondent to be killed in action.

Christiane Amanpour

Journalist Christiane Amanpour covered the Persian Gulf War in 1991 for CNN, a cable network. The Persian Gulf War was the first major conflict since Vietnam that involved U.S. troops. It was also an exciting career opportunity for

Amanpour, as she told the *New York Times:* "Clearly there is the drama, danger and immediacy. But you also see the very best and very worst of human nature."

Since the Gulf War, Amanpour has journeyed from one wartorn country to another, such as Russia, Somalia, and Haiti. Amanpour is best known, however for her coverage of the Bosnian war. She says her worst moments there were "looking into the faces of women and children caught in the shelling." Today Amanpour's services as a journalist are much sought after by all television networks.

The Internet

The latest development in human communications—and one that is still evolving—is the Internet. The Internet is the world's largest computer network. It is also a worldwide network of networks—an "inter-network."

The Internet evolved from a U.S. military research program in the late 1960s, but the government has little say in its operation today. In only a few decades the Internet has changed from a slow and complicated network for the military, scholars, and computer geniuses into a communications tool that can be used by just about everyone.

One of the most popular areas of the Internet is the World Wide Web. The Web allows anyone with a personal computer and the right software to post information that can be seen by everyone else with Web access. The difference between the Internet and other media is that messages are no longer controlled by media gatekeepers who monitor the actions of others.

Some people believe that the Internet is the beginning of a phenomenon that will change the way we communicate. They see a world where all types of information will be available on an Information Superhighway, and anyone will have access to it with the push of a button. The technology is still new, but some observations have already been made about its effects. One alarming phenomenon is that women and girls are said to be in short supply on the Internet. In early 1995 it was estimated that only 10 to 15 percent of users of computer on-line services were female. Other surveys show, however, that members of on-line services such as American Online and Prodigy are nearly 40 percent female (that is about two million women).

A Profile of Adult Internet Users

According to a recent survey, whites outnumber blacks on the Internet seventeen to one. Among whites using the Internet, more men than women are users. The profile of a typical white Internet user is a male, in his late thirties or early forties, married, with a college degree.

The situation is entirely different for black Internet users. About 51 percent of black Internet users are women. While 45 percent are single, 51 percent are under age 35, and 51 percent do not have a college degree. One explanation given for the difference is that black women may have greater access to computers at work than do black men.

How to Find Out More

Carla Sinclair is a knowledgeable Internet user who has put together a female-friendly guide to the Internet. Titled *Net Chick: A Smart-Girl Guide to the Wired World* (An Owl Original, 1995), the book gives on-line addresses for Web sites of interest to women. It also introduces the computer novice (beginner) to the world of computers. *Net Chick* bills itself as "the only guide to the stylish, post-feminist, modem grrrrl culture."

Although women have achieved some form of equality when it comes to the media, a lot of work remains to be done. Women continue to be discriminated against when it comes to hiring practices and coverage of their issues. Only when women are represented in all forms of media—print, radio, television, and the Internet—will they truly have gained the equality that has escaped them throughout history.

23

Crafts and Domestic Arts

In every known society, work has been divided between the sexes according to what the society considers appropriate for each sex. This is called the sexual division of labor. Societies have different reasons for assigning work to one sex or another. Some people believe that the work is divided between the tasks men prefer to do and the tasks men have decided to leave to women. According to anthropologist (a person who studies human behavior) Margaret Mead's book titled *Male & Female,* "Sometimes one quality has been assigned to one sex, sometimes to the other. . . . Some peoples think of women as too weak to work out of doors, others regard women as the appropriate bearers of heavy burdens, 'because their heads are stronger than men's.'"

In American society, taking care of the home has historically been the woman's assigned task. This is confirmed by the old saying: "A woman's place is in the home." Because women were shut out of the masculine world of formal art for a long time, they turned their creativity to domestic arts (home-related) such as quilting.

Timeline: Women in Crafts and Domestic Arts

1600s–1776 During the colonial period of American history, everyone, not just women, worked in the home since all work is done there.

1810–60 America becomes urbanized and industrialized. The home becomes a woman's "sphere"; and the world of work outside the home becomes a man's "sphere." Influential books published by Catharine Beecher, Lydia Maria Francis Child, and others justify the placement of women in the home.

1860–1960 The American household is transformed by "laborsaving" devices. The servant class disappears, and millions of homes contain just a wife and mother whose tasks range from menial (work considered appropriate for a servant) physical labor to highly complicated tasks, which she performs in isolation.

1960— Women leave the home to enter the work world—the man's sphere. Some men take up cooking as a result, but mostly women are left to perform all the household tasks required by their former sphere plus the job tasks required by their new sphere. Domestic arts become hobbies.

.This chapter looks at how the focus of a woman's day has changed and how it has remained the same from the colonial period (early 1600s–1776) to the present. Some of the women who have made major contributions to the traditionally female domestic arts (cooking, home economics) are profiled in this chapter. Various crafts women have developed to make the home more comfortable or more beautiful are discussed in special boxes throughout the chapter.

Domestic Arts and Crafts in Colonial America

Life and domesticity in colonial America differed from all other times in America's history in that all work was done at home. Although there was a clear-cut sexual division of labor, the colonial home was everyone's workplace, not just a woman's. The home, therefore, was not just the home—it was also the work site, the factory where all goods were produced.

Carol Hymowitz and Michaele Weissman described women's typical activities in colonial days in *A History of Women in America:*

> First came supervision of the house. Women swept, scrubbed, laundered, polished. They made their own brooms, soap, polish. They carried water and did the laundry. They made starch. They ironed. They built fires and carried firewood. They made candles. They sewed everything—sheets, clothing, table linen, diapers. Women were usually in charge of the family bookkeeping. They ordered provisions, paid bills, and made sure the books were balanced.

Showcasing Domestic Arts: Quilting

Quilts are warm blankets made of two layers of fabric with a layer of cotton, wool, or feathers in between, all stitched firmly together, usually in a crisscross design. Crazy quilts, which became popular during the late 1800s, consisted of pieces of silk of various shapes, colors, and sizes, sewn together in a random pattern.

Many people dismissed quilting as a woman's art; thus it was not considered art at all. These same people declared that quilts were nothing but a random assembling of unwanted fabric put together by many women at quilting bees. It was also believed that quilting bees were just forums for women to exchange gossip.

In her book *American Women Artists From Early Indian Times to the Present,* Charlotte Streifer Rubinstein described the quilt-making process. Quilting and sewing bees were ways for women to meet and socialize, and they were a kind of early women's network:

> The quilt artist planned the entire work with great thought, at times orchestrating hundreds of tiny pieces, and at others, making special purchases of fabric to balance a color scheme. Outstanding quilt design-

ers were well known in their communities. It should be pointed out that the very lavish and elegant quilts in certain Southern districts were often made possible by the skilled artistry of black women slaves.

A quilting bee was called when the top of the quilt was finished and was stretched on a frame ready to be sewn to the backing with thousands of tiny stitches. The quilting bee was an important social institution where women came together to work, to socialize, and to share ideas. Interestingly, the great flowering of quilting in the nineteenth century corresponds to the period of the first wave of feminism in the United States. Susan B. Anthony made her first women's rights speech at a church quilting bee in Cleveland.

In recent years (sparked, some say, by the women's movement), there has been a growing interest in quilting. That interest was celebrated in the 1995 movie *How to Make an American Quilt,* starring Winona Ryder. The best examples of quilting are often designed by one woman, who signs and dates her work of art.

However, the most important task of colonial American women was cooking.

Cooking in Colonial Days

Food preparation during colonial times was an enormous undertaking. Since there were no refrigerators and canning techniques had not yet been invented, meat was preserved by salting (using salt as a preservative), drying, or pickling (preserving food in a vinegar solution). Women made jams from berries, and they dried fruits and vegetables for winter use. These foods provided nutrients and a balanced diet throughout the year, especially in the winter months when fresh fruit and vegetables were not readily available. Although colonial women did not understand the science of a balanced diet, they could see its good effects on their families.

Evan Jones described the cooking of colonial women in *American Food: The Gastronomic Story* this way:

> To both Plymouth and Jamestown, colonial women brought the . . . British cooking style they had learned at home. . . . Nothing at all about the way they cooked . . . could be described as tricky. The kitchens they left behind were rudimentary [primitive . . . . They were women who always had done a good deal of their own work, but many of them had come from urban [city] rather than rural homes and some had to accustom themselves to the care of poultry and dairy animals and to such chores as butchering.

Colonial women were so busy contributing to the family's survival that they could not be restricted to the household. They had to go wherever their work took them. This might be to the market to buy, barter (trade), or sell handicrafts or fruits, vegetables, or other produce to bring extra income into the home. It might also be to visit and tend to the sick or women about to deliver babies.

Gardening in Colonial Times

The first women settlers in the New World (America) knew they were coming to a wilderness where they would have to grow most of their own food. Next in importance to a roof over their heads came their gardens. They tended vegetable and fruit gardens, which they grew from the seeds and plants they had carried with them from the Old World (Europe). They also found other fruits and vegetables already growing in the New World and adapted their English recipes to include them.

Besides using their gardens for food, the colonial housewives produced countless household aids—food and drink flavorings, cosmetics, insect repellents, scents for candles—from their plants. Women were also often called upon to mix medicines for the sick from the bounty of their gardens.

Domestic Arts and Crafts in Nineteenth-Century America

The Industrial Revolution was in full swing from 1709 to the mid-1800s, producing new laborsaving devices, many of which were invented by women. (See Chapter 14: Science and Exploration.)

A Return to the Home Factory?

Since the early 1800s, businesses have paid women tiny sums of money to perform work in their homes. These home-based or cottage industries included activities such as sewing and jewelry making.

In the 1880s, American social reformers began a movement to have the government regulate some of the home-based industries. These reformers said that the women who performed these jobs in their homes were being exploited by being paid too little for too much work.

Under the New Deal administration of President Franklin Roosevelt, women who worked in his Labor Department sought a total ban on work done in the home. The 1938 Fair Labor Standards Act banned home work in some clothing-related trades where the worst examples of low wages and too many hours occurred.

Efforts to regulate home labor came partly out of the desire to keep the home separate from the world of paid labor. Today we are experiencing a reversal of this attitude. Many women now want to be able to work in their homes for pay. Some politicians support home work and oppose government regulation of it. They note the advantages of home work for women who must work and also care for their children. Other politicians voice concern that women who work in the home do so to avoid paying taxes, which people who work outside of the home must pay.

Critics say that efforts to permit home work are just another way to exploit women. Eileen Boris, writing in the magazine the *Nation* in 1986, complained: "Women will now be free to type or sew [both low-paying jobs] after washing clothes and watching children." By doing so, she says, "they will limit their career prospects, pensions [retirement savings], and other benefits."

Even when their work moves into the home, many women are still solely responsible for child and elder care, will continue to earn less than men, and continue to see their work in both the family and the labor market undervalued. Furthermore, what might seem like a good option for women who seek to add to the family income can be a bad option for other women. Most immigrants and farm women who sew garments at home, for instance, are not being paid a living wage.

Because of the Industrial Revolution, American cities began to grow rapidly between 1810 and 1860. Daily life in these cities was also changing very rapidly from life during colonial days. Large numbers of single men and women moved to factory towns to work, marry, and stay rather than return to family farms. This is called urbanization.

For the women who stayed at home, urbanization and industrialization brought the separation of men's and women's worlds, which came to be known as "spheres." The woman's world shrank and she was left to perform her work in isolation in the home, while men went out into the world.

Technology promised to reduce women's domestic chores, since they would no longer have to manufacture their own cloth but could buy it factory-made. They also no longer needed to make candles or soap. The question became, how does a typical nineteenth-century woman spend her day now that she is "saving" all this time? The answer was different for urban women and those who began to head west, known as the pioneer women.

Daily Life in the East

It is difficult to describe the daily life of city women in the face of technological advances because, even in the city, women lived under a vast array of conditions. Some women were rich and some were poor. Some had many children, while others had few. Some had running water and others pumped it from wells.

In the 1850s, Gro Svendsen, an immigrant from Norway, wrote to her parents back home about what she observed in America:

> We are told that the women of America have much leisure time but I haven't yet met any woman who thought so! Here the mistress [wife] of the house must do all the work that the cook, the maid and the housekeeper would do in an upper class family at home [Norway]. Moreover she must do her work as well as these three together do it in Norway.

Author Ruth Schwartz Cowan, who provided the above quotation in her book *More Work for Mother: The Ironies of Household Technology From the Open Hearth to the Microwave,* goes on to say: "Labor-saving devices were invented and diffused [spread] throughout the country during those hundred years that witnessed the first stages of industrialization, but they reorganized the work processes of housework in ways that did not save the labor of the average housewife."

Cowan illustrates her point first by describing the preparation of a stew by a Connecticut woman living in a farm town. The labor required for that woman to prepare the stew differed very little from the labor required of a woman one hundred years before, in spite of advances in technology. Laborsaving devices took longer to reach rural (country) America, where more than one-half of America's population lived in the nineteenth century. Furthermore, not many labor-saving devices were then designed to be homemaker friendly.

Cowan further notes that a city woman living before 1800 "would have cooked and baked aplenty but [her] husband would have done much of the preparation—such as chopping wood, shelling corn . . . " and so on. With the coming of industrialization, her husband would be out working in a factory. In spite of her so-called laborsaving devices, the woman "bore the whole burden of housework" alone.

Daily Life of the Pioneer Woman

Between 1800 and 1860, millions of people moved west from the New England states. For a pioneer woman, the daily workload became even heavier than what she had left behind. For the first part of the journey, she might be able to carry out her day's activities in somewhat the same way she always had. As the journey became rougher, however, she was required to do more hard labor while at the same time trying to perform her former duties, such as cooking and washing.

When the preserved food she brought with her was gone, the pioneer woman was forced to make do with what could be found in the wilderness. Water also often became scarce. Travelers lived under constant threat of attack, accident, and illness.

Jessie Bernard, author of *The Female World,* described the pioneer woman's evening activities after a hard day's work:

At night, women often clustered together, chatting, working, or commiserating [offering sympathy to one another], instead of joining the men: 'High teas were not popular, but tatting [lace making], knitting, crocheting, exchanging recipes for cooking beans or dried apples or swapping food for the sake of variety kept us in practice of feminine occupations and diversions.'

The life of pioneer women and girls is described in detail in the *Little House* series of books written by Laura Ingalls Wilder.

Cooking in Nineteenth-Century America

If the food of colonial days was not very inspired, the situation began to change in the nineteenth century, thanks to the experiments of women. James Beard described the improvement in his book *American Cookery*:

Eventually in many small communities excellent natural cooks began to blossom, whom all the local ladies tried to emulate [imitate]. . . . It is fascinating to see, for example, how successful recipes inspired envious cooks to compete. Thus we find Mrs. Doctor Joseph Niemyer's Chicken with a Savory Sauce turning up in other cookbooks as Chicken with a Savory Sauce or Savory Sauced Chicken. Occasionally a recipe such as Mrs. Niemyer's is improved upon, perhaps by a housewife with a different ethnic background. So runs the pattern through all these remarkable paperbound cookbooks for almost two centuries. They, as much as anything, record the history of our [American] cuisine. Through them it is possible to trace the march of recipes westward and to see which of the great recipes survived through generations of change.

Furthermore, we have women to thank for preserving the history of American cooking. According to Beard:

It was difficult for women who moved west to carry out their daily duties.

The written record of [American cooking] is in many ways more complete than that of any other country. Beginning with Amelia Simmons we have the wisdom of such notables as Eliza Leslie, Catharine Beecher, Mrs. T. J. Crowen, Marion Harland, Maria Parloa, Mrs. Sarah Tyson Rorer, Mrs. Mary Lincoln, and Fannie Merritt Farmer.

Beard might also have mentioned Mary Randolph (1762–1828), whose book *The Virginia House-wife* was published in 1825. It is considered to be nineteenth-century America's finest and most influential cookbook. Until the end of the 1700s, American women had relied on cookbooks imported from England, which called for English ingredients.

Randolph, known as the best cook in Virginia, based her cooking and her book on Virginia produce (fruits and vegetables) and Virginia cooking techniques, a totally new idea at the time.

Gardening in Nineteenth–Century America

Gardening as a change from hunting and gathering began about 8000 B.C. Some say women were the first gardeners and only lost control of the fields when men gave up hunting in favor of farming. Eventually, according to Eleanor Perényi, author of *Green Thoughts: A Writer in the Garden*, women were "no longer . . . the ones to decide what was planted, how, or where; and accordingly the space allotted to them diminished [became smaller] too, until flowers and herbs were the only plants left under their direct management."

At first gardening was done to supply food for the community. Today we understand gardening to mean the growing of plants close to the home for personal use rather than garden produce to sell or trade.

The kind of gardens that developed in England during the nineteenth century have had a great influence on current American gardening style (as well as gardening styles throughout the British Empire). One of the most important names in the development of the style known as the English garden is Gertrude Jekyll (1843–1932).

Jekyll was born into a wealthy family but had little formal education. At an early age, she showed artistic talent and studied painting and other pursuits considered appropriate for the unmarried daughter of a well-to-do family of the time. When she was in her late thirties, Jekyll was forced to abandon painting because of severe myopia (nearsightedness). She then developed an interest in gardening.

During her late forties, Jekyll teamed up with the great English architect, twenty-year-old Edward Lutyens. Together they designed some of England's finest homes and gardens. Jekyll introduced many new trends in gardening, relying especially on native plants and wild gardens rather than the very formal gardens popular in her time. She wrote several books on gardening that are still consulted today. Jekyll died at age 89. Her tombstone was designed by Lutyens and on it he had inscribed: "Artist Gardener Craftswoman."

English writer Vita Sackville-West (1892–1962), author of novels, biographies, and gardening books, was influenced by Jekyll. With her husband, Sackville-West created one of England's most admired gardens at their estate called Sissinghurst in the 1930s. It is still visited today by people who appreciate fine gardens.

Among the many American landscape gardeners influenced by Jekyll was Beatrix Jones Farrand (1872–1959). She designed gardens for her aunt, writer Edith Wharton, and gardens at Dumbarton Oaks, a Washington, D.C., estate where the idea of the United Nations was formulated.

Thinking About a Woman's Place

It was during the nineteenth century that women began to question the notion of equality that was being proclaimed in the United States. They wondered how equality applied to them, since rights for white men were expanding but were growing more limited for women. The mid-nineteenth century became a turning point in women's history, however.

It was at this time that the first women's rights movement was born.

Keeping the Fourteenth-Century Home

In the late 1300s, a Frenchman who was probably between the ages of fifty and sixty married a fifteen-year-old girl who knew nothing of housekeeping. Knowing that he would probably leave the girl a widow, the man wrote her a book of moral and domestic instructions so she would make a good wife to a second husband. Eileen Power, who is an expert on the Middle Ages (500–1500), calls the book "by far the most exhaustive treatise [study] on household management which has come down to us from the Middle Ages." The book has been edited and translated by Tania Bayard and is titled *A Medieval Home Companion: Housekeeping in the Fourteenth Century.*

Many domestic arts are discussed by the husband in the book. For example, Chapter 4, titled "How to Care for a Husband," discusses these major points:

1. Cherish your husband's person carefully.

2. Take care that there are no fleas in your room or in your bed.

3. Shield your husband from all troubles.

4. Be dutiful.

However, the concept of "the lady" and the movement to put women in their place—the home—was developing simultaneously. This concept held that the domestic lady should be self-sacrificing, putting her needs behind those of all others. Many influential male writers published their thoughts about the proper "spheres" of men and women. Five women who also contributed much to the thinking about women's work in the nineteenth and early twentieth centuries were Lydia Maria Francis Child, Catharine Beecher, Fannie Farmer, Ellen Swallow Richards, and Lillian Gilbreth.

Lydia Maria Francis Child

Lydia Child (1802–1880) was a major contributor to the nineteenth-century literature describing woman's proper "sphere." Born in Massachusetts, she accepted a teaching position in Maine at age eighteen, becoming part of the growing number of New England women who were leaving home to earn their own living.

Child published her first novel, about an interracial marriage between a white woman and a Native American man, when she was twenty-two years old. Two years later she began publication of America's first educational magazine for children. Next she turned her hand to writing about women.

The Frugal Housewife was published in 1829 and proved to be one of the most successful advice manuals on household duties ever published in the United States. Child followed it with *The Mother's Book* and *The Little Girl's Own Book* in 1831.

Although she held strong opinions about the proper behavior of men and women, Child also felt strongly about the importance and dignity of "women's work." She herself was a professional woman, not a domestic one for most of her life. In 1841 Child separated from her husband of 15 years and lived independently until 1850. She then reunited with him and continued her writing career. Child regretted having no children but once wrote that her husband "serves me for husband and 'baby and all.'" The last years of her life were spent caring for her ailing father, doing housework, and writing.

Catharine Beecher

Catharine Beecher, a member of the famous family that also produced Harriet Beecher Stowe, author of *Uncle Tom's Cabin,* stepped in with her vision of the home as a woman's place. Beecher envisioned the home as woman's sphere, equally as important as the man's sphere. In her famous work, *A Treatise on Domestic Economy* (1841), Beecher explained to her readers that women were restricted to the domestic sphere for political reasons necessary to make democracy work in America.

According to Beecher, as American society expanded during the nineteenth century and immigrants arrived

Catharine Beecher's Treatise on Domestic Economy *was America's first guide to the domestic arts.*

from all over the world, there was a greater need for ways to reduce the conflict that was sure to rise between different kinds of people. Otherwise, she said, we might find ourselves self-destructing rather than coming together. Beecher led her readers to conclude that if one-half of the population—women—were to be removed from the competition and be made subservient (inferior) to the other one-half, the amount of tension that American society had to bear would be greatly reduced. If the duties of man were to be divided from those of women, "the great work of society could be better carried on."

American women, said Beecher, live in a society where "every thing is moving and changing." She meant that the flow of wealth was constantly shifting and society was in an unstable state. Beecher described the situation this way:

> Persons in poverty, are rising to opulence [wealth], and persons of wealth, are sinking to poverty. The children of common laborers, by their talents and enterprise, are becoming nobles in intellect, or wealth, or office; while the children of the wealthy . . . are sinking to humbler stations [jobs]. The sons of the wealthy are leaving the rich mansions of their fathers, to dwell in the log cabins of the forest, where very soon they shall bear away the daughters of ease and refinement, to share the privations [lack of comforts] of a new settlement. Meantime, even in the more stationary [not moving] portions of the community, there is a mingling of all grades of wealth, intellect, and education . . . . Thus, persons of humble means are brought into contact with those of vast wealth . . . [so there is] a constant comparison of conditions, among equals, and a constant temptation presented to imitate the customs, and to strive for the enjoyments, of those who possess larger means.

In this turmoil, the subordination of the wife to the husband was necessary if society was to "go forward harmoniously." The position of women in American culture was an example of how "superior and subordinate relations" contribute to "the general good of all." If women were to "take a subordinate station," it would promote the general good of the society.

The book that resulted from Beecher's ideas, *A Treatise on Domestic Economy,* was America's first complete guide to the domestic arts as well as a scientific and personal guide to female health and well-being. Beecher's volume provided simple rules allowing the reader to judge for herself how to best deal with household matters. She made medical matters less of a mystery for her audience and allowed them to think that anyone could easily know as much about them as she did by learning a few simple rules.

Beecher's *Treatise* explained every part of domestic life from the building of a house to the setting of a table. She laid out designs for kitchen plumbing systems and laborsaving devices. Before her book, women who wanted written instructions on domestic arts had to read separate books on health, child care, housebuilding, plumbing, and cooking. Beecher's was the first American volume to pull all domestic chores together and to describe their functions in the American environment. Her *Treatise* came at a time when American women were on the move westward and were being separated from their traditional sources of domestic information—grandmothers, mothers, aunts, sisters, and neighbors.

Beecher's *Treatise* was enormously influential and placed women firmly inside the home. In doing so, it asked women to help solve the problems of a society in which they were not allowed to fully participate. Beecher and the other influential nineteenth-century writers about domesticity agreed that this isolation of women in the home and away from full participation in the society would decrease the tensions of American life.

Ellen Swallow Richards, Home Economist

Home economics is defined by the *American Heritage Dictionary* as "the science and art of home management, including household budgets, purchase of food and clothing, child care, cooking, nutrition, and the like." A home economics movement developed in the early 1800s and its purpose was to prepare girls for their future as housewives and mothers.

Home economics as a profession developed in the early twentieth century. At first it attracted only women, so it was not held in high regard by society in general. The American Home Economics Association was founded in 1908 with the remarkable Ellen Swallow Richards (1842–1911) as its first president.

Richards was born in Boston, Massachusetts, in 1842 and graduated from Vassar College in 1870. Thereafter she was accepted as a special student in chemistry at the Massachusetts Institute of Technology (MIT) in Cambridge. In 1873 Richards received a master's degree in chemistry, becoming the first woman to graduate from MIT. Chemistry was considered an appropriate area of study for women of the time because it taught principles that could be used in cooking when they returned to the home.

In 1876 Richards persuaded MIT to open a laboratory where women could study chemistry. Three years later she prepared a report on sanitary conditions—the purity of air, water, and food—in the state of Massachusetts, which led the state to pass the nation's first Food and Drug Act. Food and drug acts ensure the safety and purity of the foods we buy and the prescription drugs we take. In 1881 Richards founded the Association of Collegiate Alumnae, which later became the renowned American Association of University Women. Its purpose was to promote lifelong learning and achievement by women. Richards also assisted in establishing the world's first laboratory to study sanitary chemistry in 1884.

Richards next directed her attention to the newly developing field of home economics. Her knowledge of the field was so considerable that she was named director of the model kitchen sponsored by the U.S. Department of Agriculture for the 1893 World's Fair held in Chicago, Illinois. The model kitchen focused on analyzing food for its nutrition content.

By 1899 Richards had become involved in identifying the courses of study and the standards required for an individual to be certified as a home economist. It was also at this time that the term "home economics" first began to be used. Home economists seek to apply science and technology to the home. They perform tests on food to determine calories and nutritional value. They also conduct time-and-motion studies in the home, which measure the time and motions necessary to do a given job.

Lillian Gilbreth and Modern Home Economics

Lillian Gilbreth was a pioneer in applying time-and-motion studies to the home. She wrote about her methods in *The Home Maker and Her Job* (1927). Although she was not a home economist—she had majored in English literature in college—Gilbreth's work was so respected that she became a professor of management at Purdue University in West Lafayette, Indiana, in 1935. The 1950 movie *Cheaper by the Dozen* was based on her life.

Today home economics programs, like those in the United States, exist in several industrialized nations, such as Canada and Great Britain. The United Nations is also seeking to introduce them into the poor countries of Latin America, Asia, and Africa.

Fannie Merritt Farmer, Cookery Writer

Fannie Farmer (1857–1915) was born in Boston, Massachusetts, to a poor family. She suffered either a stroke or polio when she was only 16 years old. Her illness left her with a limp considered severe enough that she temporarily gave up her dream of attending college. Nevertheless, Farmer achieved some remarkable successes that have made her name inseparable from the notion of American cooking.

Disabled and believing herself too plain for marriage, Farmer began to cultivate a talent for cooking. When lack of money forced her family to provide room and meals for strangers, Farmer's cooking was so admired that she was urged to train for a career as a cooking teacher. At age thirty, Farmer enrolled at the Boston Cooking School for a two-year course, and in 1894 she was made head of the school.

In 1896 Farmer completed the first edition of her *Boston Cooking School Cookbook.* Her publishers were so sure the book could not succeed that they asked her to pay for the costs of publication. However, the volume was an immediate success and sold many millions of copies. It also brought much unwanted publicity to its shy author.

Farmer's cookbook was distinguished by its clear recipes and instructions for measuring, timing, and preparation. Where previous cookbooks suggested the use of "heaping cups" and "rounded teaspoons," leaving it to the cook to use any cup or teaspoon she wished, Farmer sternly advised, "Correct measurements are absolutely necessary to insure the best results." Furthermore, she said, "It is the duty of every housekeeper to learn the art of soup making." But, she reassured her readers, "The art of soup making is more easily mastered than it first appears." Farmer gave her grateful audience a sense of the dignity involved in creating a delicious meal.

In 1902 Fannie Farmer founded her Miss Farmer School of Cookery with the profits from her cookbook. She also offered her services teaching nutrition to nurses and children. She wrote a cookery page for the *Woman's Home Journal* magazine and gave lectures.

Twenty-one editions of *The Boston Cooking School Cookbook* were published before Farmer's death in 1915. Today the book, called *The Fannie Farmer Cookbook,* continues to be published.

Domestic Arts and Crafts Today

As we have discussed in other chapters, American women left their home "sphere" in large numbers during World War II (1939–45) to work in factories. However, they were urged to return to the home when the soldiers returned after the war, and most women seemed to do so happily.

Many aspects of American domestic arts and crafts were lost as the country embraced mass-produced foods and other goods. Fresh and wholesome foods were replaced first by canned goods and later by frozen foods. Household items that were once lovingly crafted by hand were replaced by mass-produced items that lacked any personal touch. The people who once worked as servants found better-paying jobs elsewhere, but with the many new laborsaving devices, it was thought that a woman could do all her housework herself and did not need servants.

The book *Chronicle of the 20th Century* describes the day of a "typical American housewife" in 1948, under the headline "Appliances for electrified home, $2,274."

Morning. The typical American housewife tosses aside her electric blanket and rises. She takes a shower in water heated by an electric furnace and dries her hair under a hairdryer. The baby is crying. The woman puts the baby's bottle in an electric sterilizer and warmer.

Breakfast. The housewife prepares a scrumptious meal with the electric waffle iron, coffee maker, egg beater, egg timer and toaster. The six-cubic-foot refrigerator is opened and closed. When the meal is over, the dishes are placed in the electric dishwasher.

Cleaning. Washing machine and dryer are on. Iron is on. Upright vacuum cleaner is on. Housewife frequently glances at electric clock to ascertain [determine] the time. Baby is crying. Housewife stops cleaning to put electric heating pad below baby and vaporizer beside baby.

Evening. Wife is too tired to appreciate electric phonograph [record player], electric radio, electric harpsichord or husband. She picks up a newspaper. Reads that her electric devices cost $2,274. She wonders just how long she must wait to buy an electronic maid.

With the benefit of countless labor-saving devices undreamed of by women of the previous century, the average 1950s housewife worked 52 hours a week maintaining her home. However, her work may have seemed more like drudgery (unpleasant work) than art. Even cooking was no longer a joy. With the United States involved in a cold war with the Soviet Union, the 1950s saw a country in constant fear of nuclear bomb attack. (The Cold War was a time of political tension and military rivalry between the

United States and the Soviet Union that last from the 1950s to the early 1990s.) The March 1996 *New York Times Magazine* described the nation's new notion of food: "In the late 1950's, food seemed to be merely about the nutrient load it was capable of carrying. It was an atomic vision of food—storehoused, canned, vacuum-sealed, archived [set aside] for the day the bombs went off and it came in handy."

During the 1960s and 1970s feminists were calling for all women to get out of the kitchen. They claimed that daily cooking was not valued in our society and women ought to concentrate on work outside the home. The art of cooking fell out of favor and fast-food suppliers came into their own. Today, a typical woman must keep track of the dangerously high levels of sodium, fat, and sugar (all preservatives) in processed foods as she tries to balance the demands of her career with the responsibilities of feeding a family.

Women's lives at the end of the twentieth century are vastly different from what they were in the early days of the United States. Many of the activities we generally consider domestic arts—cooking and baking "from scratch" (using all fresh ingredients), gardening, home decorating, sewing, quilting, and food preservation (canning)—are no longer done by large numbers of women at home. Some arts, such as canning, have been made unnecessary by advances in technology. In the case of others,

women today simply have no time, and the arts are either not pursued or have moved outside the home.

Although the cry "A woman's place is in the home" is still heard from those who desire a return to the so-called good old days, the reality for more and more American women is that they must work outside the home to support themselves and their families. Statistics show that by the year 2005 nearly one-half of the total U.S. labor force will be women. Statistics also show that women spend more time performing the unappealing parts of housework—cleaning and grocery shopping, for example—in addition to their work outside the home. Still, according to the National Endowment for the Arts, 62 percent of adult women managed to find time to garden in 1992, compared to 46 percent of men.

Increasingly, modern women are beginning to realize the tremendous value to society of the domestic work they used to do. The female world is undergoing a painful reevaluation as women demand appreciation and possibly even payment in relation to the value of their services. This is reflected in movements seeking ways to pay homemakers, eldercare and child-care workers, and others who perform household functions in amounts suitable to their value. However, these movements continue to meet resistance from conservatives and those who fear that the United States cannot afford to pay women what their domestic work is worth.

Feminists Return to the Kitchen

During the 1970s feminists urged women to get out of the kitchen and into the world of work outside the home. Cooking done by women at home was looked down upon by many as a pursuit not worthy of a "liberated" (free) woman. Then, in the early 1990s, Arlene Avakian, associate professor of women's studies at the University of Massachusetts, was in the process of writing her autobiography. She found herself surprised at the way the subject of food ran throughout her book. She was inspired to begin assembling *Through the Kitchen Window,* a book about food written by feminists and published in 1996 by the Feminist Press.

"The idea behind the book," said Avakian in an interview with John Willoughby for the *New York Times* in May 1996, "is that cooking is a part of women's daily lives and has been for a very long time in most cultures. But cooking—or at least daily cooking—was always denigrated [belittled] because it was not valued in patriarchies" or male-centered societies. Avakian says this attitude is changing. "Feminist authors are all saying, "Wait a minute, there is something in this that we need to claim . . . [and] to share."

Also interviewed for the newspaper story was Carolyn Heilbrun, an author and professor at Columbia University in New York City. She remarked, "I was not always enthusiastic about the subject of cooking. I guess what I felt in the beginning was that if we were finally getting a chance to look at women's history, for goodness sake, we knew they cooked, let's look at what else they did." Now, she says, "We are further along [in women's studies] and it's a different picture. Given a choice between cookbooks and books on women athletes I might still pick athletes, but now I think that we can have them both."

The Domestic Arts Become Leisure-Time Pursuits

It is estimated that Americans in the 1990s have about forty hours a week leisure time. Nearly one-half of that time is spent watching television. If Americans go out, it is usually to movies or sporting events (either as spectators or participants). Most Americans do not use their leisure time for creative pursuits that give individual or family satisfaction, like the domestic arts of gardening or crafts.

State and county fairs demonstrate that home cooking and handicrafts have not completely disappeared. The existence of craft stores and craft fairs prove that the decorative arts are still alive.

However, these activities, once done out of necessity, have now become leisure-time hobbies. Leading the way in the small resurgence of the domestic arts is Martha Stewart.

Martha Stewart

Martha Stewart (1941–) believes there is a correct way to do everything and everyone can learn it. She has said that her goal is "to make homemaking glamorous."

Stewart credits her family and her neighbors for teaching her to love gardening and cooking. While still a child, she earned extra money by organizing birthday parties for the neighbor children. Later she learned about home construction by remodeling her own Connecticut home.

Stewart has had an interesting and varied career. She worked as a fashion model in the 1950s and early 1960s to pay for her college education. After college she worked as a stockbroker on New York's Wall Street until deciding she "wanted to sell things that were fun to sell." She began a catering business in 1976, preparing food in her home using ingredients from her own garden. She later refined her cooking skills by studying Julia Child's *Mastering the Art of French Cooking.*

In 1982 Stewart published her first book, *Entertaining,* which pulled together all her knowledge about cooking and catering. Since then she has shown millions of Americans what good taste means according to Martha Stewart, through books, a magazine and television show both called *Martha Stewart Living,* and through sheets, towels, and house paints marketed under her name. By the mid-1990s her magazine reached more than one million households and her television show reached more than five million viewers a week.

Through her books, magazines, compact discs, and cassettes, Stewart demonstrates how to do everything around the house perfectly. Stewart says she offers "stuff to dream about, even if you end up . . . not actually getting it done." Her critics charge, however, that not being able to meet Stewart's high standards makes most women feel guilty and inadequate.

The Modern Art of Cooking

As American women began fleeing the kitchen in the 1960s and 1970s to work outside the home, a strange phenomenon emerged—more men began cooking. Comic writer Nora Ephron explained the trend this way: "Men cook more [today], and we all know why. It is the only interesting household task. Getting down and scrubbing the floor is done by women, or by the women they've hired."

Another explanation for this new interest in cooking on the part of men is the influence of the incomparable Julia Child. In 1948, Child, a history major and graduate of Smith College, moved to Paris, France, the world capital of fine

Showcasing Domestic Arts: State and County Fairs

The custom of fairs came to America from Europe during the colonial period. The original purpose of such fairs was to showcase the art of the farmer and the homemaker.

By 1868 America boasted more than thirteen hundred agricultural societies, and most of them held annual fairs. Eventually the emphasis of these fairs became how to educate farmers on new methods of farming. For the farm woman, though, the fairs remained a way to demonstrate her many domestic talents. Fairs also offered entertainments typically found at carnivals and circuses, such as rides and clowns (as they do today).

Women perfected recipes and gathered up the best examples of their handicrafts to present to judges at these fairs. Those who took top prizes in fair competitions were admired by people in their communities. Sometimes food manufacturers and processors bought prizewinning recipes for mass production, providing a source of income for the winners. These fairs were also an excellent way for young people to mingle and get acquainted. Many a young woman met her future husband at the fair. The fair served as a showcase for Dad's prize pig and Mom's prize baked goods, as well as the place for son and daughter to look for their first love. This sentiment was perfectly captured in the 1933 movie *State Fair,* starring Janet Gaynor, and in the 1973 animated film *Charlotte's Web.*

Agricultural fairs are still a major industry in the United States. Des Moines, Iowa's eleven-day state fair draws nine hundred thousand people each year. Michigan boasts the oldest state fair in the country. The Big E, sponsored by six New England states, offers a taste of their foods, and it draws more than one million people annually. The fairs still focus on contests for the finest examples of crops, animals, and home-prepared foods. However, they also feature carnival rides, nationally known entertainers, and other events having nothing to do with farming, such as airplane flying demonstrations.

---

cooking, with her husband, a member of the U.S. Foreign Service. There she studied at the famous Cordon Bleu cooking school and then founded her own school, L'Ecole des Trois Gourmandes (which means The School of the Three People Who Delight in Eating Well and Heartily), with famous French chefs Simone Beck and Louise Bertholle. Together the three friends wrote *Mastering the Art of French Cooking* (Volume 1). It presented itself as the "book for the servantless

to 1973 and introduced America to a whole new style of sophisticated cookery. Across the country, French cooking became the rage. Child followed this series with one based on American cooking, *Julia Child and Company,* which ran from 1978 to 1979. In the mid-1990s, Child was still lecturing, writing, and making occasional television appearances.

The Modern Art of Entertaining

Formal entertaining today is usually thought of as the invitation of guests into one's home for a "formal" dinner—that is, a dinner where guests sit at a dining-room table and are served by someone other than themselves. This usually means the hostess.

The first person to write a guide for American entertaining was Emily Post (1873–1960). Her book *Etiquette in Society, in Business, and at Home* was first published in 1922. Etiquette used to be a set of rigid rules governing formal occasions. Today etiquette concerns itself with everyday living. The goal of etiquette is to help people get along together.

In the first edition of her book, Post declared that "it is not possible to give a formal dinner without the help of servants." Her description of a typical dinner party at the time began: "When Mrs. Worldly gives a dinner, it means no effort on her part whatsoever beyond deciding upon the date and the principal guests who are to form the nucleus [center]; every further detail is left to her subordinates [servants]—even to the completion of her list of guests."

American cook who can be unconcerned on occasion with budgets, waistlines, time schedules, children's meals, the parent-chauffeur-den mother syndrome, or anything else which might interfere with the enjoyment of producing something wonderful to eat." It was published in 1961, and that same year, Child and her husband returned to the United States and settled in Massachusetts.

In 1963 Child began her career as a television personality hosting the series *The French Chef.* Child's engaging personality won her a huge following of both men and women. The show ran from 1963

Perle Mesta: "The Hostess With the Mostes'"

Perle Mesta (1891–1975) was born in Sturgis, Michigan, and her ambition as a young woman was to be a singer. She studied voice and piano before giving it up to marry a wealthy businessman in 1915. She and her husband were both involved in politics, and after he died in 1925 she bought a mansion in Newport, Rhode Island. It was there that she began giving the series of parties that earned her a reputation as a gracious hostess.

During World War II (1939–45) Mesta owned a large cattle ranch in Arizona but gave up that life because she found it too lonely. She returned to active participation in politics and was an early supporter of the Equal Rights Amendment. Later she threw her efforts behind Senator Harry S Truman, who became her friend and was elected president of the United States in 1948. In 1949 Truman appointed Mesta to the post of U.S. Minister to the Grand Duchy of Luxembourg, a region bordered by Belgium, France, and Germany. She was only the third woman to officially represent the U.S. government abroad.

According to Mesta's autobiography *Perle,* "It's no secret that I love to give parties—lots of them. . . . It is certainly true that most of my parties have a purpose. Socializing brings people together and getting people together promotes better understanding of common problems. And since men first began to associate with one another, feasting has always been one of the most pleasant methods of finding out what is going on."

Mesta's famous parties were lively gatherings at which Truman might play the piano or actress-singer Judy Garland might stage a solo show at 3 A.M. Mesta was described as "a woman of affable [good-natured] charm, gracious and knowledgeable in the ways of pleasant living."

Irving Berlin's Broadway musical comedy *Call Me Madam* was based on Mesta's life. It starred Ethel Merman and produced the song titled "The Hostess With the Mostes' on the Ball."

Post goes on to describe what happens when all preparations for the evening have been completed by the servants:

Fifteen minutes before the dinner hour, Mrs. Worldly is already standing in her drawing-room [living room]. She has no personal responsibility other than that of being hostess. The whole machinery of equipment and service runs seemingly by itself. It does not matter whether she knows what the menu is. Her cook is more than capable of attending to it. That the table shall be perfect is merely the every-day duty of the butler. . . .

So with nothing on her mind (except a jewelled ornament and perfectly 'done' hair) she receives her guests with the tranquillity [calm] attained only by those whose household—whether great or small—can be counted on to run like a perfectly coordinated machine.

Today's dinner parties, however, are very different from how Emily Post described them. Very few women have servants, but they do have laborsaving devices to assist them as they perform all the activities necessary to accomplish a dinner party, whether it is planning, shopping, meal preparation, or cleanup.

Sometimes the hostess hires a caterer, who prepares and serves food for different people every night, unlike the servants of old.

Elizabeth L. Post, Emily's granddaughter-in-law, has updated Emily Post's *Etiquette.* In her 1984 version titled *Emily Post's Etiquette: A Guide to Modern Manners* (14th edition), Elizabeth Post gives the modern hostess permission to forego the "matching silver or fine goblets" in favor of being a "warm, relaxed and gracious party giver."

24

Fine and Applied Arts

"Where I was born and where and how I have lived is unimportant. It is what I have done with where I have been that should be of interest."

—Georgia O'Keeffe,
American painter

Women throughout the world and throughout history have been involved in creating applied and fine arts. Applied arts are those that create useful items but imbue them with (add) beauty. Applied arts include architecture, jewelry, fashion design, and furnishings such as dishes, blankets, and bags. Fine arts are those created simply to lend beauty to a room or a landscape. They include paintings and drawings, prints, glasswork, fabric hangings, sculpture, book illustration, and photography. All of these art forms, as well as some of the women artists from around the world who produce the works, are included in this chapter.

Before beginning, however, it is interesting to note that many art experts offer evidence that women's contributions to the field have been overlooked for years. Some even believe that women's contributions continue to be underrepresented in major collections and textbooks. When reading these statistics, remember that women make up about 52 percent of the U.S. population. The statistics were published in a 1995 article by Sue Marx, an

Timeline: Women in the Arts

7000 B.C. Figures of pregnant women (generally called "the goddess") are created by many Ice Age cultures to celebrate the female's ability to bear children.

5000 B.C. Egyptian wall paintings show textiles woven by a special class of servants.

A.D. 700 Pueblo and other Native American women begin weaving cotton threads into blankets.

1073-88 The Bayeux Tapestry is designed and woven by English noblewomen to tell the story of the Norman (French) Conquest of England.

1300s Women in European convents illuminate (illustrate) Bible and Church manuscripts with brightly colored and richly designed letters at the beginning of each chapter.

1614 Artemisia Gentileschi of Italy becomes the first internationally known woman painter.

1872 American Mary Cassatt moves to France and begins to paint in the Impressionist style.

1916 Georgia O'Keeffe, considered one of the greatest U.S. artists, has her first exhibit.

1932 Dorothy Dunn founds the Art Studio at the Santa Fe Indian School, creating an interest in and demand for Native American art.

1937 Margaret Bourke-White publishes her photojournalistic essay *You Have Seen Their Faces,* a collection of photos of poor farm families during the Great Depression (1929–40).

1956 Clementine Hunter paints murals on the walls of the African House and other historic buildings in Louisiana.

1979 Judy Chicago completes *The Dinner Party,* a sculpture celebrating famous women.

1981 Maya Lin designs the Vietnam Veterans Memorial.

1990 Hispanic American Judith Baca completes her mural titled *World Wall: A Vision of the Future Without Fear.*

1995 Statistics show that women are still underrepresented in the art field.

1996 Work begins on the Women of the West Museum outside Boulder, Colorado.

independent filmmaker who has done research on women in the arts.

- Forty percent of working artists in the United States are women, yet 95 percent of the artworks in museums are by men.

- Of the 2,530 paintings in the permanent collection at the National Gallery in Washington, D.C., only 5—that's 2 percent—are by women.

- At the Metropolitan Museum of Art's new Twentieth Century wing, 28 out of 411 works are by women—that's only 7 percent.

- In colleges throughout the country, *The History of Art* by W. N. Janson is the most widely used art history textbook. Prior to 1987, there was not one female artist mentioned.

- Women artists, past and present, earn 33 cents for every dollar earned by a male artist.

In spite of great obstacles, women have persisted in making their presence felt (or in this case, seen) in what has been for centuries a man's world.

A Native American woman sewing a blanket to sell.

Traditional Arts

Traditional arts include the weaving of blankets, baskets, and decorative trim, as well as the creation of pottery and other household utensils. In most ancient human societies, women were the ones who tended to the home and family. As such, they were entrusted with creating the utensils the family used and the clothing they wore. Many societies still operate under this principle, that women create the items needed for the home.

Traditional arts are sometimes referred to as "folk art." In general, folk artists know little or nothing about basic

Native American women are famous for their beautiful pottery.

principles of art, including the use of perspective (the ability to make flat surfaces, such as paper and canvas, appear to have depth and distance) and light. Instead, they create their own solutions to the problems of showing depth and sunlight in their works.

Native American Art

The Native Americans of the United States have produced a vast and colorful array of decorative and beautiful items. Navajo blankets, for instance, are the work of women weavers who have become famous for their designs. Painted buffalo hides (skins) and robes were crafted by the Indian women of the American plains states. Deerskin shirts, leggings, and moccasins were the product of native women throughout the northern portion of the United States. First they cured (prepared) the deerskin to make it as soft as velvet. Then they painted it with dyes they created and stitched it with beads, thongs (narrow strips of leather), and quills. Many of the patterns were bold, geometrical designs. Some were created through hundreds of beads carefully stitched into a design. Other clothing was decorated with feathers, hair, shells, and bones. These designs usually told an Indian legend or religious story.

In addition to clothing and blankets, Native American women are famous for their pottery. Maria Martinez, a Tewa Indian born in 1887, helped her tribe achieve economic independence through a return to their traditional craftwork. Martinez rediscovered the ancient Tewa Indian techniques of firing polychrome (multicolored) and "black on black" pottery. She taught the technique to other

Tewas and helped organize work groups. With her help, the tribe earned international fame for its beautiful ceramics. The Zuni and Pueblo Indian tribes also create unique and beautiful pottery. Their pots and vases are known for their distinctive black, white, turquoise, and red clay coloring.

Many Indian tribes are well known for their jewelry and woven baskets. The Navajo tribe, for instance, have a distinctive style that uses silver and turquoise, the elements native to their southwestern location. Navajo baskets and trays continue to be woven from marsh and prairie grasses of different colors. Women weavers use the different colors to make patterns and figures in their baskets, trays, and hats. One of the most famous modern basket-makers is Dat-So-La-Lee of the Washo tribe.

Grandma Moses has become America's most famous female folk artist.

Folk Art

Much of the early folk art was of a practical nature. This means that either the art item was useful or it was created from a medium (the materials that an artists uses, such as paint, wax, or clay) left over from another project. One of America's earliest well-known folk artists was Eunice Griswold Pinney. Born in 1770 in Connecticut, Pinney was known for her portraits, and her use of strong lines, bold colors, and background patterns. Deborah Goldsmith, another early folk artist, traveled through New England painting portraits of families. Her paintings also showed the furniture and home decora-

tions of the period and serve as an important record of these styles. Ruth Downer used watercolor paints on silk to recreate New England life in the early 1800s. Sarah A. Shafer was a Maryland woman who designed and stitched quilts in the 1850s.

Anna Mary Robertson Moses, or Grandma Moses as she is more commonly known, is probably America's most famous folk artist. Moses was born in 1860 in New York State and did not begin painting until she was eighty years old. In the twenty years before her death at age one hundred, she produced more than fifteen hundred paintings. Her works are known for their vibrant (bright) color and simple depiction of country life during the late 1800s.

African American Clementine Hunter was born in Louisiana in 1886, and is one of the best-known folk artists in the United States. By the time of her death in 1988, two dozen exhibitions of her art had taken place at prestigious commercial galleries and university shows. Hunter originally was a quilt artist, and next moved to decorative painting on household objects such as bottles, pots, and furniture. She eventually began paintings of neighborhood life and religious events. During her career, Hunter also painted murals on the walls of several historical buildings.

Decorative Arts

Glasswork, Pottery, and Ceramics

The Arts and Crafts movement of the 1870s gave many women new ways in which to express their artistic urges. The movement encouraged artists to produce items such as textiles (fabric), needlework (such as embroidery and tapestry), and glassware. Fine artists, who considered themselves "true" artists, often frowned upon these items and their creators, who became known as "craftsmen." As a result of this disproval, this artwork became a separate branch of arts known as the decorative arts.

One of the famous potters of the mid-1800s was Mary Louise McLaughlin, who was born in Ohio in 1847. She and Maria Longworth Nichols Storer, who was born in 1849, experimented with different glazing and firing techniques. (Glazing is the application of a coating to ceramics before it is fired or heated.) Among their works were vases and china dishes.

Many of the medium's finest artists are at work today. Karen Sepanski, an artist based in Detroit, Michigan, creates free-standing glass murals. One of her techniques is to create a design, make and cut the glass, and mount it in a framework of paneled hinges. Her work has been incorporated into the decorating scheme of the Royal Caribbean Cruise Lines, which has ordered pieces for three of its luxury cruise ships. Sepanski has been doing contemporary architectural glasswork since 1970. Her other works include glass doors and windows, decorative platters, and ceramics.

Viola Frey, a California-based artist, works in large-scale ceramics and is known for her enormous caricatures (a picture that greatly exaggerates distinctive features) of human beings. She has been associated with the ceramic sculpture movement that has been active in California since the mid-1950s. Betty Woodman is a ceramic artist best known for her paintings on ceramics. The Museum of Modern Art in New York has a collection of her works.

Fabric Design

Much of what we know about the Middle Ages (500–1500) today comes from the magnificent wall tapestries

Decorative Arts: Susan Soros Founds a New School

In 1991, Susan Weber Soros founded the Bard Graduate Center for Studies in the Decorative Arts in New York City. Soros sees the decorative arts as evidence of society's accomplishments. "At the Center, we don't just see objects as beautiful things to enjoy in one's home," Soros said in a 1996 *New York Times* article, "but as the documents and artifacts of history."

Soros believed enough in the value of decorative arts that she invested $20 million of her own money to start the school. Today the Bard gets its operating budget from tuition and foundation grants, as well as from the initial endowment. The Bard is only one of three schools in the United States where a student can earn an advanced degree in the decorative arts.

In 1996, the Bard graduated its first class of twenty students to earn master's degrees in decorative arts. Among the areas of study are art history, cultural history, furniture design, and contemporary (modern) decorative arts. The center also houses a library with twenty-five thousand books and magazines about the decorative arts. A journal, *Studies in Decorative Arts,* is published by the center's staff.

Soros, a native New Yorker, holds a degree in art history from Barnard College and a master's degree in Victorian decorative arts. For her master's degree, she wrote a thesis (paper) on the painter James Whistler, whose work includes the famous *Whistler's Mother.* Soros plans to do doctoral work at the Royal College of Art in London, England.

---

designed and stitched by women who lived in religious convents or castles. Even after six hundred years, the color and vividness of these fabrics remain to tell us of life in the Age of Chivalry, where knights battled in tournaments and women prayed for their safety. Besides telling stories of great battles or depicting scenes of life at the royal court, the tapestries had a practical purpose. When hung on the stone walls of castles, they helped keep out the cold drafts and dampness.

Later these tapestries were produced by weavers who belonged to guilds (formal organizations of skilled workers during the Middle Ages).

In the mid-1800s, American designer Candace Wheeler began the Society of Decorative Arts, which supported artists working in spinning, embroidery, and other fabric arts. In 1878, the success of the society led to the founding of the Women's Exchange, a store that sold these fabric works. The next year, Wheel-

Faith Ringgold creates beautiful pieces of fabric art.

designs in mosaics, lacquer (glossy) boxes, and fabrics.

In 1948, the Indian artist Kamaldevi Chattopadhyay founded the Indian Co-operative Union to help refugees struggling for India's independence from Britain. This group of weavers soon was well organized and selling Indian handicrafts around the world.

Lenore Tawney was born in Ohio in 1925. She has devoted her life to raising the status of weaving from a craft to an art form. Her huge weavings resemble paintings because she purposely exposes the warp (threads) of the cloth, which look like the strokes of a paintbrush. She has staged one-woman art exhibitions, and continues to create works that she names for the various spiritual and psychological themes they portray. Some of her works include *Dove, Bride,* and *Queen.*

American fabric artist Sheila Hicks was born in Nebraska in 1934. Her career has included rug-making in Germany and Morocco, weaving in India and Chile, and opening her own studio in the United States. She is one of the best known of the modern weavers, and her works have brought many major commissions (orders of art for a specific purpose).

African American fabric artist Faith Ringgold has become famous for developing narrative paintings and weavings, some of which also incorporate text to tell a story. One of her first such works is called *Church Picnic.* It tells the story of the love between a young woman and a minister during the 1900s. Ringgold's

er cofounded an interior design firm, and later a firm that employed only female weavers. Wheeler supervised the Women's Applied Arts Exhibition and helped decorate the Women's Building at the Columbia Exposition in 1893, a national fair celebrating one hundred years of American nationhood.

Margarethe von Brauchitsch, a German artist who worked in the early 1900s, created embroidered cushions that used stylized (restricted to a particular style) versions of elements that appeared in nature (leaves, ripples, and the like). Vanessa Bell, an Englishwoman born in 1879, experimented with geometrical

1986 work *Harlem Renaissance Party* portrays a dinner table surrounded by famous writers of the Harlem Renaissance era and celebrates the works these people left behind.

Although both Ringgold and artist Joyce Kozloff were influenced by the fabric work of folk artists, they both moved from folk art into the realm of fine art. For instance, Kozloff's fabric work *Hidden Chambers* was influenced by Islamic (Middle Eastern) and Celtic (Irish folk) decorative patterns. Kozloff is also famous for her hand-painted tiles, some of which have been done through public commissions for train stations and other city buildings.

Another artist influenced by Celtic design is Valerie Jaudon, who prints patterns of fabric based on these images. Her works appear in some contemporary museum collections. Canadian artist Dorthea Rockburne, working in Quebec, is known for folding and coloring canvas into geometric shapes such as triangles and parallelograms. Her work is also represented in museum collections.

Another fabric artist working in the mid-1990s is Miriam Shapiro, who was born in Toronto, Canada, in 1923. Now an American, in 1971 Shapiro worked with sculptor Judy Chicago to found and direct the Feminist Art Program at the California Institute of Art in Valencia. Shapiro's works are part of the collections of the Whitney Museum and the Museum of Modern Art, both in New York City, and the Hirshhorn Museum of Art in Washington, D.C. She is associated with the pattern and decoration movement and with feminism. Her best-known works are shaped patterns that resemble Japanese fans and pinwheel-like fabric collages.

National Museum of Women in the Arts

The National Museum of Women in the Arts opened in 1987 in Washington, D.C. It was then, and still is, the only major museum in the world that is dedicated to celebrating the work of women artists of the past and present. The museum's holdings include more than two thousand works by more than five hundred women artists from the 1500s to the present.

The museum has sponsored several special exhibits, which have included historical collections, New Deal (1930s) works, and American impressionists. It also sponsors a State Chapter/State Exhibit program to encourage women artists at the state level and a library and research center with more than eight thousand resources. The museum operates a store and publishes a magazine called *Women in the Arts*.

Fine Arts

Painting

Portraits first gained popularity in the late Middle Ages (500–1500), when rich patrons and noble families could afford to have their pictures painted. They would adorn themselves in their finest clothing and jewelry, strike a heroic pose, and maintain a serious expression. Many of the finest existing portraits of this time were painted in Italy, where many wealthy families lived and were able to support artists. Miniatures, however, became a popular art form in the 1700s, when people would commission an artist to create a work small enough to fit inside a small ornamental box or a locket (necklace).

Drawings, of course, form the basis for many other art forms. For instance, painters, architects, and sculptors all make drawings of their ideas before beginning work in their own medium. Some drawings, however, are created for their own sake and are themselves considered works of art.

Landscapes have been popular since the Middle Ages. They are paintings or drawing showing an area of wide open land. Some patrons wanted mementos of their trips and so they purchased paintings of travel spots to remind them of where they had been. Others wanted a visual record of their estate or belongings. In the United States, landscape painting had a special patriotic meaning, since the vast and beautiful stretches of nature beckoned to those who wanted to settle the untamed West.

Painting and calligraphy on rice paper and fabric are traditional art forms in the countries of Asia. Chinese artist Fu-Jen Kuan caught the attention of the Chinese emperor during the 1200s. He commissioned Kuan to produce many works, the majority of which depict traditional subjects such as bamboo and flower blossoms.

During the Renaissance (a period in which classical art, literature, architecture, and learning were revived) in Europe (c. 1300–1600), many famous artists were at work producing hundreds of paintings, sculptures, and public structures such as cathedrals and plazas. Because art was considered a male occupation, most of these artists were men. During this time, wealthy patrons supported artists so they could concentrate on their art works. The artists usually belonged to schools or studios, which also received money from a patron or a city government.

Women were almost entirely excluded from both the schools and studios, and few women could find patrons to finance their work. Nonetheless, even without support or encouragement, some of the finest paintings of the time were produced by women. The works include portraits, landscapes, tapestries, and illuminated manuscripts. In fact, before the 1500s, most of the artists illuminating religious manuscripts were women working in convents and schools. Although some worked as sculptors, calligraphers, and miniaturists, illumination was by far the chief occupation of women working in the fine arts.

Italian painter Artemisia Gentileschi is regarded as the most accomplished

Women Who Supported the Arts

- Giovanna Dandolo, the wife of a nobleman of Venice, supported the early printers, writers, and lace-making artists in her city.
- Isabella Stewart Gardner opened a museum in Boston, Massachusetts, in 1903 to house her collection of Oriental, Old Masters, and Impressionist art.
- Cornelia B. Sage Quinton was named director of the Albright Art Museum/Gallery in Buffalo, New York, in 1910. She was the first woman to head a museum.
- Concha Ortiz y Pino de Kleven, who was born in 1912, opened craft schools during the Great Depression (1929–40), providing employment for hundreds of people in New Mexico.
- Abby Aldrich Rockefeller cofounded the Museum of Modern Art in New York in 1929. She also recognized the value of primitive art and opened the art center named for her at Williamsburg, Virginia. The center is one of the world's largest museums devoted entirely to folk art.
- Gertrude Vanderbilt Whitney, a sculptor and heiress, founded the Whitney Museum in New York in 1931.
- Peggy Guggenheim opened the first of three galleries in 1934 and began a career of encouraging modern artists, many of whom became world famous.
- Marta Vega managed the El Museo del Barrio, a museum devoted to Hispanic art, in New York City.
- Wilhelmina Cole Holladay founded and became president of the National Muscum of Womcn in thc Arts in 1981. The museum actually opened its doors in 1987.

woman artist of the Renaissance. She used vibrant colors and huge canvases to depict Biblical scenes such as Judith slaying the Assyrian general Holofernes. Most of her paintings have female heroes, and she is considered a major influence on later generations of Italian painters. Like Gentileschi, Italian painter Sofonisba Anguissola also gained international fame. Dutch painter Rachel Ruysch, who also worked in the 1600s, is known for creating more than eight hundred works dealing with flowers and animals.

Other European artists of note during the Renaissance are Judith Leyster of Holland, known for her paintings of domestic life; Italian artist Lavinia Fontanta, known for her altarpieces; Clara Peters of Belgium, who created realistic paintings of food and flowers; and English portrait painter Joan Carlisle. Despite these few women, the fame enjoyed by female artists during the Renaissance remained small. According to *A History of Their Own:*

> Rarely given commissions for the large canvases and monumental works favored by Europe's patrons, they [women] painted subjects considered decorative but not significant. . . . The majority of female still-life painters gained little recognition. Their works became illustrations for botanical [plant] books with limited circulation, or textile and porcelain designs. Few gained access to guilds [trade unions], few were lucky enough to find their way to the attention of wealthy urban or royal patrons. Unable to make a living at their craft, they passed into the history of art as gifted amateurs.

The art world continued to operate in much the same way until the 1900s. Artists still needed patrons or some other type of sponsorship in order to have time to produce their artwork. Although they were not encouraged or supported by their societies, European women artists continued to paint.

Swiss portrait painter Angelica Kauffman was born in 1741. Subjects of her works included the famous figures of the day, as well as stories with historical and religious themes. Her use of color and the composition (arrangement) of the figures in her pictures influenced later generations of painters. French portrait painter Elisabeth Vigee-Lebrun was born in France in 1755 and was court painter to Queen Marie Antoinette. Vigee-Lebrun completed more than nine hundred works before her death in 1842.

British painter Catherine Read was the first unmarried female art student to study abroad in Paris and in Rome. By the 1770s she had become the most popular portrait painter of her time. She restricted herself to portraits because being a woman made it "inappropriate" and even impossible for her to attend public academies or even design or draw from nature.

French painter Marie Rosalie (Rosa) Bonheur was born in 1822 and sometimes dressed as a man in order to go places where she could observe animal life. She became known for her realistic animal paintings and was awarded one of France's highest awards, the Legion of Honor, by the French empress.

American painter Mary Cassatt was the first American woman to gain an international audience for her pictures. Cassatt was born in Pennsylvania in 1845, but spent most of her creative life in Paris, where she studied and worked with the Impressionists. (Impressionists were painters who watched how light illuminated forms and then used color to create that image.) Cassatt is famous for her moving portraits of mothers and children, such as *Mother and Infant* and *Sarah in a Green Bonnet.* Another American Impressionist was Lilla Cabot Perry, who studied with famous French painter Claude Monet in Paris.

Several women of note painting among the French-born Impressionists in Paris during the late 1800s include Berthe Morisot, who depicted women in domestic scenes, and Eva Gonzales, whose works were life-like portraits.

The Boating Party, *one of Mary Cassatt's paintings.*

American painter, teacher, and publisher Emily Sartain used painting and engraving as her medium. Around 1870, she became the art editor of the magazine *Our Continent,* and later taught at the Philadelphia School of Design for Women. She was instrumental in encouraging women to pursue careers in industrial (clothing, furniture, and building) design.

One of the most famous American miniaturists was Lucia Fuller, who cofounded the American Society of Miniature Painters in 1899. Fuller, who was born in Massachusetts, used watercolor on ivory to capture her subject's likeness. She also painted on a larger scale and exhibited a mural at the 1893 Columbian Exposition in Chicago, Illinois.

After the turn of the century (1900), many artists embraced a more modern style of painting. One such artist was Gwen John, an Englishwoman born in 1876. Like the Impressionists, she experimented with reproducing light on canvas, but her work had more definite lines. Vanessa Bell, another Englishwoman, was born in 1879. She developed an abstract style of painting that used geometric figures, spaces, and lines to show ideas rather than trying to represent actual images. Bell later ventured into interior design, textile design, book illustration, and pottery.

Also born in 1876, German artist Paula Modersohn-Becker produced portraits with dark colors and undefined facial features. Russian painter Zinaida Serebriakova was born in 1884 and came from a family of artists. She eventually developed her own style of realistic portraiture (making portraits). Sonia Delaunay, also Russian, was born in 1885 and is known for her abstract; boldly colored paintings, textile designs, book bindings, and costume designs. Mexican painter Frida Kahlo worked in the 1930s using a surrealistic style that creates a fantastic image by placing two unrelated objects together. Many of Kahlo's works are self-portraits such as *The Little Deer, What Water Gave Me,* and *Diego and I.*

Canadian artist Emily Carr was born in 1871. She spent much time in the forests of British Columbia, which may have been the inspiration for her vivid paintings of nature. French painter Marie Laurencin, born in 1886, worked with oil paints, water colors, and lithography (printing). She also designed wallpaper and dresses,and was known for her stage costumes.

One of America's most prominent female artists, Georgia O'Keeffe was born in Wisconsin in 1887 and began exhibiting her canvases in 1916. She is best known for her huge paintings of flowers and the desert plant and animal life of New Mexico. Some of O'Keeffe's works include *Yellow Calla, Cow's Skull: Red, White, and Blue,* and *Blue River.*

In the 1970s African American artist Alma Thomas became the first black woman to have a solo exhibition at the Whitney Museum of American Art in New York. She was also one of the first black women to receive a degree in fine arts in the United States.

Like the African American artists, Native American women such as Tonita Vigil Pena and Pablita Velarde were also making strides in the art world. Pena taught at the Sante Fe Pueblo Indian School in New Mexico and was known for her realistic portraits of people in motion. Velarde, the most famous Native American woman painter, also worked in New Mexico. She portrayed Indian life and myths in murals and paintings.

American abstract artist Helen Frankenthaler was born in 1928 in New York, and like Georgia O'Keeffe and Louise Nevelson (discussed under "Sculpture"), Frankenthaler is noted for creating new forms in her artwork. Her paintings, such as *Flood, Fireworks,* and *Scarlatti,* have large spaces and strong splashes of color.

Other contemporary painters include American Lee Krasner (born 1908), who

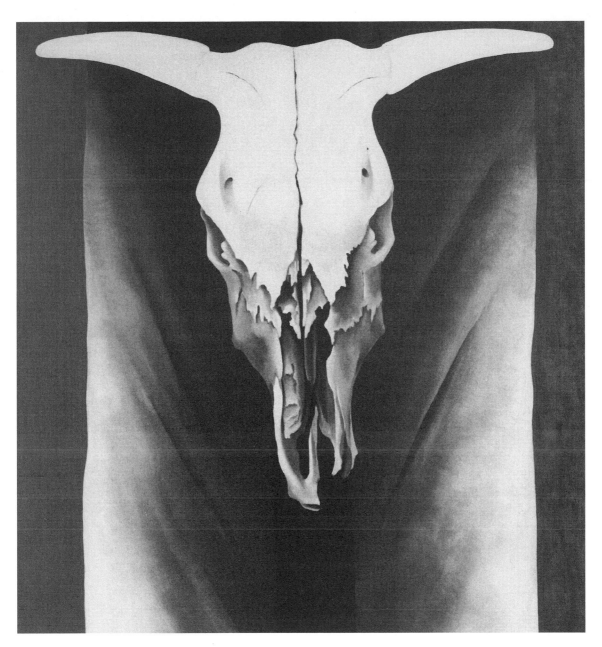

Georgia O'Keeffe's painting Cow's Skull.

worked in the middle of the twentieth century. She painted and crafted collages of paper and canvas. Krasner made a point of cutting the canvas and rearranging each work once it was done. Her reason for doing this stemmed from the idea that the act of creating the work was the art. Krasner's works appear in museum collections throughout the world.

American artist Joan Mitchell was an influential twentieth century painter who favored the abstract expressionism style. (Abstract expressionism allows the artist's unconscious to dictate the work and is considered by many to be the first uniquely American style.) Mitchell's work is part of museum collections worldwide.

Sculpture

Patience Lovell Wright was born in New Jersey in 1725 and is considered America's first professional sculptor. Her works were in wax or clay, and she was known for her ability to capture the personality of the person she was sculpting.

In Europe, Madame Marie Tussaud became famous in the late 1700s for her lifelike wax sculptures. In 1834, she established a permanent collection in London, England. Her works include death masks (casts of faces) made of Marie Antoinette and Louis XVI of France after they were guillotined. She also captured the likenesses of many of the French revolutionaries and emperor Napoleon Bonaparte. Tussaud continued to add to her collection until her death in 1850.

Sculptor Vinnie Ream, who was born in Wisconsin in 1847, was the first American woman to win a sculpting contract from the federal government. Her subjects include President Abraham Lincoln, whose full-sized marble statue stands in the U.S. Capitol Building; Admiral David Farragut, who served during the War of 1812 and the U.S. Civil War; and General George Custer, who died at the Battle of the Little Bighorn.

French sculptor Camille Claudel was the creator of several pieces that were originally attributed to the more famous male sculptor Auguste Rodin. Claudel, who was born in 1856, was the model and inspiration for Rodin. Unfortunately, much of her creative life has been overshadowed by or merged with Rodin's.

German sculptor and graphic artist Käthe Schmidt Kollwitz was born in 1867. She was a pacifist (a person who believes that disputes between nations should be settled peacefully) who opposed World War I (1914–18) and did a series of woodcuts that reflected on war, death, and poverty. Some of these works included *Bread* and *Death Seizing a Woman*. A sculpture done in honor of her son, who died in the war, was dedicated as a memorial.

Louise Berliawsky Nevelson was born in Russia in 1899 but emigrated to Maine in 1905. Nevelson is best known for her use of "found objects"—discarded bits of furniture, pieces of architectural ornamentation, old wheels, driftwood. This type of art is known as environmental

Artist Louise Nevelson poses in front of her sculpture Sky-Gate, New York.

art and is a concept Nevelson helped pioneer. She first gained recognition in 1959 for her sculpture series *Dawn's Wedding Feast*. In 1978, the World Trade Center in New York City commissioned one of her sculptures, *Sky-Gate, New York*.

Barbara Hepworth was born in England in 1903. Her early sculptures were traditional human forms crafted in stone. She later fell under the influence of the abstract style popular in the 1930s. One of her sculptures stands at the United

Artist Judy Chicago

her free-standing abstract sculptures. One such work, *Seven Poles,* is a grouping of L-shaped 7-foot aluminum wires coated with fiberglass and polyethylene (a plastic). Hesse died in 1970.

Feminist sculptor Judy Chicago was born in Chicago, Illinois, in 1939. One of her most famous sculptures is a triangular shaped table called *The Dinner Party,* which was mounted at a much-publicized exhibition at the San Francisco Museum of Modern Art in 1979. Chicago's table is set for 39 female diners whom she selected as major figures in Western history. Each of the 39 hand-painted place settings was different because Chicago designed it specifically for that "guest." The floor of the sculpture is inscribed with the names of an additional 999 women of achievement. Chicago's works have often outraged the public because of their themes of female sexuality and protest. Together with fabric artist Miriam Shapiro, Chicago cofounded the Feminist Art Program at the California Institute of Modern Art in Valencia in 1971.

Another important twentieth-century sculptor was Nancy Graves. Born in 1940 in Massachusetts, she was famous for her wall reliefs (sculptures that are carved out of a wall). Her work often contains archaeological references, such as layers with fossils and other ancient life forms. Graves's pieces are exhibited in museums throughout the world. She died in 1996.

American artist Judy Pfaff was born in 1946 in London, England, and is noted

Nations headquarters in New York City. Hepworth, who was the mother of triplets, once wrote, "My studio was a jumble of children, rocks, sculptures, trees, . . . flowers and washing."

French artist Louise Bourgeois is an important twentieth-century sculptor whose works appear in museums throughout the world. She was born in 1911 and is noted for her abstract, often human-like shapes. She also draws, and her sketches were the subject of an exhibition in Paris in 1995, and a second exhibition throughout the United States in 1996.

American Eva Hesse was born in 1936 in Germany. She was known for

for her room-scale installations. (She paints the walls, fills the room with painted wire, wood, found and fabricated objects, and incorporates the floor into the work of art.) She has room installations in museums in Tokyo, New York, and Washington, D.C.

Deborah Butterfield, who was born about 1949, is known primarily for her full-scale horses made of twigs of wood or cast in bronze. Her works are part of international museum collections. In 1996, her work was exhibited at the park alongside the river outside the Chicago Art Institute.

Jenny Holzer uses LCD display boards as her medium. These are the electronic message boards that use lighted letters to repeat the same text over and over. She uses found or created text. Her work is included in the Guggenheim Museum in New York. One of her installations was also at the Frank Lloyd Wright House, where she wrapped the spiraling interior with LCD display boards.

Book Illustration

Picture books became popular almost as soon as the printing press was invented (about 1450). The pictures were an important way in which a story was conveyed, since few people could read at that time. Illustrations also became necessary during the period of Enlightenment (1700s), when much scientific inquiry was underway. Scientists studying plants, animals, birds, and fish needed artists who could produce drawings of theses living things.

One of the earliest female illustrators on record is Herrade of Landsburg, who was a German abbess (head of a group of religious women) in the 1100s. Although her original art was destroyed by fire, it had already been traced to her. Her work includes miniature designs that illustrate the readings she set out for the nuns under her care.

American illustrator May Massee from Illinois, was known for the high standards she set while she was the editor of children's books at Doubleday, a large publishing company. She demanded high quality storytelling and illustrations from her authors and artists. In 1922 she founded the children's book department at Viking Press. Ten of the books that Massee edited won Newbury Medals and four books won the Caldecott Medal for "most distinguished American picture book for children."

One of the most beloved of children's author-illustrators is Tasha Tudor, who lives on a farm in Vermont. She published her first book, *Pumpkin Moonshine,* in 1938 and has been writing steadily ever since. In addition to creating more than eighty children's books, Tudor has also produced calendars, prints, and Christmas cards.

Photography

One of the pioneers of the artistic use of photography was English portrait photographer Julia Margaret Cameron, who was born in 1815. She received her first camera in 1863 and before her death in

1879 had photographed many of the famous people of her time. Some of her subjects included poet Alfred Tennyson, writer Anthony Trollope, and scientist Charles Darwin. She received many awards for her work.

American photographer Imogen Cunningham was born in 1883 in Oregon. She began her career as a printmaker and later applied this technical knowledge to taking and developing her photographs. Her most frequent subjects were plants and portraits of the famous people of her time, including choreographer (dance designer) Martha Graham and writer Gertrude Stein.

American documentary (true life) photographer Dorothea Lange was born in 1895 in New Jersey. She began her career as a society photographer but became famous for her moving portraits of poor people suffering during the Great Depression (1929–40). Some of her photographs of the small, hungry children were used during fund-raising appeals to earn money for relief. Lange also photographed the Japanese Americans who were imprisoned by the U.S. government in internment camps in the American Southwest during World War II (1939–45).

American photographer Berenice Abbott was born in Ohio in 1898. She used her camera to capture the spirit of New York City in such works as *Nightview, New York* and in the process created a public outcry against the destruction of many old buildings. Abbott also

photographed subjects that demonstrated the laws of physics such as a bouncing ball and the formation of soap bubbles.

Margaret Bourke-White is one of the most famous of the American women photographers. She was born in New York City in 1904 and gained international fame for her photojournalist approach to photography. She worked for *Fortune* magazine, which sent her to Russia in 1930. As a staff photographer for *Life* magazine, she covered the migration (mass movement) of the American farm workers during the drought of 1936. She also covered World War II (1939–45), including battles in Africa, Italy, and Russia. Towards the end of the war, Bourke-White was one of the first photographers to enter Buchenwald concentration camp where the Nazis imprisoned Jews before executing them. Her pictures of starved, nearly naked prisoners shocked the world. She later photographed Mahatma Ghandi in India. (Ghandi was a lawyer who led the independence movement that freed India from British rule.)

In 1954, American photographer Virginia M. Schau became the first woman to win a Pulitzer Prize for spot news photography. She won for her dramatic, real-life photos of a rescue from a truck crash in California.

German photographer Hilla Becher was born in Berlin in 1934. She has had a life long collaboration with her husband, photographer Bernd Becher. They specialize in repetitive images of architecture. Their work is seen in museums

Margaret Bourke-White prepares to leave for an assignment in 1943.

around the world and has influenced a whole generation of photographers, both in Germany and elsewhere.

Other photographers working today include Joan Meyers and Marji Silk. Meyers has published a photojournalistic book of photographs she took of the famous route of St. James (Santiago) in Spain. The route has been used by pilgrims since the Middle Ages (500–1500). St. James, the Roman Catholic apostle, is said to have returned from the grave to help the Spanish drive the Moors (Arabs) out of Spain and back to the Middle East. Silk is an internationally known fine arts photographer and instructor. She has received two International Gold Medals, a prestigious photography award. She specializes in photographs of scenes, both indoors and out.

Tina Barney, who was born in New York in 1945, is a documentary photographer who captures the images and feelings of families at home. Her work is in the collection of the Smithsonian Museum in Washington, D.C. Jan Groover, born in New Jersey in 1943, is a surrealistic photographer whose works are in the collection of the Museum of Modern Art in New York City. Barbara Kruger, born in 1945 in New Jersey, has works in museum collections around the world. Her medium is text and photography based on advertising. Cindy Sherman, born in 1954 in New Jersey, disguises and costumes herself, and then takes self-portraits. Her works also appear in museums throughout the world.

Architecture

Architecture is the design of buildings. Louise Blanchard Bethune was the first American woman to gain fame as an architect. She was born in New York in 1856 and designed a variety of buildings that included schools, hotels, factories, and homes. Bethune was one of the first architects to design structures with steel beams and poured concrete slabs. Between 1892 and 1893, she was one of several women architects to exhibit at the Columbian Exposition in Chicago. The exposition celebrated the four-hundredth anniversary of Columbus's landing and drew thousands of visitors. Bethune was also elected a member of the American Institute of Architects.

Born in 1900, Polish architect Helena Niemirowska Syrkius and her husband led the movement toward a more modern, functional style of architecture. They helped rebuild Warsaw, Poland, after World War II (1939–45) and created housing developments that blended the social needs of the residents with the environmental needs of the community.

Italian architect Gae(tana) Aulenti was born in 1927 and is known for her comprehensive approach to architecture. Rather than design just single homes or schools, she considered how entire neighborhoods and cities should be constructed.

Canadian architect Eva Hollo Vecsei was born in 1930 in Vienna, Austria. She lived in Budapest, Hungary, before emigrating to Canada. She is famous for designing large sites used for commercial and business purposes.

Greek architect Suzana Antonakakis was born in 1935. She is best known for her modern tourist buildings and for her interest in ancient buildings. Antonakakis and her husband excavated and documented many structures from the time of ancient Greece.

British landscape artist Brenda Colvin was born in 1897. She helped found the profession of landscape art, which included working with natural elements such as hills and trees and carefully adding man-made structures. Sylvia Crewe was working in England at the same time. Her works included gardens and public grounds.

Public Art

Public art includes landscape design, monumental sculpture, mobiles, murals, and bas relief (a slightly raise engraving). Harriet Goodhue Hosmer is considered the finest American woman sculptor of monumental art. She was born in Massachusetts in 1820 and learned about human anatomy by working with a local doctor. Her first works were of gods and other figures from classical mythology (ancient Greek and Roman legends). She went on to sculpt a larger-than-life bronze statue of Senator Thomas Hart Benton from Missouri, who served in the U.S Senate from 1821 to 1851 and opposed the use of paper money. Her other subjects included a marble statue of Queen Isabella of Spain for the 1893 World's Columbian Exposition in Chicago, Illinois.

Edmonia Lewis was born in New York State in about 1843. The daughter of a Chippewa Indian mother and an African American father, Lewis is generally considered the first major black sculptor in America. Her early subjects were the heroes of the antislavery movement. Later statues by Lewis depict heroines of color such as Hagar, the maidservant of the Biblical figure Abraham, and Cleopatra, queen of ancient Egypt.

Elisabet Ney was born in Prussia (now Germany) in 1833 and studied at art academies in Berlin and Munich. She went on to sculpt the famous leaders of her time, including kings, generals, and revolutionaries. Ney eventually settled in Texas, where there is a museum named for her in Austin.

In 1937 American artist Jean Goodwin Ames began an ambitious wall mural whose subject was the girls who made a living by fishing off the coast of Southern California. She later created public art for churches, department stores, and government buildings.

Beverly Stoll Pepper, born in Brooklyn, New York, in 1924, was a famous sculptor of outdoor art. Her media included trees and painted steel triangles. A later phase took her into environmental art, which creates a piece of art out of landscape. Her *Amphisculpture* uses concrete and other material to cover a large area of ground in a series of huge circles. It was completed in 1977 in New Jersey.

American sculptor Nancy Holt was born in Massachusetts in 1938. She creates environmental sculptures of stone, water, and earth. The land upon which she sculpts becomes an important part of her work. Her *Architectural Tower Structure* became a permanent installation at the site of the 1980 Winter Olympics in Lake Placid, New York.

Alice Aycock, born in Pennsylvania in 1946, creates large-scale, machine-like structures of wood and metal. Her works often incorporate wheels, ladders, and towers. Aycock had a solo exhibition at the Museum of Modern Art in New York in 1977, and had an installation at Battery Park in New York City in 1980.

Asian American Maya Lin is known worldwide as the sculptor of the Vietnam Veterans Memorial in Washington, D.C. Lin designed the memorial in 1981, when she was a twenty-year-old architecture student at Yale University in New Haven, Connecticut. Lin's idea was very different from typical war memorials. She created a long, black, V-shaped wall that hugged the rolling hill of a meadow near the Washington Monument. The names of the fifty-six thousand Americans who died in the Vietnam War (1954–75) are carved into the wall. At first, the public and veterans' groups hated the design because it was so different. Today, however, "The Wall," as it has become known, draws tens of thousands of visitors. Lin's other famous sculpture is the Civil Rights Memorial in Montgomery, Alabama, which she completed in 1989. She used the words of civil rights leader Martin Luther King Jr. as her inspiration. King's

statement that seekers of equality would not be satisfied until "justice rolls down like waters and righteousness like a mighty stream" moved Lin to create a circle of granite designed to allow a continuous stream of water to wash over it.

Mexican American artist Judith Baca's works include the *Great Wall of Los Angeles,* which is one-half mile long. This mural tells the story of California from the Ice Age to modern times. Baca is famous for involving teenagers in her work. The *Great Wall* took five summers to complete and used the help of hundreds of teens from different races and ethnic backgrounds. Her *World Wall: A Vision of the Future Without Fear* mural contains the artwork of many international artists and can be disassembled and shipped to other countries for showing.

Fashion Arts

Clothing Design

The fashion arts include clothing design, fashion illustration, and jewelry (a category which usually includes decorative pieces made from metal). According to Doretta Davanzo Poli, the history of fashion is a fairly short one. Poli is the curator (director) of an exhibit called "Serenissima," which shows the fashions of Venice from the 1200s to the 1700s. Poli says that prior to the 1700s, fashions did not change much because clothing had to last a long time. Then, in the late 1700s, artists in Paris and Venice began to design shoes and ornaments that were meant to go out of style in a short time.

One of the most famous fashion designers in history was not an artist at all. Her name was Amelia Bloomer, and she was a suffragette (a person who worked to win the right to vote for women). Bloomer gave her name to a pair of loose trousers she admired that combined comfort and freedom of movement with modesty. Unfortunately, Bloomer was ahead of her time; trousers for women never became popular during her life. Bloomers did make a comeback, however, around the turn of the century (1900) when they became part of a movement toward "rational dress" for women. The attire included a pair of knickers (long bloomers) that made it possible for women to ride a bicycle.

Women's dress fashions have always caused some amusement among the public. In 1913, a London brain specialist sought to explain "why women love clothes." Their motives are self-display and/or a love of the beautiful and delicate, he theorized.

In the 1920s, women's dress underwent a drastic change. For the first time in history, women cut their hair and wore it in a short curled style called a "bob." Women openly wore makeup. Hemlines rose to mid-calf and then to the knees. The constricting undergarments of the 1890s (corsets and petticoats) gave way to skimpy, sheer items called "teddies." Material clung to the female form instead of disguising it. Among the dress design-

Amelia Bloomer

ers creating these styles was Coco Chanel, who first became famous for making sportswear a staple in the female wardrobe. Later Chanel became famous for her perfume, Chanel No. 5.

Edith Head was born in 1913 in Los Angeles. She was the chief costume designer at the Paramount movie studios during the 1930s. Head won several Academy Awards for costume design, the last in 1973 for the film *The Sting*.

Englisher designer Mary Quant was born in 1934 and revolutionized women's fashion when she introduced the miniskirt in the mid-1960s. Her designs were casual and colorful, and she has won

Folk Costumes: Everyday Art

For centuries, women have been involved in making the beautiful clothing worn on special holidays. For instance, in Hungary, many women use embroidery (needlework) to enhance the vests of both men and women. They also embroider jackets, scarves, and table linens. The color and detail of their designs have made Hungarian folk costumes famous throughout the world.

In the Middle East, women also use embroidery to lend color, beauty, and value to their clothing. The embroidery is done in the geometric patterns common to Arabic cultures. Women also weave in coins, beads, sequins, and other objects.

In ancient Japan, a woman's kimono was a work of art. It combined many panels of different colored fabric and was crafted to hang properly at the shoulders and arms. Many fabrics were enhanced by intricate embroidery.

In Africa and South America, folk costumes are crafted of native grasses, animal hides, bone fragments, beads, and metal disks. The costumes are meant to be enhanced by the face- and body-painting of the wearer. They are worn on ceremonial occasions, such as preparation for a hunt, victory over an enemy, or a wedding.

---

many fashion awards. Another designer, Diane Von Furstenberg, became famous in the 1970s for her simple dress design. The best known was a simple wrap-style that fell to the knee. These dresses were made of the new synthetic materials such as polyester, which clung to the person's figure.

Some fashion designers create costumes for theaters and movies. Barbara Karinska, who was born in the Ukraine (Russia) in 1886, was both an engineer and an artist. She designed ballet costumes that would allow the dancers to move but that would also create a beautiful scene when viewed from the audience. Karinska created costumes for productions of *The Nutcracker, Joan of Arc,* and the *Ice Capades.*

American fashion designer Anna Sui is famous for her clothing styles and for repopularizing the "Hush Puppies" brand of shoe. Hush Puppies are known for their comfortable, low-key styling. Sui revitalized the shoes by ordering them in a variety of fashion colors. She is also one of several high-powered fashion artists who have been sought out by the automotive manufacturers to produce fabrics and designs for use in automobiles.

Aline Bernstein: Scenic Artist

One of the areas reluctantly opened to women artists was the design and creation of scenery for stage productions. The first woman admitted to the Brotherhood of Painters, Decorators, and Paperhangers was Aline Bernstein, who gained her membership card in 1926 after repeated applications. The set designers in this union eventually left and formed their own union called The United Scenic Art Union of the AFL (American Federation of Labor). This union now admits women members without discrimination.

Bernstein had the credentials when she first applied for membership. She had designed scenery and costumes for the Neighborhood Playhouse in New York City and had created sets for other plays. She went on to become a respected costume and scenery designer whose work supported Hollywood films and playwrights such as Lillian Hellman. In 1949 she won a Tony Award for her work in the theater. Bernstein is also known as one of the founders of the Museum of Costume Design in New York City and as an instructor of costume design.

Jewelry

In the 1700s, wives often helped their husbands pursue their craft by doing the book work and, in some cases, by learning the craft themselves. This was true of metalworker Hester Bateman, one of the greatest eighteenth-century silversmiths (a person who makes or repairs items made of silver). Her work included teapots, spoons, and tableware such as platters.

Jennifer Swartz is a metal artist working today to create jewelry, small decorative objects, and home decor. Her Detroit MetalWorks imprint can be found on objects sold at more than five hundred art galleries and boutiques throughout the United States. Her metalsmithing background helps her create five thousand pieces each year, ranging from the jewelry line she began in 1992 to one-of-a-kind masks and objects produced in a variety of media.

Art Exhibits: Where Are the Women?

Exhibits are public shows of an artist's work. The shows are held at art galleries or in libraries or universities. The exhibits are reviewed by art critics who write for the media and are a major way in which an artist gains a reputation and a following. They also serve as a way for an artist to sell her or his work. However, according to the National Museum of Women in the Arts: "Although nearly 50% of all practicing artists in the United States today are women . . . 95% to 98% of the works in our nation's art museums are by men."

Eleanor Dickinson is a professor at the School of Fine Arts at the California College of Arts and Crafts in Oakland. In 1995 she published a study called *Statistics: Gender Discrimination in the Art Field* that looked at female art professionals working in the United States in the period from 1960 to 1995. From her data, Dickinson concludes that:

• more than 50 percent of the visual artists in this country are female

• at least one-half the trained artists and art historians are women

• women artists and art teachers tend to earn less than men

• before 1990, government and other major funding agencies gave more grants to men artists than to women artists; after 1990, the distribution became more even

• female artists are poorly represented in the art history books most widely used as references

• women artists are underrepresented in major art exhibits

• exhibits by women artists are reviewed less in the media

Dickinson concludes her report by saying that "change in exhibition policies can be brought about by pressure, public exposure, or protests." The same tactics may work to win women more representation in art gallery and museum management and in university professorships.

25

Religion

"What would have been the effect upon religion if it had come to us through the minds of women?"

—Economist and writer
Charlotte Perkins Gilman

Many of our customs, attitudes, and beliefs are influenced by two ancient traditions: the Greco-Roman and the Judeo-Christian. The term "Greco-Roman" refers to the great cultural influence that the ancient Greek and Roman empires have had on Western (European and American) civilization. Our notions of democracy, justice, social order (the systems by which we run society, including our legal, governmental, and educational systems), and art may all be traced back thousands of years to the Greeks and Romans. Our ideas about God, goodness, salvation, and our place in the universe can be traced back to the ancient Jewish and early Christian (Judeo-Christian) religions. These ideas are the foundation not only of many of our churches, but of our justice system and our ideas about individual and community responsibility and social morality.

One of the most influential stories of all time is the Biblical story of Eve, the first woman. She and her husband, Adam, the first man, lived in the Garden of Eden. God provided Adam and Eve with all they needed to live, but they chose to disobey his one rule: not to eat the fruit of the tree of knowledge. A snake tempted Eve to try the fruit, and she did. She then convinced Adam to try it. The rest is history. For Christians, this act of introducing sin (the violation of religious law) into the world meant that God, in his anger, drove Adam and Eve from Eden. They and their descendants spent the rest of their days asking for forgiveness and awaiting salvation, or the saving of their souls from punishment. Salvation came to Adam and Eve's descendants thousands of years later when Jesus Christ, the Son of God, came to earth in the form of a man. Through his death and resurrection, he made it possible for humans to enter heaven upon death.

The story of Eve and the Tree of Knowledge or Tree of Life had its beginnings in the ancient civilizations of Asia Minor (Turkey). Although many ancient religions have similar stories of a fall from grace, few laid the sole blame on the woman the way that Christian faiths tend to do. Ancient peoples blamed both Adam and Eve but worried less about the predicament of salvation. These ancient peoples tended to live in the present, looking for their gods' guidance in day-to-day activities. It was only during the relative ease of the Middle Ages (500–1500) that people had enough leisure time to become especially worried about the future state of their souls.

At any rate, this view of woman as temptress and as having a weaker character than men is present throughout both Jewish and Christian scripture since before Christ was born two thousand years ago. It was this view of women that helped create what has essentially been a male hierarchy (power structure) in Judeo-Christianity. This hierarchy had a major impact on American culture. Until very recently, the pope, bishops, and priests of the Christians, the rabbis of the Jews, the swamis of Hinduism, the imams of Islam, and the Dalai Lama of Buddhism have all been men. Few of these men addressed the special needs of women, whether they were nuns living a religious life or wives raising families and caring for their homes.

Other faiths that have persisted into modern times also tend to be male-centered. The founders of all the major religions were men and their chief deities (gods) have been formed in their own likenesses. While some faiths do have female goddesses or saints, they usually serve a secondary role.

In order to better understand what formal religions offer women of today, let us look at the five major religions in the order of their membership: Christianity has the most followers throughout the world, followed by Islam, Hinduism, Buddhism, and finally Judaism. This chapter also offers a look at the special role played by female saints, mystics, founders of religions, and missionaries. An excellent general source for religions is *The Encyclopedia of Religion,* edited by Mircea Eliade and published by Macmillan in 1987.

Timeline: Women in Religion

26000 B.C. Ancient people create statues as part of their worship of "The Goddess," a female deity celebrated for her fertility (ability to bear many children).

700 B.C. The ancient Greeks develop an elaborate religion where goddesses have major positions of power.

c. 6–5 B.C. Mary gives birth to the infant Jesus.

A.D. 858 A woman disguised as a man is elected pope of the Roman Catholic Church and takes the name Pope John VIII. When her identity is revealed, she is called Pope Joan, a French nun, and founds the Daughters of Charity, an order of nuns devoted to nursing.

1635 Anne Hutchinson defies the Puritan elders of Massachusetts Bay Colony and is exiled (sent away) with her followers.

1774 Mother Ann Lee leads the English Shakers to a new home in America.

1845 Ellen Gould Harmon White founds the Seventh-Day Adventists.

1853 Antoinette Brown Blackwell becomes the first female minister ordained in the United States. As a member of the Congregational Church, she works to abolish slavery and gain women's rights.

1866 Mary Baker Eddy founds the Church of Christ, Scientist.

1930 Sarah E. Dickson is named the first elder (a governing officer) in the Presbyterian Church.

1970 St. Catherine of Siena is named a Doctor (distinguished student of religion) of the Roman Catholic Church.

1985 Mother Theresa of Calcutta is called a "living saint" for her work among the poor of Calcutta, India.

1988 Reverend Barbara Harris becomes the first woman named a bishop in the Anglican Communion (the U.S. Episcopal Church).

Ancient Religions

Archaeologists (people who study ancient life and cities, usually by digging up and examining ruins) have unearthed figurines and other artifacts from an ancient Czechoslovakian civilization dating back to 26000 B.C. The figurines are of a woman, and scientists believe that the owners of the figurines used them as fertility symbols. That is, these ancient people believed that these figurines had power to help them conceive children. In a time when the death rate was extremely high for all age groups, the ability to bear numerous children was a real advantage.

These Stone Age figurines are not unique to the Czech Republic. (The Stone Age began about two million years ago and ended in various places between 40,000 and 10,000 years ago.) They have been found at archeological sites around the Black Sea in eastern Europe and as far west as Spain. Figurines of a later date are also believed to be fertility symbols used to increase crop yields. Some scholars called these figurines "Venuses." (In Roman mythology, Venus is the goddess of love and physical beauty.) Most of the statues are remarkably alike, even though they are found thousands of miles apart.

Greece and Rome

Many years later, from about 1000 B.C. to A.D. 100, Greece was in its Iron Age. That is, the tools and weapons used during this time were made of bronze. In the 800s B.C. ancient Greek culture began to evolve as the Greeks borrowed bits and pieces of stories and customs from other peoples they encountered. The pantheatic religion (worship of nature) we know today as Greek mythology was being formed during this time. The Greeks were also polytheistic; that is, they believed in more than one god. The Greeks combined their pantheism and polytheism by giving different parts of nature a name and a set of human qualities. Like many ancient peoples, they explained events and things in nature by attributing them to the actions and moods of their deities (gods). Thus the sun became Apollo driving his fiery chariot across the sky, and lightning bolts showed the displeasure of Zeus, the king of the gods.

The Greeks also had many powerful female deities called goddesses. For example, Earth was known as the goddess Gaea. She married the god of the heavens, whose name was Chaos. Their children were Rhea and Cronus. Since the Greek gods have no prohibitions against family members marrying one another, Rhea and Cronus gave birth to the generation of gods and goddesses whom we most commonly associate with Greek mythology. One of their daughters was Demeter, the goddess of the harvest, who had control over feast and famine. Their other daughters include Hera, who became the queen of heaven and the protector of marriage, and Hestia, who guarded the home and family life. Hestia's grandchildren include Artemis, the goddess of the moon, women in childbirth, and hunting. All woodland creatures are also under her protection. Another of Hestia's granddaughters was Persephone, who embodied springtime and the beginning of the planting season. Aphrodite, the goddess of beauty and love, was also a relative.

The Greeks celebrated their deities by building temples in which to worship them, by telling stories about them, and by depicting them in Greek art and music. Unlike more modern ideas of God, the Greek gods and goddesses had distinctly human failings such as jealousy, ambition, and greed. For example, although Hera was the queen of heaven, she is generally remembered for the retribution (punishment) she inflicted upon the unfortunate human females with whom her husband, Zeus, flirted.

Nevertheless, the Greeks loved their gods and goddesses. A favorite was Athena, who was said to have sprung full grown from the forehead of her father, Zeus, the king the gods. Athena was the goddess of wisdom, warfare, and artisans (skilled tradesmen). She was also the patron of the most famous of the Greek city-states, Athens, which was named for her. Athena is usually depicted as a tall woman dressed in armor and having a noble brow and a thoughtful expression.

In addition to their major gods and goddesses, the Greeks had a large number of lesser deities. Among these were the three Graces, sisters who embodied beauty and charm. There was also the nine Muses, who presided over the arts, literature, and history. The nymphs were nature goddesses. However, not all the minor deities were friendly to humans. The Gorgon sisters, for instance, were so frightful that their appearance could turn men to stone. The most famous of the Gorgons was Medusa, whose hair was a nest of snakes.

The Greeks also had their collection of witches and human women who used their power for evil ends. One of the more famous of the witches is Circe, who figures prominently in the legend of Odysseus. The tale of Odysseus's twenty-year journey home from the Tro-jan War is told in *The Iliad.* In this story Circe turns Odysseus's men into swine (pigs) but later gives them directions for returning home. Another woman with witchlike power was Medea, who helped Jason win the Golden Fleece (the wool stolen from a golden ram) but almost killed him during a later quarrel.

Under the leadership of Alexander the Great, the people called Macedonians conquered Greece in about 340 B.C. They adopted the Greek religion and spread it through their empire, which straddled the Mediterranean Sea. Eventually, many of the Greek gods and goddesses were adopted by the Romans and given Latin names. Thus Hera became Juno, Athena became Minerva and so on. It is interesting to note how much power these ancient peoples gave their female deities. Since much of Western civilization is based on the concepts and cultures of Greece and Rome, we still see the influence of these goddesses. Their names appear in literature and their faces on carvings and statues. One goddess's name, Gaea, was given to a scientific theory, which is discussed in Chapter 14: Science and Exploration.

Many Native American religious beliefs also center on female deities. Among these deities are Sedna of the Inuit (Eskimos). Sedna, originally a human woman, became the goddess of the sea and sea creatures. The Cheyenne people tell of Quillworker, a maiden whose adventures led her to be transformed into one of the stars in the Big Dipper. The Cherokee pray to Selu, the corn mother.

Major Religions of Today

There are hundreds of religions practiced throughout the world today. For the purposes of this discussion, however, we will focus on the five religions with the most followers in the mid-1990s:

- Christianity, with 1.5 billion followers
- Islam, with 817 million followers
- Hinduism, with 647 million followers
- Buddhism, with 295 million followers
- Judaism, with 18 million followers.

Christianity

The cornerstone of Christian religions is the belief in one God, an idea called monotheism. Christians believe that Christ is the son of God. Christ came to earth in the form of a man (Jesus Christ) in order to redeem (save) humankind from Adam and Eve's original sin. Some Christian religions believe in a God that is actually three persons: God the Father, God the Son (Jesus Christ), and God the Holy Spirit. Most Christian religions also recognize the special role of Mary, the mother of Jesus, and of the apostles, the twelve men chosen by Jesus to be his students.

The majority of Christian faiths share a common belief in baptism, communion, and the forgiveness of sin (reconciliation). Most also regard marriage as holy and do not approve of premarital sex or divorce. The final resurrection (rising) from the dead and a belief in a joyful life in heaven for those who die in a state of grace are also fundamental beliefs among Christians. The basic text of Christian religions is the Holy Bible, which has two parts, the Old and the New Testaments.

Christianity began about 5–6 B.C., with the birth of Jesus Christ in Bethlehem, a city in the Holy Land (now the country of Israel), at that time a part of the Roman Empire. After the death of Christ in about A.D. 33, Christianity spread throughout the countries ruled by Rome. The Roman Empire eventually accepted Christianity as the official state religion in A.D. 381, and it soon became the major religion in Europe.

The Christian church, however, experienced several challenges from within that led to divisions and the formation of other major religions. The first challenge came in A.D. 1054, when Eastern European countries split from the Catholic Church to form the Eastern Orthodox Church. The remaining branch, which continues to be based in Western Europe, was then called the Roman Catholic Church. The second challenge came from Martin Luther in 1517. Luther, a German and a Roman Catholic ex-priest, founded the Lutheran church, the first of the major Protestant religions. The third challenge came from the English king, Henry VIII, who formed the Anglican religion in 1534. Henry's daughter, Queen Elizabeth I, made Anglicanism the official state religion when she ascended to the throne. However, some English people thought Anglicanism was still too fancy and formal, and as a result, became Puritans and eventually settled in the New World (America).

Women of Faith: Mary

Mary, the mother of Jesus Christ, was born in the first century B.C. somewhere in what is now called the state of Israel. As a young, unmarried Jewish girl, She received a vision in which an angel told her that she would conceive a child and become the mother of the Messiah. Jewish religion held that the Messiah would come to return the Jews to their rightful place as a separate, free nation. (The Jews have a history of being conquered by other nations.)

Mary believed her pregnancy was miraculous, since she had never before had sexual relations with a man. Joseph, the carpenter to whom she was engaged, had been advised in a dream to accept Mary even though she came to the marriage already pregnant. The virgin conception fulfilled one of the prophecies about the Messiah that had been made in the Old Testament.

Just before it was time for Mary to give birth, the ruler of the land called for a census to be taken. In order for the census count to be accurate, each man had to travel to the town of his birth. Since Joseph had been born in Bethlehem, Mary traveled there with him, and it was in the town of Bethlehem that her son was born. The birth in Bethlehem also fulfilled one of the prophecies made in the Old Testament.

Much has been written about Mary, and these works are assembled in a body of study called Mariology. Little about her is contained in the New Testament following the birth of Jesus. She is mentioned during his childhood, when he taught in the temple, and she plays a minor role in Jesus's first miracle, turning water to wine at the wedding in Canaan. Mary is again mentioned during Jesus' crucifixion (execution).

Catholics believe that Mary was born without original sin. She is the first and only human born without sin after Adam and Eve brought it into the world. Mary's body had to be holy in order to be a fit resting place for the Son of God. Catholics also believe that, because of the sanctity of her body, Mary was not buried when she died but was lifted bodily into Heaven.

Mary's state of grace has earned her a special place in the Roman Catholic Church. Many churches are named after her, most nuns have added her name to their own when they become sisters, and millions of Catholic women have followed her example of faith in the will of God.

Today, there are many different Christian religions. In the United States, the major ones are Roman Catholicism, Southern Baptist Convention, and Methodism.

Catholicism

Roman Catholics differ from other Christian sects in several ways. First, they concentrate their belief and worship much more on the New Testament, the latter half of the Bible which tells the story of Christ's life. They regard Jesus Christ as the savior of the world and the son of God. Catholics also believe that Christ meant what he said literally when he said that communion would consist of his sacred body and blood. Mary, the mother of Jesus, is also revered by Catholics. Unlike some other Christians, Catholics believe that Mary remained a virgin throughout the conception and birth of Jesus because the conception was through the Holy Spirit. Finally, Catholics celebrate seven sacraments (rituals believed to have a sacred meaning): baptism, penance (reconciliation), Eucharist (communion), confirmation, marriage, priesthood, and last rites. The pope is the spiritual head of the Roman Catholic Church. He lives in Rome and traces his authority back to St. Peter, the leader of the apostles (the original 12 followers) of Jesus Christ.

Attitude Toward Women

In its early days, before a formal theology (the study of God and religious writings) was developed, Christian women served as prophets, priests, and bishops. After the writings of St. Paul and St. Augustine appeared, however, the role of women became more narrowly defined. One famous remark attributed to St. Paul read: "[Women] must learn in silence and with all submissiveness. I permit no woman to teach or to have authority over men; she is to keep silent." Some later scholars even questioned whether women had souls. (Without a soul or spirit, women could not hope to enter heaven.) In 1995, Pope John Paul II attempted to publicly change the Church's attitude toward women. In a letter, he acknowledged and thanked women for the work they had done and continue to do. He apologized for centuries of overlooking women's contributions, and he also pledged to raise the status of women in the Roman Catholic Church. (See Chapter 1: Words, for an excerpt from the letter.)

Mystics

In the early church, worship was community-based. By the Middle Ages (500–1500), people were mostly concerned with their own personal salvation. They worried more about sin, penance, and entering heaven after death. It was during the Middle Ages that Europe saw a great flourishing of people called mystics. Mystics spent their lives in contemplation (thinking) and prayer. They also had visions in which God or his angels told them what to do or interpreted certain signs for them. One of the most famous of the mystics was Gertrude von

Helfta, a German nun and mystical writer. Her visions led her to begin a special worship of the Sacred Heart (the symbol of Christ's sacrifice on the cross).

Hildegard of Bingen was a German abbess (the leader of a convent, a place where nuns live and worship) who was also a visionary. She wrote sacred texts, including hymns, poems, and a morality play, and she also studied science and medicine. Hildegard gave advice to kings and popes and was influential in helping launch the Second Crusade in 1147. The Crusades were a series of Medieval wars waged by the Christian knights of Europe to free the Holy Land from Muslim influence.

In 1858, Bernadette of Lourdes, a fourteen-year-old French girl, had her first vision of Mary, the mother of Jesus Christ. Bernadette had her visions in a cave near the town of Lourdes, and miraculous cures from illness were attributed to Mary's presence in this cave. Bernadette was canonized (made a saint) in 1933. In addition to Lourdes, the Virgin Mary is said to have appeared at Guadalupe, Mexico, in 1531 and Fatima, Portugal, in 1971.

Witchcraft Persecution

During the late Middle Ages and even into the 1700s, the witch hunts of Europe destroyed about 100,000 women by burning, stoning, hanging, and other grisly forms of execution. The Middle Ages were a time of great hardship for many people. Unending wars between

The Blessed Mary is said to have appeared to many women.

small kingdoms meant that fields did not get planted and that famine was common. In addition, unsanitary conditions meant that disease was widespread. The Middle Ages were marked by the bubonic plague, or the "black death," that killed 1 in 4 people in Europe. It was also a time of little education and much superstition. The combination of misery, hunger, pain, and superstition set the stage for the great witch hunts.

Women who lived outside the rules of society were the ones most likely to be accused of being witches. These women might be healers, whose knowledge of

An artist's rendition of a women standing trial for witchcraft.

herbs was appreciated during peaceful times when people needed help with cures and treatments. In less peaceful times, however, people saw this knowledge of herbs as a potential source of poisoning. As a result, the respected healer could easily be thought of as a witch with powerful tools. Religious women who were outspoken or had strong opinions might also be considered witches. In some cases, the accusation of witchcraft was accurate. Because some women became frustrated with their lack of power in the church, they turned to the old religions of their ancestors. These religions allowed women positions of power as priestesses (women who preside over non-Christian ceremonies), sorceresses (women who practice magic for evil purposes), and witches. A brief description of some of the more famous cases follows.

Marguerite Porete was a French mystic who believed that salvation could be earned through faith and was not necessarily dependent upon attending church services or following the Church's teachings. The church fathers considered her teachings heresy (against established teaching) and put her on trial in 1310. Porete was eventually accused of being in league with the devil, condemned, and burned at the stake in Paris. Her book *Mirror of the Simple Soul* was a forerunner of the beliefs of Anne Hutchinson, the great American religious leader. Like Porete, Hutchinson believed that a faith in God could save people and that attendance at church and obedience to church fathers was optional. (Hutchinson is discussed in greater detail later in this chapter.)

The Scottish healer Agnes Sampson was executed in 1592, after being accused of consorting with two hundred other witches at fantastic ceremonies attended by the devil. The fact that she confessed after being tortured means nothing, since most people would do anything to stop the pain of torture. Sampson is notable because her trial fascinated the public with details of the occult. The occult is a set of ancient, secret beliefs in which the devil has great power. Sampson's trial also illustrated the link that many made between witchcraft and threats to established power, such as the church and the government.

Renata Saenger von Mossau was a German nun accused by her fellow sisters of being a witch. Mossau confessed after robes, poisons, and ointments were found in her room. She then detailed a life of witchcraft practices and was eventually burnt at the stake as a witch in 1749. Witchcraft trials continued throughout Europe until 1782, when Anna Goddi, a Swiss woman, became the last person executed as a sorceress.

Doctors of the Church and Spiritual Leaders

St. Catherine of Siena and St. Teresa of Avila are the only women who have been declared doctors of the Catholic Church. According to the 1996 *Catholic Almanac,* "The Doctors of the Church were . . . writers of eminent [distinguished] learning and sanctity who have been given this title because of the great advantage the Church has derived from their work." In simple terms, doctors of the church were religious people of deep faith, learning, and reputation. Their work and lives are believed to be inspirational to others, even after the passage of centuries.

Catherine of Siena was born in 1347 in Italy and joined a convent at age sixteen. She led a life of service, prayer, visions, and writing. Some of her visions

St. Teresa of Avila

led her to experience stigmata, a phenomenon in which the person is so much in tune with Christ that she or he exhibits the wounds of Christ inflicted at his crucifixion. (The wounds of Christ include those on his head from the crown of thorns, the nails pounded into his hands and feet, and a lance wound in his side.) Catherine was influential in persuading the pope to return the seat of the papacy (headquarters of the Roman Catholic Church) from France to Rome, Italy, where it continues to be located. Many of her letters have been preserved, as well as her major document, *Dialogo* ("Dialogue"). She died in 1380 and was can-

onized (made a saint) in 1461. In 1970, she became the second female named a doctor of the church.

Teresa of Avila lived in Spain during the 1500s. She was a nun who experienced many visions that called her to help reform religious life. In response, Teresa traveled throughout Spain, showing both nuns and priests how to live a simpler, more prayerful life. Her writings include an autobiography that has served as a spiritual inspiration for other Catholic women, and books about how to save one's soul through prayer. She died in 1582 and was canonized in 1622. She was named the first female doctor of the church in 1970.

Queen Isabella I of Spain was born in the kingdom of Castile in 1451. She is remembered for three contributions to world history. First, her marriage to Ferdinand of Aragon helped unite two of the most powerful Spanish kingdoms and paved the way for a united Spanish peninsula (modern Spain covers most of the Iberian peninsula). Second, her religious beliefs persuaded her to fund Christopher Columbus's expedition in 1492. Columbus was looking for a shortcut to the Indies, and his men were looking for gold. But Isabella was looking for converts to Christianity. She funded Columbus's expedition in order to save the souls of the heathens (non-Christians) of the Indies. Third, her religious zeal led her to approve of the Spanish Inquisition.

The Inquisition, as it came to be known, had its roots in the Medieval

Christian's suspicion of the Jews, their hatred of the Infidels (Muslims or followers of Islam), and their fear of witchcraft. Established in Spain in 1478, the Inquisition spread throughout Europe. However, it remained strongest in Spain, where it had the blanket approval of Isabella to proceed as it saw fit. The Inquisition was run by Jesuit priests (an order founded by St. Ignatius of Loyola) who established religious courts throughout Spain. Hundreds of people worked for the Inquisition, spying and reporting on their neighbors. Jews were forced to convert to Christianity or be executed. Muslims were executed instantly. Hundreds of people accused of witchcraft were tortured into confessing their sins and were then executed.

Some scholars believe that the Inquisition stifled any type of independent thought in Spain and that this stranglehold lasted for several centuries. By the time Spain abolished the Inquisition in 1834, most other European nations had experienced the great artistic period called the Renaissance and were entering the period of scientific inquiry called the Enlightenment. Although Isabella may have converted some Native Americans to Christianity, she may also have cost her country its chance to become a major world power in modern times.

American-born Saints and Leaders

Kateri (Catherine) Tekakwitha was an Algonquian-Mohawk Indian living in New York State when she was baptized a Catholic in 1676. Her decision to become a Christian was not popular among the members of her Mohawk tribe, so she moved to a Catholic mission in Canada. Tekakwitha devoted her life to prayer and good works, always trying to increase the understanding between the Indians and Europeans. She was proposed for sainthood in 1932 and was declared "blessed" in 1980. "Blessed" is the first step toward canonization, the process of officially declaring a person a saint.

Elizabeth Ann "Mother" Seton was born in New York in 1774. Seton was converted to Catholicism during a trip to Italy and was baptized in 1806. After the death of her husband, Seton became a nun and, in 1809, established the Sisters of Charity of St. Joseph. This was the first U.S. order (group) of nuns. The order was based in Maryland, and it was here that they opened the first free parochial (church-run) all-girl school. Seton also cofounded the Society for the Relief of Poor Widows with Small Children, an organization thought to be the first charitable institution in the United States. Seton was canonized in 1975, becoming the first American-born woman to be declared a saint. She is also credited with founding the parochial school system in the United States. Today, "parochial" refers to schools that have any religious affiliation.

In 1829, four black women became nuns and founded one of the oldest congregations of black American nuns in the United States. They were Mary Rosine Boegues, Mary Frances Balas, Mary Theresa Duchemin, and Mary Elizabeth

Women of Faith: Mother Waddles

Charleszetta "Mother" Waddles was born in Missouri in 1912 but has earned the respect of millions of Americans because of her missionary work in the poor areas of Detroit, Michigan. Waddles, an ordained Pentecostal minister, is a visionary who believes that God reveals his grace through the good works of people.

When Waddles opened her first soup kitchen on Detroit's west side in 1950, all meals cost just thirty-five cents. She ran the restaurant almost singlehandedly, doing the cooking, laundry, shopping, and cleaning. Her restaurant offered real dishes, napkins, and other refinements so that every person could feel that he or she was being treated with dignity. This respect for people is one of Waddles's basic beliefs.

The restaurant evolved into the Perpetual Help Mission in the mid-1950s, and Waddles has operated it for more than forty years. The mission includes a soup

kitchen and cupboard for needy families, and provides job training, health care, financial counseling, and clothing. In addition to the Detroit mission, Waddles has opened ten urban missions, including two in cities in Africa. Each year, her missions service more than one-hundred thousand people. In 1989, Waddles was the subject of a thirty-minute PBS documentary called *Ya Done Good.*

Lange, and they came from the United States, Cuba, and Haiti (an island in the Caribbean Sea). Their order was called the Oblate Sisters of Providence, and they were located in Baltimore, Maryland. Lange was named mother superior (the woman in charge of a religious group of women), and the order received official approval from the pope in 1831. These four women accomplished a remarkable feat. In the face of sexual, racial, and religious prejudice, they founded a convent in the American South. The Oblate sisters opened a school for girls, a school for boys, and an orphanage. The group eventually expanded and opened schools in other southern states, as well as in Cuba. The order celebrated its one hundred-fiftieth anniversary in 1976.

Frances Xavier "Mother" Cabrini was born in Italy in 1850 and became a nun in 1877. Three years later, she founded a religious order, which she called the Missionary Sisters of the Sacred Heart. In 1889, the pope asked Cabrini to open a convent in the United States where she would work with poor Italian immigrants. Cabrini's U.S. work included establishing convents, schools, orphanages, and hospitals in New Orleans, Louisiana; New York, New York; Seattle, Washington; Denver, Colorado; and Los Angeles, California. She also founded convents in Europe, Central America, and South America. She became a naturalized (full) U.S. citizen in 1909. Cabrini died in 1917 and was named the first American saint in 1946.

Mary Katharine "Mother" Drexel was born in Pennsylvania in 1858. She was a millionaire who used part of her fortune to found a religious order. In 1891, she became a nun and founded the Sisters of the Blessed Sacrament for Indians and Colored People in Pennsylvania. The order opened day and boarding schools and social service agencies in New Mexico, a school for black girls in Virginia, and Xavier University in New Orleans, Louisiana. At the time of her death in 1955, the order had grown to include 51 convents and more than 500 sisters. In 1964, Drexel was proposed for sainthood.

Frances Xavier "Mother" Cabrini

Baptists

Baptists are a Christian denomination whose history dates back to about 1500, when the Reformation was taking place in Europe. The Reformation was a time of great questioning regarding the power and teachings of the Roman Catholic Church. Many people broke away from the Catholic Church at this time, during which the major Protestant religions were formed. The word "Protestant" came from the word protest. Today the Baptists are the largest Protestant group in the United States and are concentrated mostly in the southern states. Their basic teachings include the belief

Window on History: Missionaries

A missionary is a person who leaves her or his own country to travel to a distant land to spread the word about God, salvation, and repentance. Among the first missionaries were the Buddhists who left India to spread enlightenment throughout Asia. Their work helped make Buddhism one of the five major religions in the world today.

Many missionaries follow Christian-based religions. An early missionary was Marie Guyard, a French nun whose visions told her to journey to Quebec, Canada, to work with the European settlers and native tribes. Guyard did so, opening a girls' school. Her writings have been valuable sources of early Canadian history, Native American customs, and the Algonquian language.

During the late 1800s, many European women became missionaries for a number of reasons. In large part, they felt a spiritual call to preach in foreign lands. To some degree, becoming a missionary allowed them to escape from the rigid confines of late Victorian society. At that time, society had a very narrow definition of women's roles. Their place was in the home, and their occupation was managing the house, being a wife, and doing church work.

Two sisters who chose to do their church work abroad were Evangeline and Francesca French. They were also joined by Mildred Cable. These three British women became missionaries for the China Inland Mission, an evangelical Protestant society founded in 1865 to bring Christianity to China. Their travels took them across the Gobi Desert, and in 1942 they published an account of their experience, titled *The Gobi Desert*.

---

that a person makes a choice, through baptism, to embrace the Lord and thus achieve salvation. Children are not baptized in the Baptist religion until they reach the age of reason (about seven years old). Baptists also interpret the Bible in a strict sense, believing that the stories in the Bible can and should be used to make decisions in everyday life. In addition, Baptists stress missionary work. More African Americans belong to Baptist churches than any other type of religion. In the mid-1990s, there were about 36 million Baptists in the United States (of those, 15 million belonged to the Southern Baptist Convention).

Attitude Toward Women

Baptist teachings place a great emphasis on evangelicalism (converting people to a religion). Many Baptist women and men spend time organizing events in the community such as concerts, dinners, and religious programs. They invite

Susie Carson Rijnhart was a Canadian missionary who traveled through eastern Tibet in the late 1890s. Rijnhart was a physician and learned both Chinese and Tibetan to help her communicate with her patients and potential converts. While in China, she and her husband worked with both Buddhist monks and Muslim imams (holy men) to establish clinics and exchange ideas about religion.

Annie Royle Taylor was the first European woman to travel to Lhasa, Tibet, the holiest city of the Buddhists. Lhasa is called the "forbidden city" because in the 1700s Europeans were barred from going there. Taylor was born in England in 1885 into an upper-class family but chose to work with the poor in the slums of London. She became a missionary for the Inland China Mission in 1884 and, after her journey into Tibet, returned to England to found the Tibetan Pioneer Mission. She recruited several English women and returned to the border of Tibet in 1893 to set up her mission.

Another missionary to China was Lottie Moon, a representative of the Southern Baptists. Moon arrived in China in 1873 and set up a girls' school, where she taught the Bible to village women and girls. When famine struck the area in 1911, Moon, moved by the spirit, gave away her food to the less fortunate. She died of starvation that year.

Mary Mitchell Slessor was a Scottish missionary who traveled to west Africa in 1876, working on behalf of the United Presbyterian Church. Her ambition was to challenge some of the tribal customs—such as human sacrifice and the ritual murder of the weaker of twin babies—that she had heard about.

non-Baptists to the events in the hopes of winning them over as new members. Other Baptists choose to live the life of a missionary. Baptist missions have been set up in the slums of urban cities and in the rural areas of Asia and Africa.

Traditionally, Baptists tended to rely on the Old Testament of the Bible for guidance in daily living. Since the family structure described in the Bible is strongly patriarchal, so are many Baptist families. In a patriarchal family, the husband rules the household and makes most of the major decisions. His will is not questioned by his wife or his children. His wife's duty is to keep the home, raise the children, and live a good life.

Methodists

The Methodist religion dates back to the 1700s, when John Wesley challenged the authority of the Anglican Church in England. Methodism is an offshoot of the Church of England. (Members are called Anglicans or, in America, Episcopalians.) However, Methodists differ from Episcopalians in the great emphasis they place on reading and studying the Bible. Methodists believe in the sacraments of baptism, marriage, communion, and ordination. In the United States, about two-thirds of all Methodists belong to the United Methodist Church. Many African Americans belong to a special branch of the church, which is called the A.M.E. or African Methodist Episcopal church. In the mid-1990s, about 14 million Methodists lived in the United States.

The basic beliefs of Methodism are described in the *Sermons of John Wesley* and in his *Explanatory Notes Upon the New Testament*. These beliefs include the need for salvation through faith, the need to do good works, and the possibility of triumphing over temptation.

Attitude Toward Women

Methodism was founded as a reaction against the excesses of the Roman Catholic Church and the Anglican Church. Methodists wanted a return to simple family values such as goodness, obedience, honesty, faithfulness, and the reading of the Bible for spiritual inspiration. Traditional Methodism emphasized the role of the woman as wife and mother. Her spiritual pursuits were confined to her home, children, and the Bible. She was not encouraged to seek further learning or enlightenment (although neither were the women in other Protestant denominations). Since Methodism relied on the Old Testament of the Bible for guidance, most Methodist families were patriarchal. That is, the husband and father ran the household and made decisions.

Protestant Visionaries

Many women and men of Christian faiths other than Catholicism had visions of God, angels, and the saints or prophets. Sometimes the visions helped them interpret the events of their times. In other cases, the visions guided them to a new course of action.

One such visionary was Mother Shipton, who lived in England during the 1500s. Legend has it that Shipton sold her soul to the devil in exchange for the ability to tell the future. Many of her predictions came to pass, including the persecution of Catholics in England and the execution of Mary, Queen of Scots.

Mary Jane Ward lived in England during the 1600s. Inspired by visions, she began an organization of women who would work in the community rather than live away from society in convents as nuns did. Ward was a woman born before her time, however. Many men in the community objected to her free movement throughout the community and to her interference in the home lives of those in the villages. Ward and her followers were eventually excommunicated (banned) from participating in the sacraments of the Church.

Born in England in 1750, Joanna Southcott began life as a Methodist. She broke away from this church, however, when she became convinced that she had a major role to play in the Second Coming of Jesus Christ. (The Second Coming refers to the reappearance of Jesus Christ and signals the end of the world.) At the age of sixty-four, she claimed to be pregnant with Jesus. Soon after, she died of brain disease. Her autopsy revealed no pregnancy. Nevertheless, Southcott attracted many followers who were anxious for the reappearance of Christ on Earth.

Rebecca Cox Jackson was born in Philadelphia, Pennsylvania, in 1795. This free (nonslave) African American woman was a religious leader who was inspired by a vision to leave the Methodist Church of her upbringing to join the United Society of Believers in Christ's Second Appearing (more commonly known as the Shakers). The Shakers, a branch of the Quaker religion (who opposed rituals and wars), earned their name by the intensity of their prayer, which led them to tremble. Jackson became an important religious leader for African Americans because of the social message contained within her faith. She formed her own Shaker community of like-minded African Americans in protest against the segregationist (separation of the races) practices of the white Shakers. She also emphasized the value of reading and writing as a way to gain independence and insight into Scripture (sacred writings). Jackson popularized the Shaker belief that in the Second Coming, Christ would appear as a woman.

Evelyn Underhill was an English woman who lived during the late 1800s. She became a Christian as a young adult, and her studies led her to explore the question of faith. She wrote for many years and published her book on mysticism just before World War I broke out in 1914. Mysticism is the belief that spiritual truth can be revealed through prayer and meditation. Underhill is credited with popularizing an evangelical (missionary) movement in England. Her goal was to avoid or end the war by working with the Germans on a Christian-to-Christian basis. When her plan failed, she and her followers became pacifists (people who oppose war) and refused to participate in the war.

Not all visionaries are legitimate. Some are people who claim a special relationship with God in order to collect donations of money and property from their followers. One such imposter was Aimee Semple McPherson, a Canadian who brought her religious show to Los Angeles, California, in 1919. McPherson's charisma (appeal) was so intense that, within five years, she was preaching to crowds of five thousand people. She named her religion the International Church of the Foursquare Gospel. Although she had many romances, used donation money to make trips to Europe, and lived the life of a wealthy woman, her followers continued to believe in her message and her ability to do "faith healing." Faith healing utilizes a burst of spiritual insight to heal a sick or handicapped person. By the time of her death, McPher-

Religious leader Aimee Semple McPherson.

son had set up four hundred churches, two hundred missions, and a radio station to spread the word.

Islam

Islam is the name of the religion practiced by the followers of the Prophet Muhammad, who lived in the Middle East around A.D. 570. Those who follow Islam are called Muslims. In the religious sense, "Islam" means "surrender to the will of God." Islam shares some of the Biblical history of the Jews and Christians, but its real emphasis is on the revelation of God to Muhammad. These revelations are contained in the Islam sacred text, which is called the Koran. Followers of Islam believe in one God and the need for a life of prayer and fasting (not eating certain foods). They pray five times each day, facing to the east toward Mecca, the birth place of Muhammad. They fast at least once each year, give money to the poor, and try to make at least one holy pilgrimage (visit) to Mecca during their lifetime. In the mid-1990s, about three million Muslims lived in the United States.

Attitude Toward Women

Islam places a special importance on the idea of modesty in women. Protecting a woman means protecting her family honor as well. If a woman loses her honor, then the family loses its honor, or good name. Muslims believe that in order for women to protect their honor, they must wear a veil to cover their faces when they are in public. In some strict Muslim communities, women are covered from head to foot, with only their eyes exposed, in a large robe called a chador. It is believed that the coverings protect women from the unwanted attentions of men who are not related to them, although modesty is also maintained within the home. In earlier times, women lived separate from the men in the family. If the family was wealthy and the home large enough, separate rooms called a harem were set aside for the woman's use. Modern Muslim women may inherit property, but only half as much as the men in the family. Men also control divorce and the custody of children.

Muslim women are required to be dressed modestly at all times.

Islamic priests are called imams. Women may not become imams but they may become nuns. Nuns are women who leave society and devote their life to religious thought. One such woman was Rabiah al-Adawiyyah, who was born in 712 in what is now Saudi Arabia. She became a scholar of Islam, rejecting society and living in a cave near Basra. She is credited with performing many miracles and with introducing the idea of mystical love into traditional Muslim writings. Her teachings led to the founding of a separate branch of Islam called Sufism (Islamic mysticism). She died in 801 at age 89.

Hinduism

Hinduism dates back to about 3000 B.C. The basic teachings of Hinduism are contained in the Veda, scriptures containing poems, instructions, hymns, and prayers. Hinduism is a polytheistic (having more than one god) religion, and each of its major gods has several personalities. Among its gods are Brahma, who is male and is the creator; Vishnu, who is male and is the savior; and Siva, also male, the god of destruction. These three gods make up the Hindu trinity, or three-person god. Durga, a goddess with ten arms, portrays one of Siva's wives' personalities, the avenging warrior who

Women of Faith: Fatimah

Fatimah was the daughter of the prophet Muhammad, who founded the religion of Islam. Fatimah lived from about A.D. 606 to 632. She was born in Mecca, which became the holy city of Islam because it was the birthplace of Muhammad. Fatimah is revered among Muslims because of the care she gave to her father and her family (she had four children). When Muhammad was being persecuted, she followed him from Mecca to Medina, and she nursed him tenderly during his final illness. Fatimah was the wife of Muhammad's chief pupil, his nephew Ali. When Muhammad died, another disciple became the caliph (leader) of Islam. Fatimah objected, believing that her husband had the more legitimate claim as the spiritual leader of Islam.

Fatimah is regarded with special reverence by a group of Muslims called Shi'ites. They have many legends about her. Fatimah is also important because she was the only one of Muhammad's children to produce a long line of descendants. Some of these descendants claimed the throne (caliphate) in the ninth and tenth centuries based on this relationship. They were called Fatimids, after their ancestress.

destroys demons and saves humankind. In the mid-1990s, Hinduism was practiced by a very small population of Indian Americans in the United States.

Hindus believe in reincarnation—that the souls of the dead are reborn into animals or humans, depending on how virtuous (sin-free) a life a person has led. A bad life leads to reincarnation as a lower life form, such as an animal or insect. A good life could lead to rebirth in a person of a higher caste. (Traditional Indian society was divided into five castes, or social classes. People who belonged to the highest or most prestigious caste were called Brahmans. Those at the lowest level were called untouchables. People did not mix with members of other castes, which is one reason why arranged marriages [in which a man or woman's spouse is chosen by family leaders] were the norm.) Hindus also value family life, prayer, and meditation.

Attitude Toward Women

The most common image associated with Hindu women is the custom of suttee. When a Hindu man dies and is burning on his funeral pyre (bed), his wife is expected to commit suicide by joining him there. The idea is that the woman's life is no longer worth living without her husband, and that they will gain happiness as a couple in heaven.

Actually, this custom has been outlawed since about 1820.

In fact, many traditional practices that discriminate against women have been outlawed in India, where Hindu is the major religion. However, many Hindus choose not to follow these legal reforms. Village life, for instance, remains much as it has for the last several hundred years. The majority of Indians still live in one of the country's more than 500,000 villages and farm the land. This is some 660 million people, about ten percent of the human race, and the rural population continues to grow. Education is limited, since most students drop out in grade school to help their families farm the land.

In the villages, women do the jobs they have done for centuries. They haul water from the well, wear veils in the presence of strangers, and allow their fathers to select their husbands for them. Since the caste system is alive and well in these villages, these women's husbands are chosen from a small group within the eligible caste. To help their fathers chose a good husband, the village girls pray to Gangur, a Hindu goddess.

Other examples of traditional Hindu family life in India illustrate that women hold a lower religious and social status than men. Not all Indians practice these customs, and it is increasingly rare to find them practiced in the larger cities. In the villages, however, life remains unchanged in many respects. Men, for instance, may have several wives but a woman may have only one husband. The need for multiple wives was explained as the need for a male heir. Men own the property and are the heads of their families. Female infanticide (killing of female children) was practiced since a daughter was less desirable than a son. Most women were illiterate (unable to read and write) before 1900, and many village women continue not to learn to read or write.

Buddhism

Buddha was an Indian philosopher who lived about 500 B.C. close to the border between India and Nepal. (Nepal is a country that shares a southern border with India and a northern border with Tibet, a region of China). Buddha was originally a prince born into one of the highest castes in Indian society. One day while traveling, he had a revelation. He realized that suffering was the fate of humankind and that earthly riches did not have lasting value. This realization is called the "Great Enlightenment." Some scholars regard Buddhism as an offshoot or refinement of Hinduism. Today Buddhism is practiced throughout Asia. In the United States, Buddhists belong to the Buddhist Churches of America. In the mid-1990s, about 19,000 Buddhists lived in the United States.

The major beliefs of Buddhism are collected in the Tripitika, which means "three baskets." Buddhists believe in reincarnation. Buddha taught that if one lived a truly holy life, she or he could reach nirvana, which is an end to the

A statue of Buddha.

was adopted and sometimes combined with elements of the local religion and culture. The result is that Buddhism in Japan is similar to but also slightly different in some respects from the Buddhism practiced in Malaysia, Sri Lanka, Vietnam, and even the United States. For instance, in the United States, women may become senior members at Buddhist monasteries (religious houses), while in Sri Lanka only men may do so.

One custom remains consistent, however. Buddhists operate schools in many villages, and both boys and girls attend. The result is a higher literacy rate among Buddhists than among the general population. Another custom is that both women and men may enter holy life, women as nuns and men as monks. While both nuns and monks are respected in Buddhist communities, the monks are more revered because they are considered the direct inheritors of Buddha's teachings (and the Dalai Lama, the spiritual leader of the Buddhists, has always been a man). A woman who wishes to remain a nun for her lifetime may be ordained a nun; otherwise, she remains a novice (a person who enters a religious order but has not yet taken final vows). Buddhists have a formal set of social obligations that they must follow, such as the rules that govern the interaction between husband and wife, between employer and servant, and so on.

cycle of reincarnation and comparable to the Christian idea of heaven. To reach nirvana, Buddha recommended a "middle way," which meant not overindulging in pleasure or worldly goods nor being overly strict. The road to the middle way is reached by following the "eightfold path." This path contains advice for correct speech, correct action, and so on.

Attitude Toward Women

While Buddhism originated in India, it is now based in Nepal and practiced on a much wider scale in other eastern Asian countries. As Buddhist missionaries reached new countries, the religion

Judaism

Judaism is the faith of the Hebrews or, as they are known today, the Jews.

Demographics: Women and Religion Around the World

Christian women are clustered in these areas:

United States • Canada • Europe • Central America • South America • Philippines • Australia • Africa

Muslim women are clustered in these areas:

Middle East • North Africa • Turkey • Central Asia • Iran • Afghanistan • Pakistan • India • Bangladesh • Malaysia • Philippines • Indonesia China • Europe • United States

Buddhist women are clustered in these areas:

Japan • Malaysia • Korea • Sri Lanka

Hindu women are clustered in these areas:

India • Bangladesh • Sri Lanka • Fiji • Mauritius (Africa)

Jewish women are clustered in these areas:

Israel • Europe • United States

Judaism originated in the Middle East, among tribes of peoples who wandered the desert tending flocks of animals. The beliefs of Judaism are contained in the first part of the Holy Bible, called the Old Testament, which tells the stories of the prophets and how the Hebrews came to know God. Jews call the first five books of the Old Testament the Torah. They do not use the second part of the Bible, the New Testament, which tells the life of Jesus, because they regard Jesus as only a prophet, not as the Messiah (God's son).

Judaism teaches a belief in one God, adherence to the Ten Commandments (a code of good behavior), and a belief in an afterlife. The faithful also believe in supporting the poor, a custom called tithing (giving 10 percent of your income to support the community). In the mid-1990s, about six million Jews lived in the United States.

Attitude Toward Women

The history of the Jews is traced through the patriarchs (father or ruler of a family or tribe) and prophets, most of whom were men. The Jews trace the passage of time by reciting the names of the prophets in order. This interest in lineage (descendants) is important because from Abraham, the father of the Hebrews, would descend the Messiah, the person who would redeem the world from sin. Interestingly, Jews trace their Jewish ancestry through the female line. Only if the mother is Jewish can the child be considered Jewish.

The Old Testament does celebrate some women because of their feats of bravery or faith. Deborah was a prophetess and a judge of Israel. Her story is told in Judges (verses 4 and 5), a book of the Old Testament. Sarah was the wife of Abraham and the mother of Isaac. Rebecca was the wife of Isaac and the mother of Jacob and Esau. Through Jacob, the lineage of Abraham continued unbroken. Through Sarah, God fulfilled his promise to Abraham that he would become the father of a nation now known as Israel. Sarah's story is told in the Book of Genesis. Judith was a heroine whose story is told in the Book of Judith, a portion of the Bible not accepted by strict Jews. Ruth was the daughter-in-law of Naomi and the wife of Boaz, a wealthy Hebrew farmer. Ruth's story of her conversion to Judaism is told in the Book of Ruth. The heroine Esther's story is also told in the Book of Ruth.

Deborah was a prophetess, judge, and the savior of her people in the twelfth century before Christ. She worked in the Temple, helping to resolve quarrels and making prophecies (foretelling future events). One of her visions led her to declare that a needed military victory would come at the hands of a woman, but not many people gave credit to this particular vision. Then the Canaanites (another Middle Eastern tribe) threatened the Hebrews. At Deborah's urging, the Hebrew commander attacked the invaders. God sent a thunderstorm and the Canaanite leader fled the battle. He sought shelter with Jael, a loyal Hebrew woman who killed him. Thus Deborah's prophecy came to pass.

One of the teachings of Judaism is that all people are created equal. This includes women, poor and diseased people, and those who are evil. Jews believe that people have free will, or that they make a choice about how to behave. Orthodox (strict) Jews do not accept women as rabbis (teachers), and most Jewish sects do not make special provisions for women of deep religious faith. However, Jewish marriage law does treat women and men fairly. Divorce may occur, but only after the husband repays his wife the amount specified in their marriage contract. Thus, a wife cannot be easily set aside. Although a man may initiate a divorce, a woman must ask her rabbis to begin a divorce action for her. Intermarriage with people of other religions is discouraged, but those who do so are not shunned. In 1822, some members of the Jewish congregation in Hamburg, Germany, introduced a new practice called Bat Mitzvah. The traditional Bar Mitzvah is a coming of age ceremony for boys. The Bat Mitzvah is the coming of age ceremony for adolescent girls and takes place in the synagogue, just as the boys' ceremonies do.

Modern Judaism has three branches: Orthodox, Conservative, and Reform. Orthodox Jews believe that men and women should be segregated (kept apart) in public. So, while men and women may attend the same synagogue (Jewish house of worship) and weddings, they sit separately and do not mingle. Some Orthodox women do not wear make-up or jewelry and hide their hair under scarves or wigs to hide their attractiveness from men other than their husbands. Orthodox couples do not practice birth control, so an Orthodox woman usually has a large family to care for. Orthodox Jews also follow strict dietary laws, which forbid them to eat pork and to mix milk and meat products. Today, however, most Orthodox synagogues offer a wider range of programs for female members and include girls in Hebrew lessons. Hebrew instruction is necessary to read the Torah, the first five books of the Old Testament, which state the laws and customs that Jews must follow.

In the mid-1800s, a reform movement swept through Jewish communities that led to the formation of a new branch of Judaism, called Reform Judaism. One of its teachings is that women should have equal rights in the synagogue. Today, some Reform congregations even have female rabbis. Conservative Judaism developed in response to Reform Judaism and created a middle road for Jews. Conservative Jews are less strict than Orthodox Jews and more strict then Reform Jews. Women and men do mix in the synagogue and at social functions. More American Jews follow Conservative teachings, followed by Reform teachings, and then Orthodox teachings.

Religions Founded by Women

Antinomians

Anne Hutchinson was born in England in 1591. She journeyed to the "New World" (America) with her husband in 1634 and settled in the Massachusetts Bay Colony, which was a Puritan community. The Puritan religion was an offshoot of the Anglican church, and its followers believed in strict morality. Hutchinson, an outspoken and opinionated woman, soon questioned the amount of power held by the elders (the religious leaders) of the community. As men, these elders objected to Hutchinson's challenges. Nevertheless, her arguments convinced others to join her. In 1635, she formed the Antinomian party, a religious group, and had meetings in her home. By 1638, however, Hutchinson had been tried and banished from the colony for her boldness in defying the Puritan elders. She and her family settled in what would become New York and were killed in an Indian attack in 1643.

Hutchinson is remembered as the first American woman to begin her own religious group, the first to openly ques-

Anne Hutchinson was exiled from her home because of her religious beliefs.

tion the authority of the Puritan elders, and the first woman to preach in public. Some historians believe that Thomas Jefferson was remembering the trials of Anne Hutchinson when he made freedom of expression and religion the First Amendment to the U.S. Constitution.

Shakers

"Mother" Ann Lee was born in England in 1736. Her family were Quakers, a religious group devoted to nonviolence and a simple way of life. Lee journeyed to America in 1774 with a small group of friends and relations and settled near Albany, New York. Their particular group became known as "Shakers" because they trembled when they prayed. Soon other Shaker communities were founded throughout New England.

A major belief of the Shakers was that of the Second Coming (the end of the world) when Christ would appear in the form of a woman. This appearance would help erase the sin of Eve, who ate the apple from the forbidden Tree of Knowledge in the Garden of Eden and thus introduced sin into human society. Some Shakers believed that Lee was the second Christ. Because the Shakers were committed to undoing Eve's sin, they sought salvation by not marrying and by not having sexual relations. They lived in single-sex dormitories, and men and women even worshiped separately.

The Shakers believed so strongly in nonviolence that they became the nation's first conscientious objectors when they refused to take part in the American Revolutionary War (1775–83). Lee died in 1784. Today, Shaker music, furniture, and crafts are valued for their simplicity and beauty. There are few Shakers today since the religion must rely on converts to keep going, and few modern people are interested in the low-technology, nonsexual lifestyle that the Shakers require.

Seventh-Day Adventists

Founder of the Seventh-Day Adventists religion, Ellen Gould Harmon White was born in Maine in 1827. Ill health and an accident in her adolescence left her time for meditation and reading. She first became a Methodist and then a Baptist, but still she found herself spiritually dissatisfied. Although White had visions and began preaching as early as 1845, she did not formally found the Seventh-Day Adventists until 1863. Her religion stressed healthy and moral living in preparation for the Advent or Second Coming of Jesus Christ. Her followers celebrate the Sabbath on Saturday (the seventh day) and refrain from eating meat and using tobacco or caffeine products. The Seventh-Day Adventists were based in Battle Creek, Michigan, where a publishing house they operated produced White's many writings about the church. Her major work is *A Sketch of the Christian Experience and Views of Ellen G. White,* which was published in 1851. In the mid-1990s, there were eight million Seventh-Day Adventists, although fewer than 10 percent live in the United States and Canada. The group operates missions and hospitals.

Christian Scientists

Mary Baker Eddy of New Hampshire is renowned as the first woman to found a major religion. Eddy first became interested in theology when she was recovering from an accident in 1866. She credited prayer and reading the Bible with curing her. This belief in self-healing through prayer became the basis of her faith. In 1875, Eddy published *Science and Health With Key to the Scriptures,* which became the major work of those who belong to the Church of Christ, Scien-

Mary Baker Eddy, founder of the Christian Science Religion

tist. In 1876, she founded the Christian Science Association. Three years later, she opened the First Church of Christ, Scientist, in Boston, Massachusetts.

Eddy used personal appearances, lectures, and writings to spread her message of the healing power of prayer. By 1900, her church had 22,000 members in more than 400 churches. However, the church has experienced a drop in membership since 1979, as modern society becomes more secular (nonreligious) and more dependent on medical technologies. Today, there are 700,000 Christian Scientists in the United States.

Theosophy

Helena Petrovna Blavatsky was born in Russia in 1831. Her marriage took her on travels throughout Europe, America, and Asia, where she became interested in spiritualism and the occult (the practice of magic). In 1875, she established the Theosophical Society, a sort of mystical American religion with ties to ancient Tibet (the home of the Dalai Lama, the spiritual leader of the Buddhists). Her version of theosophy combined elements of Eastern and Western religion with science and philosophy. The major emphasis of Blavatsky's religion was a belief that people should work to find the source of unity that binds them together, rather than focusing on ways in which they are different. Her major work, published in 1889, is *The Secret Doctrine.* At the time of her death in 1891, she had more than 100,000 followers.

Issues for Women of Faith

During the 1990s, many women were experiencing a crisis of faith. They questioned their churches' traditional stands on many issues having a direct impact on women. This section considers three of those issues: the churches' stands on the use of birth control, abortion, and the ordination of women to the priesthood. These issues are considered by looking at the doctrine of some of the world's major religions.

Birth Control

Christianity

Among Christians, the Roman Catholics have the most formal guidelines about the use of birth control. The Roman Catholic Church does not view the issue as one of a personal choice made by a person with an informed conscience. Rather, the church has issued an encyclical (holy writing), which it expects all Catholics to follow. The encyclical, called "Humanae Vitae" or "Of Human Life," was published by Pope Paul VI in 1968, and it remains the church's official teaching on birth control. It specifically bans the use of any type of artificial birth control, but it does permit the use of abstinence and natural family planning as means of birth control. Both abstinence and natural family planning are discussed in Chapter 16: The Family.

In the United States, the National Conference of Catholic Bishops sometimes offers a more liberal interpretation of doctrine than that issued by the church in Rome. Some priests and bishops counsel American women to search their conscience and make their own choice about the use of birth control. Many other Christian groups also believe that birth control is a moral choice made by a couple.

Judaism

Orthodox Jews do not permit the use of birth control. They point to the Old Testament writings as proof that God wanted man to be fruitful and multiply.

Abortion

Roman Catholicism

The Roman Catholic Church opposes abortion under any circumstances. This stand was explained in a 1995 encyclical (holy writing) issued by Pope John Paul II, titled "Veritatis Splendor" or "The Splendor of Truth." This encyclical linked abortion to murder and blasphemy (speaking against God).

Islam

Islamic theologians (people who study the nature of God and religious truth) are called muftis. In general, the muftis agree that ensoulment occurs forty days after conception (this means that the fetus is thought to be human, with a soul, at about six weeks into a woman's pregnancy). Although the muftis agree that abortion is a sin, they do believe that abortion before the sixth week is a lesser sin. They also agree that abortion is acceptable in the case of a pregnancy resulting from rape or incest.

In a 1995 article in the *Los Angeles Times,* Benazir Bhutto, prime minister of Pakistan—where Islam is the official religion—explained her country's almost total ban on abortion. "Islam lays a great deal of stress on the sanctity of life. The Holy Book [Koran] tells us: 'Kill not your children on a plea of want. We provide sustenance for them and for you.' Islam, therefore, except in special circumstances, rejects abortion as a means of population control."

Pakistan is a theocracy, a country where religion and government are intertwined and influence one another. Many other countries with huge Muslim populations, such as Egypt, containing the largest Muslim population, also have strict laws against abortion in most circumstances.

Hinduism

Traditional Hindus point to writings in the Veda (their holy book) to declare that abortion is a sin. While Hindu scholars have a strict interpretation of the Veda, most Hindu priests do not offer specific spiritual guidance about abortion. Today, many modern Hindus believe that a person has a soul only after it is born, and that abortion is an acceptable medical practice.

Buddhism

Many Buddhists believe that human life begins fourteen days after conception. However, abortion is not banned outright. It may be considered if the needs of the living are greater than those of the unborn.

Judaism

Some rabbis teach that abortion is not a good act but that it is not morally wrong either. They point to a passage in the Book of Exodus (in the Old Testament of the Bible) that states that a man who causes an abortion should be fined. Since early Jews believed in the death penalty for the worst sins, rabbis see the reference to a

Pauli Murray: Religious Pioneer

One of the pioneers in the expanded role of women within traditional churches was Pauli Murray, a multitalented woman whose religious beliefs led her to work for social justice. During her 75-year life, Murray was a lawyer, poet, scholar, author, educator, administrator, religious leader, civil rights activist, and women's rights activist. An African American with European and native American ancestors, she was born in 1910 and grew up in the segregated South. Murray had applied to a southern college that refused to admit her because of her color. Since she would not attend an all-black college, she headed north to enroll in Hunter College in New York and was one of four black students in a class of 247. There, and throughout the remainder of her long life, she continued to protest against segregationist practices. Murray was attending Hunter in the 1930s, more than twenty years ahead of the Civil Rights movement launched by Martin Luther King Jr.

After graduating from Hunter, Murray applied to the graduate school at the University of North Carolina, where she was denied entry because of her race. Her case became a national news story and led to the opening of public colleges to African Americans.

In 1940, Murray's interest in civil justice heightened when she was arrested in Virginia and jailed for three days. Her "crime" was her refusal to occupy a broken seat to which she was directed by a white bus driver. Murray entered law school in 1941 and began her legal battle against segregation. Her discussion of the unfairness of the "separate but equal" basis of segregation was used in *Brown* v. *Board of Education of Topeka,* the 1954 court case that overthrew segregation in public schools.

Murray befriended Eleanor Roosevelt, the First Lady, and advised her for twenty years on racial issues. Some of these issues were equal opportunity in employment, an end to the practice of lynching (illegal hanging, usually of blacks by whites), and an end to discrimination against women. Murray became active in the

man receiving a fine instead of being executed for performing an abortion as proof that the fetus is not considered human while it is still in the mother's womb. Rabbis agree that the health of the mother, both physical and emotional, takes precedence over that of the fetus.

Ordination

Ordination is the preparation and ceremony in which a person dedicates his or her life to God as a priest. Priests have special status in most religions and, in many cases, are the only ones permitted to perform certain rituals. In

women's rights movement of the mid-1960s and was one of the founders of the National Organization for Women (NOW).

In 1977, Murray became an Episcopal priest—and the first black woman ordained in the two-hundred-year history of the Protestant Episcopal Church. She continued her priestly duties until her death in 1985. Her many writings include religious contemplations, real-life stories, legal arguments, poetry, and discussions of social issues. Murray's greatest contributions were her ability to put anger aside and open the lines of communication between the black and white races. She was also an influential role model to several generations of young black women.

In 1990, the University of North Carolina (which had once refused Murray entry because she was black) established the Pauli Murray Scholarship. The scholarship was to be awarded annually to an undergraduate student who was poor but had participated in activities which promoted racial harmony on campus.

Christian religions, for example, only priests may perform sacraments such as marriage and death rites. (It is preferable for a priest or deacon to preside over a baptism, but, in an emergency, any baptized person may baptize someone else.)

In most traditional religions, women are not permitted to become priests. They may dedicate their lives to God and serve in a secondary capacity, as nuns. They remain celibate (not engaging in sexual activity) and usually take vows of poverty. Their work may include teaching, nursing, grief counseling, and missionary work. Some nuns live in cloistered convents, apart from the world so they can spend their time in prayer and thought. This is called a contemplative life. Certain cloistered nuns take a vow of silence and do not speak, even among their own religious community.

Many religions have orders of nuns. Each order of nuns has its own name, its own calling, and its own set of rules. A woman joins an order because its way of life has a particular appeal for her. For instance, in the Roman Catholic Church, the Sisters of Charity in India are dedicated to working among the poor and diseased in the city slums, Dominican nuns teach, and Carmelite nuns live contemplative lives or do missionary work.

Most religions regard their nuns and other holy women as special people doing the work of God. The community helps support the nuns by contributing to the upkeep of their convents, schools, and hospitals. However, while these holy women and their work are admired, very few religions allow women to take what many consider a natural next step. They do not permit women to become ordained as priests.

The reason for this is that many religions believe that God is a male deity and that priests should be the physical representative of God. The Christians worship a God whom they call "Father" and "Son," both masculine terms. Traditionalists (people who look to long-held rules for guidance) also point to the fact that the twelve Apostles chosen by

Jesus Christ to follow him were male, and that they are used as the models for priesthood. The Jews worship "Yahweh," a fatherly figure, and have great respect for their prophets, all of whom were male. Hindus revere Krishna, a male. Muhammad, the great prophet of Islam, was a man, as was Buddha.

Only the ancient Greek and Roman religions sometimes pictured their deity as a woman. The worship of the goddess dates back to 20,000 B.C. The ancient Greeks built temples that were operated by priestesses, as did the ancient Egyptians. But the major religions of today are all male-centered. That is, they revolve around a male deity. Women have a role in the church, but they are subordinate or lesser roles.

Other objections to female ordination or positions of authority in the church are that such jobs would undermine a woman's first duty, which is to her home and family. Some believe that women are emotionally unsuited to become leaders in their church communities. Others believe that women, because Eve introduced sin into the world (according to the Bible), are morally unfit to be spiritual leaders. This belief is called "Eva rediviva," or "Eve reborn."

Modern women have begun to question their inability to become priests and hold other positions of authority within their religions. Here are some recent examples of women challenging the male-dominated hierarchies (structures) of power within their churches.

In the United States, Seventh-Day Adventist women are challenging their inability to be ordained as priests. Although the church authority continues to deny ordination to its women members, one congregation has chosen to disregard this ruling. In 1995, the Sligo community in Maryland held ordination services, at which three women were ordained. They are now ministers working with Seventh-Day Adventist congregations.

Some religions, such as the Anglican, do ordain women as priests, and even allow women to hold higher positions, such as bishop. In 1989, Reverend Barbara Harris was elected as the first female bishop of the Anglican Communion (the American Episcopal Church). A bishop is the spiritual leader of a diocese, a district of churches. Harris, an African American, was the first woman to hold the position of bishop in any of the three major branches of Christianity (Anglicanism, Roman Catholicism, and Eastern Orthodoxy). She was ordained as an Anglican minister in 1980 and served as the pastor of a church before being elected a suffragan (assistant bishop) of the diocese of Massachusetts in 1988.

Rethinking the Role of Women in the Church

Partly because of the activities of their members, traditional churches are heading in new directions in their treatment of women and women's concerns. Some are reconsidering their stands on the ordination of women. Others are including

Barbara Harris become the first female bishop in the Episcopal Church.

women in leadership positions and inviting them to teach in seminaries. Some religions are also rethinking their stands that birth control and abortion are always wrong, and that child care and care of the elderly are primarily women's work.

In 1993, a Gallup Poll questioned American Catholics about their religious beliefs. The results of this poll and several others are captured in a book titled *Laity: American and Catholic.* Among the practices reported are:

- Eighty percent of those polled say they would "never" leave the Catholic Church

- American Catholics tend to follow their own consciences when confronted with sexual questions rather than rely solely on the teachings of the Church

- Three-quarters of those surveyed believe that lay (nonordained) people should help choose their priests and even the pope

- Young Catholic women are more religious than young Catholic men, and these women are interested in a more democratic structure for the Church.

Catholics are seeing other trends that indicate women want to be more involved in decision-making roles in the Church. In 1995, a religious law organization, the Canon Law Society of America, agreed that women could be ordained as deacons. A deacon has most of the duties of a priest, including performing baptisms and marriages and giving communion. Another trend is an increase in the number of older women who want to become nuns. The National Religious Vocation Conference in Chicago reports that divorced women, mothers, grandmothers, and widows have inquired about entering a religious order.

In Islam, women are also questioning the traditional roles they have played. Since the early 1900s, when the Egyptian Huda Sharawi began writing, women have challenged the custom that says they must be veiled from head to toe. Women have also demanded that they be allowed a larger role in public life, including receiving education and holding decision-making posts in the community. Muslim women have even joined their husbands and sons in their holy wars (called jihads) which have been fought in Afghanistan, Iran, and Pakistan.

Although women have not been at the forefront of many of the world's major religions in the past, this is a trend that is gradually changing. Religious leaders are now offering women more opportunities to participate in services and decision-making processes. However, women must continue to demand that the world's religions allow them to participate fully in the direction these churches will be taking in the future.

Index

*Italic indicates volume numbers;
(ill.) indicates illustrations*

Daughters of the Dust 3: 609, 628

David-Neel, Alexandra *2:* 395; *3:* 522

Davies, Marion *3:* 612

Davis, Alice Brown *1:* 117

Davis, Bette *3:* 608, 613, 616

Davis, Geena *3:* 623, 624 (ill.)

Davis, Marguerite *2:* 376

Davis, Paulina Wright *1:* 127

Day, Doris *3:* 620

DDT *2:* 374

Deacons *3:* 752

Dead Man Walking 3: 624

Deborah *3:* 742

De Civi ("The City") *1:* 9

Declaration of Independence *1:* 10

Declaration of Rights and Sentiments *3:* 500

Delano, Jane *1:* 109

Delaunay, Sonia *3:* 702

Delay, Dorothy *3:* 540, 545

Delta Kappa Gamma Society International *2:* 296

Demesieux, Jeanne *3:* 540

Denmark *1:* 19

Desai, Anita *3:* 522

The Descent of Man 1: 14

Desperately Seeking Susan 3: 566

Devi, Phoolan *2:* 328; *3:* 623

Dewson, Molly *2:* 283

The Dial 3: 651

Dialogo 3: 728

Diaphragm *2:* 462

The Diary of Anne Frank 3: 512

Dickerson, Nancy *3:* 643

Dickinson, Amy *1:* 222

Dickinson, Eleanor *3:* 716

Dickinson, Emily *3:* 501, 584, 594

Dickson, Sarah E. *3:* 719

Didion, Joan *3:* 609

Dieting *2:* 474

Dietrich, Marlene *3:* 610

A Different World 3: 593

Dillard, Annie *3:* 518

Dinesen, Isak *3:* 523 (ill.)

The Dinner Party 3: 690, 706

Disabled Womyn's Educational Project *2:* 310

A Discourse on Political Economy 1: 10

Discrimination *1:* 146

Divorce *1:* 153; *2:* 437, 439

Dix, Dorothea *1:* 169; *2:* 266, 327 (ill.), 391

Dixie to Broadway 3: 604

Dmitryevna, Yelena *1:* 210

Dobbins, Georgia *3:* 568

Dole, Robert *2:* 420

A Doll's Life 3: 602

Domestic History of the American Revolution 3: 502

Domestic violence *1:* 134; *2:* 446

Dominican nuns *3:* 750

Donovan, Erin *2:* 339

Donovan, Marion *2:* 401

Don Quixote 3: 581

Dorman, Caroline *1:* 106; *2:* 372

Double Indemnity 3: 618

Douglas, Helen Gahagan *2:* 284

Dove 3: 696

Dove award *3:* 560

Dover, Connie *3:* 547

Down Argentine Way 3: 616

Downer, Ruth *3:* 693

Dowry murders *1:* 79

Dreifus, Claudia *3:* 649

Drexel, "Mother" Mary Katharine *3:* 731

Dr. Quinn: Medicine Woman 3: 638

Drugs *2:* 472

Du Chatelet, Emilie *2:* 370

Duchemin, Mary Theresa *3:* 729

Duerk, Alene B. *1:* 160, 163

Du Maurier, Daphne *3:* 520

The Dumb Girl of Portici 3: 629

Dunaway, Faye *3:* 618

Duncan, Isadora *3:* 582-83

Dunham, Katherine *3:* 574, 586-87, 587 (ill.), 598

Dunn, Dorothy *3:* 690

Dunn, Irene *3:* 613

DuPre, Jacqueline *3:* 540

Durga *3:* 737

Duse, Eleanora *3:* 574, 591-92

Dworkin, Andrea *3:* 514

Dwyer, Doriot Anthony *3:* 540

Dying Swan 3: 578

Dynasty 3: 593, 634

E

Earhart, Amelia *1:* 116; *2:* 395

Earle, Sylvia *2:* 263, 386

Eastern Orthodox Church *3:* 722

Eberhardt, Isabelle *3:* 523

Ecofeminism *3:* 518

Eddy, Mary Baker *1:* 100, *3:* 719, 745 (ill.)

Edelman, Marian Wright *2:* 440-41, 441 (ill.)

Eden, Barbara *3:* 632

Ederle, Gertrude *1:* 195

Edinger, Tilly *2:* 373

Edmonds, Sarah Emma *1:* 159, 169

Educational Equity Act *1:* 124, 144

Edwards, Amelia *2:* 395

Edwards, Cecile Hoover *2:* 386

Edwards, Helen T. *2:* 379

Edwards, Julia *3:* 663

Eighteenth Amendment *3:* 507

Elderly woman *2:* 475 (ill.)

Eliade, Mircea *3:* 718

Elion, Gertrude Belle *2:* 376

Eliot, George *3:* 520

Elizabeth I *1:* 8; *2:* 289 (ill.); *3:* 722

Elizabeth II *2:* 289

Ellet, Elizabeth Lummis *3:* 502

El Saadawi, Nawal *3:* 523

Elvebakk, Anne-Elinor *1:* 209

Emerson, Gladys Anderson *2:* 386

Emily Post's Etiquette: A Guide to Modern Manners 3: 688

EMILY's List *2:* 301

Emma 3: 519

Ender, Kornelia *1:* 212

Endometriosis *2:* 468

England, suffrage movement *2:* 254

English Common Law *1:* 123

The Englishwoman in America 2: 395

Enlightenment *1:* 8

Ephron, Nora *3:* 684

Episcopal Church *3:* 719

Episcopal Women's Caucus *2:* 308

Equal access *1:* 144

Equal Credit Opportunity Act *1:* 125, 128

Equal Employment Opportunity Act *1:* 124

Equal Employment Opportunity Commission (EEOC) *2:* 409

Equal Pay Act of 1963 *1:* 148; *2:* 258, 407-8

Equal pay demonstrator *2:* 405 (ill.)

Equal Rights Advocates *2:* 298

Equal Rights Amendment (ERA) *1:* 21, 151; *2:* 260; *3:* 687

Esquivel, Laura *3:* 516

Estefan, Gloria *3:* 570

Esteves, Sandra Maria *3:* 514

Estrin, Thelma *2:* 387